本书系2019年海南省高等学校教育教学改革研究项目“网络多模态教学模式在大学英语听说教学中的应用研究（编号：Hnjg2019－42）”的阶段性研究成果

天涯论丛

二语写作中的错误分析与中介语研究

Error Analysis and
Interlanguage in
Chinese Second Language Writing

马玉红　著

暨南大學出版社
JINAN UNIVERSITY PRESS

中国·广州

图书在版编目（CIP）数据

二语写作中的错误分析与中介语研究 = Error Analysis and Interlanguage in Chinese Second Language Writing ：英文 / 马玉红著. —广州：暨南大学出版社，2024.2
（天涯论丛）
ISBN 978-7-5668-3750-9

Ⅰ.①二… Ⅱ.①马… Ⅲ.①第二语言—写作—研究—英文 Ⅳ.①H05

中国国家版本馆 CIP 数据核字（2023）第 150202 号

二语写作中的错误分析与中介语研究
ERYU XIEZUO ZHONG DE CUOWU FENXI YU ZHONGJIE YU YANJIU
著　者：马玉红

………………………………………………………………………………………………

出 版 人：阳　翼
项目统筹：杜小陆
责任编辑：康　蕊
责任校对：苏　洁　黄亦秋　王燕丽
责任印制：周一丹　郑玉婷

出版发行：暨南大学出版社（511443）
电　　话：总编室（8620）37332601
营销部（8620）37332680　37332681　37332682　37332683
传　　真：（8620）37332660（办公室）　37332684（营销部）
网　　址：http://www.jnupress.com
排　　版：广州良弓广告有限公司
印　　刷：佛山市浩文彩色印刷有限公司
开　　本：787mm×960mm　1/16
印　　张：14
字　　数：280 千
版　　次：2024 年 2 月第 1 版
印　　次：2024 年 2 月第 1 次
定　　价：59.80 元

PREFACE

This book is written from the perspective of Chinese college English writing, concretely, mainly investigates the problems that Chinese college students encounter in English writing with the aspects of error analysis theory and interlanguage theory, and also examines other possible reasons that affect students' writing, such as writing attitude, writing difficulties, and teachers' feedback. In the book, conceptions of error analysis and interlanguage are introduced and illustrated with specific examples. Furthermore, the theoretical framework is also derived from the previous studies which also focus on the same topic. The concrete data are collected through three kinds of methods, testing, questionnaire and semi-structured interview. The research demonstrates the writing errors students commit in their English writing with different frequencies, the reasons contributing to the errors and the methods to investigate the data.

This book is composed of six chapters. Chapter one provides information on the background of the study and the teaching context and situation of English writing in China. Chapter two reviews the literature on error analysis, contrastive analysis, and interlanguage, and provides the several theoretical frameworks demanded in this dissertation. Chapter three focuses on the methodology adopted in thesis study. It provides comprehensive information on the research design, the participants, the instruments adopted to conduct the research and the pilot study. Chapter four presents the results of the data analysis which are related to different errors, questionnaires and interviews. Chapter five discusses the five research questions. Chapter six reports the conclusion about the findings and the implications of these findings for the L2 writing teaching instruction and learning regulations.

The audience of this book might be the college English majors, or the postgraduates who are interested in Second Language Acquisition and try to do the research in this domain. Some statistical devices adopted in this study are friendly to the beginners who would like to conduct teaching experiments. The duration of writing this book, from collecting the data to the final draft, is about one and a half year. During this process, lots of data are provided by college students of non-English majors in Hainan Normal University. Meanwhile, my colleagues also offer me much precious information. More importantly, my gratitude should go to my supervisor professor Sunhee Kwon who supervises the whole process, from selecting the data to analyzing it with some concrete computer software.

This book is funded by College of Foreign Languages, Hainan Normal University, and I am so grateful for such action. Without the publication fund, this book may never come out. Besides, I also show my gratitude to the editors in Jinan University Press, Guangzhou. They audit the draft book many times, which makes the book fit to the standard of publication.

In all, the publication of this book is the outcome of the writer, supervisor, assistants and editors. In the future, I will dedicate myself fully to the English language teaching and teaching experiments, try to solve the practical problems, and contribute to the career of English teaching.

Ma Yuhong
Haikou, China
September 30, 2023

LIST OF TABLES

Table 2 – 1　Examples in Interlingual and Intralingual Transfer
Table 3 – 1　An Overview of the Research Design
Table 3 – 2　An Overview of Participants Information
Table 3 – 3　Inter-rater Reliability of the Three Raters
Table 3 – 4　Interpretation of Cohen's Kappa
Table 3 – 5　Grammatical Errors That Chinese Students Are Faced with
Table 3 – 6　Substance Errors That Chinese Students Are Faced with
Table 3 – 7　Lexical Errors That Chinese Students Are Faced with
Table 3 – 8　Syntactic Errors That Chinese Students Are Faced with
Table 3 – 9　Semantic Errors That Chinese Students Are Faced with
Table 3 – 10　Background Information of Questionnaire Participants
Table 3 – 11　KMO and Bartlett's Test
Table 3 – 12　Results of Factor Analysis of Piloting Questionnaire
Table 3 – 13　Inter-rater Reliability for the Errors Identified by All Three Raters
Table 3 – 14　Steps to Analyze Writing Errors
Table 3 – 15　Background Information of Questionnaire Participants in the Main Study
Table 3 – 16　Interview Schedule for Students
Table 3 – 17　Interview Schedule for Teachers
Table 4 – 1　The Differences among Three Proficiency Groups in Different Types of Errors
Table 4 – 2　Frequency and Percentage of Errors
Table 4 – 3　Different Types of Pronouns and Their Forms
Table 4 – 4　Correlation of Final Exam Score and Composition Score
Table 4 – 5　Correlation of Error Number and Composition Score
Table 4 – 6　Correlation of Error Type and Composition Score
Table 4 – 7　Pearson Correlation of Five Error Types
Table 4 – 8　The Frequency of Interlingual and Intralingual Transfer Made by Students of High, Fair and Low Proficiency Level

Table 4 – 9 The Comparison of Interlingual Transfer and Intralingual Transfer Made by High, Fair and Low Proficiency Levels
Table 4 – 10 Examples of Interlingual and Intralingual Transfer
Table 4 – 11 Errors in Three Groups Caused by Interference of L1
Table 4 – 12 Compared Differences in Writing Errors Caused by Interlingual and Intralingual Transfer
Table 4 – 13 Errors Caused by L1 Interference
Table 4 – 14 Errors Caused by Overgeneralization, Incomplete Application of Rules, Ignorance Rule of Restrictions and False Concept Hypothesis
Table 4 – 15 KMO and Bartlett's Test
Table 4 – 16 Results of Factor Analysis, Descriptive Statistics and Cronbach's Alpha in Questionnaire
Table 4 – 17 Final Coding Scheme
Table 4 – 18 Pearson Correlation among Writing Variables
Table 4 – 19 Results of ANOVA of Three Different Groups with WA, WD and CF
Table 4 – 20 Descriptive and Correlation Coefficients of Variables ($n = 292$)
Table 4 – 21 Results of ANOVA of Different Writing Proficiency with WA, WD and CF
Table 4 – 22 Multiple Regression Results of Writing Attitudes, Writing Difficulties and Corrective Feedback on Writing Errors

LIST OF FIGURES

Figure 2 – 1　The Notion of the IL
Figure 2 – 2　The Notion of Dialect Relation
Figure 2 – 3　The IL Continuum
Figure 3 – 1　The Mixed Research Methods in This Study
Figure 3 – 2　Theoretical Framework of EA Cited from Ellis (1994)
Figure 3 – 3　The Procedure of Conducting the Interview
Figure 4 – 1　The Frequencies of the Linguistic Errors Made from the Year 2013 to 2020
Figure 4 – 2　The Changes in Total Error Numbers of Each Year in Terms of Proficiency Levels
Figure 4 – 3　The Changes in Errors in Terms of Each Category from the Year 2013 to 2020
Figure 4 – 4　The Types and Frequencies of Linguistic Errors
Figure 4 – 5　Frequencies of Each Type of Errors

LIST OF ABBREVIATIONS

ANOVA	Analysis of Variance
CA	Contrastive Analysis
CET	College English Test
CN	Chinese non-English Majors
EFL	English as a Foreign Language
EA	Error Analysis
ELT	English Language Teaching
ESL	English as a Second Language
FLT	Foreign Language Teaching
IL	Interlanguage
L1	First Language/Native Language
L2/SL	Second Language/Foreign Language
MOOCs	Massive Open Online Courses
POS	Part-of-Speech
SLA	Second Language Acquisition
SI	Student Interviewee
TL	Target Language
TI	Teacher Interviewee

CONTENTS

PREFACE /001

LIST OF TABLES /001

LIST OF FIGURES /001

LIST OF ABBREVIATIONS /001

CHAPTER 1 INTRODUCTION /001

1.1 Research Background and Purpose /002

1.2 Research Questions /006

1.3 Objective and Significance of the Study /009

1.4 Organization of the Research /011

CHAPTER 2 LITERATURE REVIEW /013

2.1 Errors and Error Analysis /013

2.1.1 Defining "Error" /014

2.1.2 Errors and Mistakes /016

2.1.3 The Significance of Learners' Errors /018

2.1.4 Categorization of Errors /022

2.1.5 Contrastive Analysis and Error Analysis /025

2.2 Error Analysis and Second Language Acquisition /030

2.2.1 Error Analysis and Second Language Learning /030

2.2.2 FL/L2 Writing Research in China and Abroad /031

2.2.3 Error Analysis and Second Language Writing /041

2.3 Interlanguage /044

2.3.1 Interlanguage Hypothesis /045

2. 3. 2 Interlingual Transfer /048
2. 3. 3 Intralingual Transfer /049
2. 3. 4 Applications to Teaching /049
2. 4 Error Correction /053
2. 4. 1 What is "Correction"? /053
2. 4. 2 Pros and Cons towards Correction /055
2. 4. 3 Rules and Principles in Error Correction /059
2. 5 Previous Studies on Error Analysis from the Perspective of Interlanguage /064
2. 6 The Development of Learner Language and Error Analysis Research /066
2. 7 Error Analysis and Corpus Linguistics /068
2. 7. 1 Learner Corpora /068
2. 7. 2 Strengths of the Computer-aided Error Analysis of Learner Corpora /069

CHAPTER 3 METHODOLOGY /070
3. 1 Research Design /070
3. 2 Participants /072
3. 3 Instruments /074
3. 3. 1 Writing Proficiency Test /076
3. 3. 2 Error Analysis Categorization /076
3. 3. 3 Questionnaire /077
3. 3. 4 Semi-structured Interview /078
3. 4 The Pilot Study /079
3. 4. 1 Data Collection Procedures /080
3. 4. 2 Data Analysis /081
3. 4. 3 Piloting the Questionnaire /084
3. 4. 4 Piloting the Category of Error Types /088
3. 5 The Main Study /091
3. 5. 1 The Sampling Method and Description of the Samples /091
3. 5. 2 Data Collection Procedures /091
3. 6 Data Analysis /097
3. 6. 1 Scoring the Writing Proficiency Test /097
3. 6. 2 Calculating Frequencies of Writing Errors /098
3. 6. 3 Implementing the Questionnaire /098

3.6.4 Transcribing and Analyzing Interviews /099

CHAPTER 4 RESULTS AND DATA ANALYSIS /100

4.1 Descriptive Statistics in Chinese L2 Students' Writing Error Patterns /100
4.1.1 Frequencies and Percentages of Writing Errors /103
4.1.2 Levels of Error /107
4.1.3 The Relationship between Students' Writing Errors and Their Writing Proficiency /126
4.2 Linguistic Factors Causing Writing Errors /129
4.2.1 The Frequencies of Interlingual and Intralingual Transfer /129
4.2.2 Correlation of Writing Errors with Interlingual and Intralingual Reasons /135
4.2.3 Errors Caused by Interlingual Transfer /136
4.2.4 Errors Caused by Intralingual Transfer /136
4.3 Questionnaire Statistics /140
4.3.1 Factor Analysis /140
4.3.2 The Three Topic Factors /141
4.3.3 Students' Writing Errors and Writing Attitudes, Writing Difficulties, and Corrective Feedback /147
4.3.4 Predicative Effects on WA, WD and CF /148
4.4 Semi-structured Interview /150
4.4.1 Students' Perspective on Their Writing Errors /150
4.4.2 Teachers' Perspective on Students' Writing Errors /152
4.5 Writing Instructions in the Non-English Major Class /155

CHAPTER 5 DISCUSSION /157

5.1 Writing Errors in Eight Years /157
5.2 Relationship between Writing Errors and Writing Proficiency /160
5.3 Linguistic Causes of Writing Errors /162
5.4 Non-linguistic Causes of Writing Errors /163
5.5 Other Particular Variables Affecting Writing Proficiency /164

CHAPTER 6 CONCLUSIONS /168

6.1 Summary of Findings /168
6.2 Research Implications /170
6.2.1 For Teaching L2 Writing /170
6.2.2 For L2 Learners /172
6.2.3 For School Administrators /173
6.3 Limitations /174
6.4 Future Studies /175

ACKNOWLEDGEMENTS /177

REFERENCES /179

APPENDICES /194

Appendix 1 The Writing Proficiency Test /194
Appendix 2 Scoring Scheme for the Writing Proficiency Test /195
Appendix 3 List of Codes Used to Analyse the Errors in English Writing /197
Appendix 4 Items in Piloting Questionnaire (English Version) /198
Appendix 5 Items in Piloting Questionnaire (Chinese Version) /201
Appendix 6 Items in Semi-structured Interview (English Version) /203
Appendix 7 Items in Semi-structured Interview (Chinese Version) /204
Appendix 8 An Example of Transcription in an Interview (English Version) /205
Appendix 9 An Example of Transcription in an Interview (Chinese Version) /206
Appendix 10 Questionnaire Consent Form /207
Appendix 11 Interview Consent Form /207
Appendix 12 The Cutting Point of Three Different Proficiency Groups /208
Appendix 13 Item in Questionnaire of the Main Study /209
Appendix 14 Items in Questionnaire of the Main Study (Chinese Version) /211

CHAPTER 1 INTRODUCTION

Errors are a crucial aspect of learners' lives, referring to incomplete learning in the language learning process (Corder, 1974). It is inevitable to make errors during second language acquisition (SLA). Different scholars (Corder, 1974; Ellis, 1995; James, 1998) categorized the types of errors from different perspectives, providing different methodologies in the process of error analysis (EA). Meanwhile, EA can be considered as a fundamental tool in language teaching to reorganize teachers' points of view and re-address his/her methodology for fixing and fulfilling the students' gaps (Vasquez, 2007). On the other hand, language learning unfolds in various forms related to a wide array of underlying causes (Darus & Subramaniam, 2009). Historically, the causes were attributed to the concept of separation of language system in learners' minds . But Corder (1974) thought the partial knowledge of the language was attributed to the influence of the first language on the process and product of second language learning. Many scholars (Darus, 2009; Ellis, 1995; He, 2009; Richards, 1974) have identified different reasons for errors which include first language interference, overgeneralization, incomplete application of rules, ignorance rule of restrictions and false concept hypothesis, etc. , which belong to the concept of interlanguage (IL). This dissertation, based on the above two theoretical frameworks: error analysis and interlanguage, investigates the patterns of writing patterns in Chinese L2 writing and explores the possible linguistic reasons for committing these errors. Meanwhile, some non-linguistic factors affecting students' writing errors are also examined through a questionnaire survey. The whole study adopted a mixed-method study with three methods to investigate the data. The findings of this research will not only enrich the understanding of theories of error analysis and interlanguage but also provide the pedagogical practice for teachers and learners in foreign language (FL) or second language (L2).

1.1 Research Background and Purpose

Regarding the factors which influence L2 writing, Brown (1994) and Littlewood (1998) ever mentioned that "language learners' errors come from systematic and non-systematic sources". Systematic sources mainly refer to interlingual errors of interference from the native language and intralingual errors within the target language, while non-systematic sources focus on the psycholinguistic cognitive strategies, sociolinguistic context of communication and countless affective variables (Littlewood, 1998). Therefore, a comprehensive understanding of learners' motivation, writing attitudes, and language level through committing errors is crucial for second language learning (Takac & Berka, 2014). Chinese students in one university are equipped with similar teaching environment and facilities, also with similar scores enrolled, but their English proficiency and application of English language vary from each other. With the development of globalization and the opening of China, the enhancement of English writing abilities has become a key objective for university students.

However, English writing teaching is considered a fruitless job even though the administrators attach great importance to it. According to the official statistics issued by College English Test Band 4 (CET-4) and College English Test Band 6 (CET-6)—two official standardized exams implemented in 1987, more than half of non-English major students at the top Chinese universities failed the writing section of the test (Qiao & Yu, 2017). The test results of non-English majors at average universities were even less impressive. Even the writing performance of English majors on the same national exam were judged to be below satisfactory. Thus, this question attracted much attention from teachers, that is, is it worth spending so much time on teaching English writing?

With the development of globalization, China inevitably participates in international exchanges in the fields of economy, science, culture, technology, and many other aspects. To meet the demand of Chinese development, competent talents are the most important part to stimulate the academic professions. Among these, English in higher education has become an important discipline in China. Education Ministry of PRC issued a series of policies to foster talent training improvement. The latest version is The Guidelines on College English Teaching (2022) (hereinafter referred to *Guidelines*) and The English Syllabus for Non-English Majors (Ministry of Education, MoE, 2022).

At present, college English is still a compulsory program for universities all over the country, even different universities with different requirements. College English courses in top level universities, like Tsinghua University, Peking University, etc., usually provide some professional lessons for their non-English majors, like *English Linguistics*, *English and American Literature*, *Chinese-English Translation*, etc. The hypothesis based on this policy is that those students have grasped the basic information of English language, and they all got quite high score in their English exam in National Entrance Examination. Hence, it is unnecessary to open the general English course for them. The courses usually opened for English majors can broaden and deepen their vision in English learning. The rest of universities usually adopt such a policy of college English teaching, that is, students receive 3 hours of instruction in English per week during a 16-week course. *New College English Course Textbook* and *New Horizon College English* are two popular textbooks adopted by most universities in China for college English course in speaking, listening, reading and writing. Course texts, like *New College English Course Textbook* series, are expected to provide instructional material for a one-semester course covering 1.5 hours per week of reading and writing plus 1.5 per week of listening and speaking. Course textbooks are different from one university to another. In some universities, students are required to take four semesters of College English courses while others take two semesters and the rest two semesters with selective English courses. Language proficiency for non-English majors is measured by CET – 4 and CET – 6, like we have mentioned before, these are two official standardized examinations in China. The objective of college non-English major is to earn the certificates of CET – 4 or CET – 6 because many universities regard these two certificates as the necessity for their graduation qualification and employment prospects.

Classroom size is usually large in most Chinese universities because the ratio of students and teachers is large. Especially since the year of 1998, Chinese government issued the policy of "increasing enrollment of college students", so there are 45 to 60 students in one class on average. Despite the large class size, college English teaching also made great progress over the past two decades. However, the traditional teaching methods still dominate English classes, which is also challenged by social and international development. Besides, lots of aspects are neglected in English teaching process. For example, most teachers still neglect student-centered learning, or students' ability to apply the knowledge. Meanwhile, teachers are used to control the whole teaching process but neglect releasing openness-centered teaching and learning.

Students' uniqueness is also omitted, and little inspiration and exploration students get from English class (Liu & Wu, 2008).

To deal with the challenges mentioned above, administrators, experts, researchers, and teachers have tried their best to improve the condition by carrying out many kinds of teaching reforms across the country. These reforms include a mixed-teaching model, flip class, Massive Open Online Courses (MOOCs), and Production Oriented Approach (POA). However, these new teaching methods failed to deal with the present problems in college English teaching and were also questioned by many researchers and experts (Hu, 2015; Zheng & Zhang, 2014). The above analysis on such issues suggested that even though English is highly valued by Chinese students, teachers and experts, the problems which are grounded in English teaching and learning are still lingering.

College English writing has an embarrassing situation in college English teaching, because for most universities, there is no fixed time for students to learn and practice. Writing is usually regarded as a selective course provided for college students. However, the EFL writing curriculum is still influenced by national guidelines/syllabus. The guidelines/syllabus of 2022 for college English writing part stated that the students should be able to describe experiences, emotions, events, and perceptions in English. Students should also be capable of writing short passages or general topics or outlines with complete language structure, clear ideas, appropriate words, and coherent semantics (MoE, 2022). CET – 4 and CET – 6 still have the required standard for English writing, such as in CET – 4, it is said that the students should write a relevant composition on a given topic with at least 120 but no more than 180 words. And of course, CET – 6 has a higher requirement than CET – 4, not only in the word number but the word choice, the coherence of the passage and the overall level of the compositions.

With the development of technology, more and more online marking systems for English writing have flourished, such as *Grammarly. com* and *Pigai. org*. It is said that there are more than 400 universities that have adopted this kind of online system. The reasons to adopt this is due to the large size of English class and the overall students numbers English teachers should take. Taking my university as an example, English teachers should take four or five classes, with an average of 50 students in one class, and there are more than 200 students for each teacher. Apparently, teachers need much time and energy to accomplish their task, so online checking system is created and applied. With this system, students can upload their compositions online and get their scores and feedback from the Internet. Definitely, online writing checking system is also questioned by students, teachers, and experts since its creation. This kind of system has its disadvantages and advantages. On the one hand, it relieves teachers of tons of students' writing compositions, and students can upload their compositions repeatedly. The system will supply feedback repeatedly, too. From this feedback, students can correct their improper expressions and upload the revised compositions. On the other hand, teachers cannot see the overall view of students' compositions. Thus, it is impossible to adjust their writing strategies timely. What's worse, these programs can only identify spelling errors and grammatical mistakes. The content, structure or any other elements of assessing a good writing cannot be recognized and checked. Last but not least, without feedback from their teachers for a long time, students' interest in English writing might be impaired, which is also a problem worth noticing.

Under the guidance of the syllabus and guidelines, non-English majors only receive writing instruction during their first two years of undergraduate study. However, writing skills development is involved in other broader compulsory courses, like listening, speaking, grammar, vocabulary, and reading. The courses are designed to improve students' overall English skills. The time allocated to English writing depends on the teachers' individual choice, and there is no equivalent standardized syllabus. Therefore, according to English teaching reforms, some universities encourage teachers to open the optional writing course for students who want to enhance their writing abilities.

Regarding the direction of English writing, most teachers like to teach according to the CET – 4 composition reference books, which, they think, can help their students to pass the test. CET – 4 composition has its form and model. Thus, students tend to memorize the model-led essays before the exam. As a result, students acquired the pattern with highly structured paragraphs and passages with fixed opening and concluding sentences. Chinese college English teachers often noticed similar sentences or structures when marking student compositions. In such situation, statistics showed that most students fail the writing section in CET – 4 (Cai & Fang, 2006; Deng, 2002).

Many studies conducted in Chinese L2 writing suggest it is not optimistic on the current state of English writing instruction in Chinese universities. Most students report that they have low interest and low satisfaction towards inefficient English writing instructions and learning outcomes (Feng & Zheng, 2016; Wang, Xuan & Chen, 2006; Zhang, 2008; Zhao, Hao & Gao, 2010). One possible reason for such phenomenon is that test-oriented writing teaching and learning. The focus on test preparation might exert a negative impact on helping students with an active role in writing. Because the writing should be acquired in a natural way, from surface to deep root, to explore the writing interest. Such a writing acquisition model explodes students' exploration in English writing, and provides a shortcut for English writing. Eventually, students lose interest in various writing styles and are reluctant to write at all.

Reichelt (2009) argued that environmental factors significantly shape Foreign Language (FL) writing instruction based on what he investigated in China, Japan, and Spain. Therefore, non-linguistic factors, like motivation and writing attitudes, also play very important roles in fostering students' L2 writing.

1.2 Research Questions

Five research questions are proposed to fulfill the research purpose at two perspectives—theoretical and pedagogical aspects. To be concrete, this study adopted many theoretical frameworks in order to ensure the scientificity of the research. A framework of categorizing errors proposed by James (1998) is adopted to find out the patterns of errors committed by Chinese L2 writers while the framework of procedure of error analysis proposed by James (1998) is employed to conduct the procedure of error analysis. Interlanguage hypothesis developed by Selinker (1972) explained the linguistic reasons to cause these errors, while a questionnaire cited from many scholars (Alivernini & Lucid, 2008; Payne, 2012; You & Dörnyei, 2016; You, Dörnyei & Csizér, 2016) examined the relationship between writing errors with writing attitudes, writing difficulties and corrective feedback. Those are quite important factors influencing students' writing errors. Regarding semi-structured interview part, the methods and the procedure are mainly quoted from the scholar Yang (2009) who provided an overall methodology in qualitative study, in which semi-structured interview is usually adopted because of its flexibility in exploring deeper reasons after conducting the questionnaire.

As we have mentioned in the previous section, many scholars (Corder, 1974; Ellis, 1995; James, 1998) developed their own ways to categorize the writing errors. Compared with other scholars' framework, the categorization of James (1998) in writing errors is quite clear and the error patterns fit to what these Chinese L2 learners committed in their writing. Therefore, this framework is quoted as the main structure of this study in descriptive part of writing errors. This categorization consists of five main categories and 25 sub-categories, which refers to different layers of the passage, from single words to sentences. Thus, this kind of category in writing errors can help this study to investigate the patterns of writing errors in two levels.

In addition, this study will employ a questionnaire which is composed of many other scholars' questionnaires (Alivernini & Lucid, 2008; Payne, 2012; You & Dörnyei, 2016; You, Dörnyei & Csizér, 2016). The purpose of this questionnaire is to investigate the relationship between writing errors and writing motivation, writing attitudes, writing difficulties and corrective feedback. To investigate the scientificity of the questionnaire, a pilot study is conducted to categorize the factors with the participants from a normal university. After the pilot study, this questionnaire will be more suitable for the participants, which can conclude with the accurate statistics.

Last but not least, to investigate deeper about the writing errors and the possible causes to commit these errors, a semi-structured interview will be adopted to achieve the above goals. The semi-structured interview is widely used in qualitative research (Edwards & Janet, 2013). Qualitative methods, such as interview, are believed to provide a "deeper" understanding of social phenomena than would be obtained from purely quantitative methods, such as questionnaires (Silverman, 2020). In semi-structured interview, the interviewee can express their ideas or opinions freely, and ask the interviewer questions during the interview. They could more easily supply the reasons for their answers during the interview (Keller & Katharina, 2020). The flexibility in semi-structured interviews makes it possible to cross-check and validate information from previous interviews (Bryman & Bell, 2015).

Based on the theoretical framework and empirical studies discussed above, five research questions were formulated to guide the investigation into Chinese L2 writer's error types, error analysis and its causes:

Research question one: How many errors of each type occur in each group? What are the patterns of errors in Chinese L2 learners' writing? And what are the differences among proficiency level groups?

Research question two: What is the relationship between Chinese L2 learners' writing errors and their writing proficiency?

Research question three: To what extent are linguistic factors (interlingual or intralingual transfer) responsible for Chinese L2 learners' writing errors? Is there a difference among different proficiency groups?

Research question four: What is the relationship between Chinese L2 learners' writing errors and writing attitudes, writing difficulties and corrective feedback? What are the differences among different proficiency groups?

Research question five: What any other particular variables can affect Chinese L2 learners' writing errors?

Research question one is the descriptive analysis on the collected compositions, which will identify the total numbers of writing errors of each year, the number of errors in each type, the writing patterns of writing errors, and the differences of writing errors in three proficiency groups. Through the first question we can have an overview of the writing errors in the past eight years in Chinese L2 writing, which can provide implications to avoid such errors as much as possible and for the future teaching.

Research question two tries to explore the relationship between Chinese L2 learners' writing errors and their writing proficiency. The results will show to what degree students' writing errors are related to their writing proficiency. Meanwhile, the results will verify the previous literature we will review in Chapter 2.

Research question three intends to investigate the causes of writing errors, which is very important for teaching implications. If students' writing errors are caused mainly by interlingual transfer, the differences between Chinese and English language should be revealed and taught in English class, which can raise students' awareness of differences of two languages. Otherwise, if intralingual transfer is responsible for the main writing errors in Chinese L2 writing, the concrete analysis of English rules or more practices are needed to make students familiar with these rules.

Research question four examines the relationship between Chinese L2 writing errors and writing attitudes, writing difficulties and corrective feedback. Non-linguistic reasons can still be the main causes to writing errors, which implies that when teachers conduct their teaching, students' learning attitudes, the difficulties of composition and the corrective feedback should be taken into account. Thus, students' writing proficiency can be improved to a quite high degree.

Research question five explores the other particular variables that can affect Chinese L2 learners' writing performance, indirectly affecting the writing errors in their composition, such as teachers, teaching material and the school administrations. These elements will be concluded from the semi-structured interview, which also provides effective suggestions to improve students' writing performance.

1.3 Objective and Significance of the Study

This research was conducted to investigate the error types committed by Chinese L2 writers and the effect of the non-systematic factors on their writing, which intends to find the possible reasons to cause such errors. The respondents are divided into three groups according to their writing proficiency. This research also aims to shed light on the roles that different proficiency groups utilize different strategies to meet the demand of making errors. This study also examines the linguistic challenges that three groups encounter when they compose English. With the literature we have reviewed before taking writing, the writing situation in China has been presented. This study is based on the theories of error analysis, interlanguage and motivation. With the final exam compositions as the samples, this study can explore further on the relationship between errors and interlanguage and the other factors influencing the writing proficiency.

The primary objective of the study is to explore: ① the numbers and the patterns of errors in Chinese L2 learners' writing; ② the correlation between Chinese L2 learners' writing errors and their writing proficiency; ③ to what extent linguistic factors (interlingual or intralingual transfer) are responsible for Chinese L2 learners' writing errors; ④ the relationship between Chinese L2 learners' writing errors and writing motivation, writing attitudes and writing behavior; and ⑤ any other particular variables that can affect Chinese L2 learners' writing errors. Generally, the present study has employed multiple research techniques to provide a holistic and comprehensive view of EA, IL and writing attitudes in the EFL context.

This research is significant for learners to take English as FL and particularly for Chinese learners of English for several reasons. First, this study investigated in depth on the error types and their possible reasons in L2 writing. It demonstrates the process of analyzing errors and linguistic and non-linguistic factors which affect Chinese L2 writing. To the best of my knowledge, few studies conduct their research in the different groups for a long time while most of them investigate the same group in a short period of time. Previous studies (Jung, 2013; Liu & Wang, 2022; Zafar, 2016) in the field either examined the application of error analysis in L2 writing or the interlanguage (Ellis, 1985; Han & Tarone et al., 2014) or the relationship between interlanguage and L2 writing (Yan & Kang, 2021). Those studies only attempted to examine the phenomenon of writing errors, or tried to find out the possible causes of committing errors, or the relationship between the two elements. The results of focusing on one aspect cannot provide a full view of such issues. Therefore, in order to compensate the above issues, this research would not only examine the writing errors in Chinese L2 writing, but also explore the possible reasons committing to these writing errors.

Besides, this study deepens our understanding of the role played by error analysis, interlanguage, and writing attitudes in EFL writing through a full and deep exploration of Chinese university students writing. The project also develops from the theory part into practical part, which is from abstract to concrete. From the angle of theory, this study enriched the content and the view to empirical research of college English writing. Moreover, through the literature of the relevant researches, it was found that many studies focused on English writing rather than the relationship between error analysis and L2 writing. Secondly, this experimental study provides a mixed method, that is, a combination of descriptive analysis, questionnaire and semi-structured interview. From the perspective of practical meaning, firstly, it helps teachers understand the difficulties and requirements of students, make clear of puzzles and confusions of students to arouse their interest in L2 writing. Secondly, teachers can see clearly the error types committed by students and adjust their teaching strategies. Thirdly, this study provides the results of horizontal experiment of the participants, and reveal the regulation of main errors, which can provide the experiences for Chinese L2 writing. Finally, this current research is expected to provide the effective information to a holistic understanding of how linguistic, behavioral, environmental and psychological factors influence the L2 writing in Chinese context.

However, when conducting this research, there are some challenges encountered from the selecting participants to the semi-structured part. Selecting the samples or participants is the first and foremost step in the experiment because the scientificity of samples decides the rationality of the results. The relevant data is about 32,000, from which the samples should be selected. This is a big challenge for me at the beginning of the experiment. Even though I have learned the ways to select samples in SLA, which method is most suitable for this research is my concern. Random selection is easy to carry out but the samples are not representative, while the stratified selection is more rational but with complex procedure to select samples. With the help of my supervisor, the guidance of SLA books, and the relevant references, three proficiency groups were decided in this research. However, how to define the proficiency groups is another challenge I met. I reviewed lots of research papers and books, in which some experiments selected the same number of group members because it is easy to compare the results, but some others selected samples with different numbers in each group according to the normal distribution. After assessing the results of other experiment, I think the normal distribution possesses the statistical meanings. Therefore, the number in each group was decided.

Another challenge for me is how to collect the questionnaires of the participants. The time I began to conduct the experiment is when I was in Busan, but the participants were in China. I had to ask my colleagues to inform their related students to answer the questions online. Fortunately, nowadays, there are many online questionnaire tools, which solve the problem of distance. With the help of my colleagues, the questionnaire are selected and input into the statistical software.

The following challenge for me is to import questionnaires into SPSS and get the useful information for my study. Actually, I seldom used SPSS before I conducted my research for I never wrote the papers on teaching experiments. Therefore, I read some books and watched lots of video clips to make clear of some conceptions and the meaning of them.

The last challenge in teaching experiment is the semi-structured part, because this study examines the opinion of teachers and students. Therefore, how to let teachers and students talk what they know is the key section. Most students can get into the point while others cannot express their real feeling. Moreover, I should listen to the recordings and transcribe them into passages for a number of times so that I could explain how errors came about. This task was really demanding and time consuming, but it was very important to obtain the accurate and reliable data.

Definitely, conducting an experiment is a process full of challenges, but from which the acquisition for SLA can be clearer than before with a series of data and results. Challenges can become the driver to develop.

1.4 Organization of the Research

This book consists of six chapters as follows:

Chapter 1 provides information on the background of the study and the teaching context and situation of English writing in China. It also demonstrates the five research questions we would like to explore in this study. Meanwhile, it also discusses the objectives of the study, the significance of the study both theoretically and practically, and the challenges encountered.

Chapter 2 reviews the literature on error analysis, contrastive analysis, and interlanguage, and provides the several theoretical frameworks demanded in this dissertation. Last, it examines relevant studies on the error analysis from the perspective of interlanguage.

Chapter 3 focuses on the methodology adopted in thesis study. It provides comprehensive information on the research design, the participants, the instruments used to conduct the research and the pilot study. It also describes how the data is analyzed, including how to divide the three groups, the procedure of analyzing the errors, selecting interview participants, and analyzing interviewing data.

Chapter 4 presents the results of the data analysis which are related to different errors, questionnaires and interviews. It tries to demonstrate the overall view from different angles of students' error types, their non-linguistic reasons, and the direct feedback from English teachers and their students.

Chapter 5 discusses the five questions raised in Chapter 1, the main questions conducted in this research. These questions were clarified and illustrated with the results we have presented in Chapter 4. With the help of these results, the main characteristics of error types L2 learners committed are revealed, and the possible reasons to cause such errors are also differentiated. Thus, the five questions explain the confusions and puzzles of the research in English writing errors.

Chapter 6 reports the conclusion about the findings and the implications of these findings for the L2 writing teaching instruction and learning regulations. It also discusses the limitation of the study and provides constructive recommendations for future research.

CHAPTER 2 LITERATURE REVIEW

This chapter will first focus on the definitions of errors and error analysis from the perspective of SLA. It will then provide a literature review on the relationship between error analysis and L2 writing, while the differences between contrastive analysis and error analysis are also revealed through a comparison of some related works. Another key conception of interlanguage is also provided in the following part, and at the same time, the interlanguage hypothesis depicts the concrete situation of L2 language development. Furthermore, two kinds of linguistic reasons for committing writing errors, interlingual transfer and intralingual transfer, will be demonstrated and reviewed with literature on their relationship with L2 writing. Last but not least, this chapter also examines critically the ever-meaningful studies on error analysis from the perspective of interlanguage.

2.1 Errors and Error Analysis

Errors are a crucial aspect of learners' lives, which refer to incomplete learning in the language learning process (Corder, 1974). It is inevitable to make errors during second language acquisition (SLA). Different scholars (Corder, 1974; Ellis, 1995; James, 1998) categorized the types of errors from different perspectives, providing different methodology in the process of error analysis (EA). Meanwhile, EA can be considered a fundamental tool in language teaching to reorganize teacher's point of view and readdress his/her methodology for fixing and fulfilling the students' gaps (Vasquez, 2007). On the other hand, language learning unfolds in various forms related to a wide array of underlying causes (Darus, 2009). Historically, the causes were attributed to the concept of separation of language system in learners' minds (Iqbal, 2019). But Corder (1974) thought the partial knowledge of the language was attributed to the influence of the first language on the process and product of second language learning.

Many scholars (Richards, 1974; Darus, 2009; Ellis, 1995; He, 2009) have identified different reasons for errors which include first language interference, overgeneralization, incomplete application of rules, ignorance of the rule of restrictions and false concept hypothesis, etc. , which belong to the concept of interlanguage (IL). This dissertation, based on the above two theoretical frameworks: error analysis and interlanguage, investigates the patterns of writing patterns in Chinese L2 writing and explores the possible linguistic reasons for committing these errors. Meanwhile, some non-linguistic factors affecting students' writing errors are also examined through a questionnaire. The whole study adopted a mixed-method study with three methods to investigate the data. The findings of this research will not only enrich the understanding of theories of error analysis and interlanguage but also provide the pedagogical practice for teachers and learners in foreign language (FL) or second language (L2).

Regarding the factors which influence L2 writing, Brown (1994) and Littlewood (1998) ever mentioned that "language learners' errors come from systematic and non-systematic sources". Systematic sources mainly refer to interlingual errors of interference from the native language and intralingual errors within the target language, while non-systematic sources focus on the psycholinguistic cognitive strategies, sociolinguistic context of communication and countless affective variables (Littlewood, 1998). Therefore, a comprehensive understanding of learners' motivation, writing attitudes, and language level through committing errors is crucial for second language learning (Takac & Berka, 2014). Chinese students in one university are equipped with a similar teaching environment and facilities, also with similar scores enrolled, but their English proficiency and application of English language vary from each other. With the development of globalization and the opening of China, the enhancement of English writing abilities has become a key objective for university students.

2.1.1 Defining "Error"

Learners commit errors whichever language they acquire or learning stages they are in, which is a necessary process in SLA. However, there is no agreement on the conception of "errors", different scholars define the term with their own understanding. Therefore, in the field of SLA, there is no agreed definition on the term "errors". The following part will discuss the conception of errors from different perspectives.

Corder (1967) believed that, according to their nature, errors could be divided into two types, in Chinese "错误" and "失误" while the English expression *errors* and *mistakes*, in which mistake is an occasional and self correcting problem caused by fatigue, etc., while the error is the opposite. Corder describes errors as the result of learners' insufficient mastery of language knowledge, and the problem of deviation from the use of native speakers. Errors are caused by learners' insufficient ability, which is difficult for learners to correct these errors by themselves. Corder also thought Error Analysis (EA) has two objectives: one is theoretical objective which concerns what and how learners learn a language, while the other is the practical one which is closely related to how to help learners learn a language by making use of the knowledge they have already had. Hence, he asserts that EA is very useful and he also proposed the five-stage process of EA: the collection of errors, the identification of errors, the description of errors, the explanation of errors and the evaluation of errors (Corder, 1974 cited in Wu & Garza, 2014). Richards J. C (1971) believes that errors are aroused by the differences in foreign language learners' expressions (including vocabulary, structure, etc.) and the expressions in the native speakers or those who have grasped the target language. It is considered by Norrish (1983) as a systematic deviation which happens when a learner has not acquired something, and consistently gets it wrong. However, the attempts made to put the error into context have always gone hand in hand with either language learning and second-language acquisition process. In linguistics, an error is "the use of a word, speech act or grammatical items in such a way that it seems imperfect and significant of an incomplete learning" (Richard et al., 2002: 184). Carl James (2001) summarized the errors into a simple sentence, "the part of speech that failed to express". Dulay, Burt and Krashen (1982) made the statement that the error analysis is the method to analyze errors made by EFL and ESL learners when they acquire a language. It can not only help reveal the strategies adopted by learners to learn a language, but also it can assist teachers to know what difficulties learners encounter during the process to improve their teaching. Another scholar Hinnon (2014) also confirms that EA is beneficial after her long period of study of literature related to error analysis. She states that EA can help teachers prepare accurate and precise teachings that are suitable for their students. Crystal (1999) defines Error Analysis (EA) as the study of language learners' language forms, and those forms deviate from those of the target language. Rod Ellis (1995) believed that the error not only refers to the content different from the target language expression, but also includes using the correct expression in an inappropriate language environment. Hendrickson (1987:357) mentioned that errors are "signals" that indicate an actual learning process taking place and that the learner has not yet mastered or shown a well-structured linguistic competence in the target language. According to James (1998:77) an error may arise "only when there was no intention to commit one". Errors are systematic, consistent deviance which is characteristic of the learning produced by learners' linguistics system at given stage of learning. Errors are typically made by learners who do not yet fully control the systematic rules of the target language; they arise due to the imperfect competence in the target language. In China, some scholars usually posed their own ideas on the conception of "errors" or "mistakes". Dai and Shu (1994) defined the error as a result of the use deviation caused by the lack of understanding of language rules. They thought compared with the errors caused by language rules, deviations or errors caused by cultural reasons are difficult to change. Another Chinese scholar Gui (2005) describes what learners have committed in English writing as speech errors. He believes that speech errors should be viewed from two perspectives, one is "mistakes", mainly manifesting in two aspects. On the one hand, it is due to the failure of language processing, that is, sudden memory blurring, staged errors, etc. On the other hand, mistakes are caused by inadequate communication skills, that is, the inability to use the target language well to express what you want to explain. The above two kinds of mistakes can be corrected by themselves after being instructed by others or discovered by oneself. The other is errors, which reveals that language learners do not have relevant language knowledge or ability and cannot correct themselves. He proposed that it is difficult to distinguish different types of errors or mistakes, so they generally call them "errors", including "mistakes" and "errors".

Experts and scholars at home and abroad have different interpretations of the concept and characteristics of "errors". It is not difficult to see from the explanations of the above scholars that although there are differences in the content of language expression, the understanding of its essence is basically the same, that is, errors are objective and inevitable in language learning. But the error is not completely negative, the correction of which has a positive effect on language learning, so the study of errors can make better use of the positive aspects of errors.

2.1.2 Errors and Mistakes

All the definitions seem to stress either on the systematic deviations triggered in the language learning process, or its indications of the actual situation of the language learner themselves, which will later help to monitor, or help particularly the language teacher to solve the problem, respecting one of the approaches argued in the Error Analysis (Anefnaf, 2017). The occurrence of errors doesn't only indicate that the learner has not learned something yet, but also it gives the educators the idea of whether the teaching method applied was effective or it needs to be changed.

But one thing should be noticed is that we should make a clear difference between mistakes and errors, they are usually confused as one conception. According to Brown (1994), "it is crucial to make a different definition between mistakes and errors, technically two very different phenomena. A mistake refers to a performance error that is either a random guess or a 'slip', in that it is a failure to utilize a known system correctly. On the other hand, an error refers to idiosyncrasies in the interlanguage of the learner that is operating at the time in the second language speech" (p. 205). There is difference between making mistakes and making errors (e. g., a mistake is accidental and known to the author; an error is made deliberately without understanding it is wrong). However, it would be difficult to distinguish the difference between mistakes and errors in learners' writing subjectively.

According to James (Corder, 1967), he stated that "mistakes are of no significance to the process of language learning". However, the problem of determining what is a learner's mistake and what a learner's error is one of some difficulties and involves a much more sophisticated study and analysis of errors than is usually accorded them. Richard et al. (2002) ever stated that people may have the competence to produce an infinitely long sentence but when they actually attempt to use this knowledge (to "perform"), there are many reasons why they restrict the number of adjectives, adverbs, and clauses in any one sentence (2002). But Brown (1994) ever stated that sometimes, distinctions between error and mistake may be not obvious enough as "their expressions are too short and not typical enough, while the differences can be found when learners convey adequate information. Furthermore, the inevitability of errors makes it possible to observe, analyze, and classify errors in order to make clear the process of learners' application of language" (p. 206). To distinguish between an error and mistake, Ellis (1997) suggested two ways. The first one is to check the consistency of learner's performance. If he sometimes uses the correct form and sometimes the wrong one, it is a mistake. However, if he always uses it incorrectly, it is then an error. The second way is to ask learner to try to correct his own deviant utterance. Where he is unable to, the deviations are errors; where he is successful, they are mistakes. But Corder (1967) introduced the distinction between mistakes and errors. He pointed out that there are two kinds of errors, one is unsystematic errors and the other is systematic errors. Corder calls these mistakes unsystematic errors which occur in one's native language while he keeps the terms "errors" for the systematic ones, which occur in a second language. In this study, we just examined the writing errors of second language learners, so all the problems occur in their writing will be categorized in the scope of errors.

This study also adopts Gui's view (2003) on the definition of error, but whether it is "mistake" or "error", it is collectively referred to as "error". That is, as long as errors occur in L2 writing, no matter what reasons, maybe learners do not have relevant language knowledge or ability, or they are caused by learners' insufficient language processing and communication processing, they will be collectively referred to as "errors" in this study. This defining is very important for later experiment in error analysis of L2 writing.

2.1.3 The Significance of Learners' Errors

When one acquires the second language or foreign language, it comes as a surprise to find how the authors deal with the question of learners' errors and their correction. However, during the language acquisition, it seems not particular importance, even sometimes it becomes annoying, distracting and inevitable byproducts of the learning a language. Of course, with the application of linguistic and psychological theory into error research, people believed that they had a quite scientific method to explain these errors. These errors are mainly caused by the interference in the SLA from the habits of the first language. The linguist contributes himself to language teaching is that in the intensive contrastive study of the systems of the second language and the mother tongue of the learner. However, teachers do not always regard linguist's contribution as great thing for their practical experience which has usually shown them where these difficulties lie and they don't think the contribution of the linguist provides them any newly significant information. They take the example that many of errors they encounter in their teaching were not mentioned or discussed by the linguist. Teachers and educators are concerned more with how to deal with these errors and effective ways to solve such problems.

In the field of methodology, there have been two schools of thought in respect of learners' errors (Corder, 1967). The first school mainly supposed that if we were to achieve a perfect teaching method, the errors would never be committed in the first place. Therefore, the occurrence of errors is merely a sign of the insufficient teaching techniques. While the second school holds the philosophy that we live in an imperfect world, and errors will always occur despite of our best efforts. Our attention should be paid on techniques to deal with errors after they have occurred.

These two points of view are compatible with the same theoretical standpoint about language and language learning, psychologically behaviorist and linguistically taxonomic (Corder, 1967). Audiolingual and fundamental skills are the two kinds of language teaching applications based on such points of view.

In the previous section, Corder (1967) pointed out that there are two kinds of errors, one is unsystematic errors and the other is systematic errors. The use of the term systematic in this context implies that there might be errors which are random, or we call it non-systematic. The opposition between systematic and non-systematic errors is important. We are all aware that we native speakers continuously commit errors of one sort or another. These errors are usually caused by memory lapses, physical states, such as fatigue and psychological conditions such as strong emotion. We are normally immediately aware of them when they occur and can correct them with more or less complete assurance. However, it would be quite unreasonable to expect a L2 learner not to show such slips of the tongue (or pen). We should make a distinction between the two errors we just mentioned. One type is closely related with the chance circumstances, and the other reveals the underlying knowledge of the language to, or we call it transitional competence. The errors of performance will characteristically be unsystematic and the errors of competence, systematic. As Miller (1966) puts it, "it would be meaningless to state rules for making mistakes". Corder (1967) thought errors of performance as mistakes, while the term error refers to the systematic errors of the learners. However, mistakes are of no significance to the process of language learning. The problem of determining what is a learner's mistake and what a learner's error is one of some difficulties and involves a much more sophisticated study.

According to Corder (1981), a learner's errors can provide evidence of the system of the language that he is using at a particular point in the course. They are significant in three different ways. Firstly, it is meaningful for teachers because when the teacher undertakes a systematic analysis, he will know how far towards the goal the learner has progressed and, consequently, what remains for him to learn. Secondly, it is significant for researchers because they can prove how language is learned or acquired, and what strategies or procedures the learner employs in his discovery of the language. Thirdly and most importantly, they are indispensable to the learner himself, because making errors can be regarded as a device the learner uses in order to learn. It is a way for learners to test their hypotheses about the nature of the language he is learning. The making of errors is a strategy adopted by children to acquire their mother tongue and those who are learning a second language.

The following dialogue is quoted from Corder (1981), which was recorded during the study of child language acquisition. The recording bears unmistakable similarities to dialogues which are a daily experience in the second language teaching classroom:

Mother: Did Billy have his egg cut up for him at breakfast?
Child: Yes, I showeds him.
Mother: You what?
Child: I showed him.
Mother: You showed him?
Child: I seed him.
Mother: Ah, you saw him.
Child: Yes, I saw him.

The dialogue describes a child within a short exchange. Corder claimed that this dialogue has tested three hypotheses:

"One relating to the concord of subject and verb in a past tense, the second one about the meaning of *show* and *see* and a third about the form of the irregular past tense of *see*. It only remains to be pointed out that if the child had answered/*saw* him immediately, we would have no means of knowing whether he had merely repeated a model sentence or had already learnt the three rules just mentioned. Only a longitudinal study of the child's development could answer such a question. It is also interesting to observe the techniques used by the mother to 'correct' the child. Only in the case of one error did she provide the correct form herself: You saw him. In both other cases, it was sufficient for her to query the child's utterance in such a form as: *You what*? or *You showed him*? Simple provision of the correct form may not always be the only, or indeed the most effective, form of correction since it bars the way to the learner testing alternative hypotheses. Making a learner try to discover the right form could often be more instructive to both learner and teacher. This is the import of Carroll's proposal already referred to."

Of course, the expression of a correct form cannot prove the learner has acquired the language system which would generate that form in a native speaker. He might just repeat a heard utterance, which case is just behaviour, not a language. Spolsky (1966) calls it "language-like behavior". On the other hand, we cannot overlook the fact that the utterance which is superficially non-deviant is not the evidence of the learning of the language systems. Because the utterance is semantically related to the situational context. For example, in the sentence "I want to know the English", it might express an unexceptionable sentiment, and it is more likely that he expressed his wish to know the English language. Therefore, when we examine errors in the language, the situation context should be taken into account.

Although some references and literature suggested that the strategies of learning a first and second language may be the same, the distinction between them is still to be noted. It may suppose that the first language learner has an unlimited number of hypotheses about the nature of the language (Corder, 1981), while the second language learner has a quite simple task, that is, "Are the systems of the new language the same or different from those of the language I know? And if different, what is their nature?" The evidence shows that most of his errors are related to his mother tongue.

The above section talks about the significance of the errors that is very crucial for teachers and learners in the Chinese context. For a long time, errors and mistakes mean a failure in the acquisition of the foreign language, so teachers and students regard such writing as not a good one if errors can be checked from the text. This chapter can clear some puzzles and confusions on this aspect, which provides the information that the error itself has the significance in language learning. With those errors, teachers and students can reflect what they should do to the following learning. After reading the the comments and quotations from Corder, the attitude toward errors might change in Chinese teachers and students, which will play a very important role in language learning.

In this chapter, we talked about the definition of errors, the differences between errors and mistakes, and the significance of errors to teachers and learners. Through the introduction of the first chapter, readers can have a general idea on the term *errors* in SLA. More importantly, learners can have a clear distinction of errors and mistakes that are confused by lots of teachers and researchers. The significance of errors provides an overview of the positive aspects of the negative information in language learning. I believe, through the above three aspects, the readers will have a preliminary cognitive knowledge on learners' errors. For the next chapter, we will continue to explain the theories behind the errors in L2 learning, provide the development process of error analysis, and the relationship between error analysis and L2 writing in SLA.

2.1.4 Categorization of Errors

When categorizing errors, the categorization is quite different because of different criteria in methods of categorizing, research participants, research directions, and so on. Therefore, in the past decades, many scholars show their different classifications of errors according to their own findings in this aspect. However, one thing should be noted that the following error types are categorized from a micro perspective, not a macro one, so it just obtained a generality.

Richards (1971) categorized error types according to the methods of language effects: interlingual errors, intralingual errors and developmental errors. Interlingual errors are caused by the linguistic and cultural differences between mother language and target language, while intralingual errors and developmental errors are aroused by the misunderstanding and misuse during the process of language learning because of the differences between mother language and target language. The differences between intralingual and developmental errors lie in that the former is unavoidable in using language while the latter is caused by the hypothesis of learners with unclear expression ways.

In 1967, Corder explained the concept and classification of errors, and then in 1974, Corder and Allen worked together to improve and supplement the classification of errors. According to the different stages of language systematism, Corder divides errors into the following three types: Pre-systematic errors: learners have a certain language foundation and have the ability to use target language. However, due to the limited mastery of the target language, learners can only learn as much as possible from their own language system to look for ways to express their ideas. At this stage, learners' response to language errors mainly includes two aspects: first, learners' free expression is strong and difficult to explain; the second is that learners lack ability to correct themselves, even if they are pointed out the mistakes, it is hard to correct them. Systematic errors: Learners have mastered the target language systematically and have certain expressive ability. However, due to learners' incomplete understanding of the expression of the target language, errors will occur in the expression. At this stage, when pointing out errors, learners can make reasonable explanations for the errors, but it is difficult to correct them without guidance. Post-systematic errors: Learners have a good understanding of the grammatical concepts of the target language, but in the absence of language practice, the expression of ways has not reached the stage of unconscious behavior, so in application, inexperience causes mistakes. At this stage, learners can make reasonable explanations for errors and also correct themselves.

In 1973, Dulay and Burt investigated the errors of language learners and collected a large amount of error information. Based on the concept of psycholinguistics, four categories can be classified: interference errors, development errors, uncertainty errors, and special errors. Among them, interference error refers to the error caused by L1 structure interference, and development error refers to the error similar to the process of L1 learning. The uncertainty errors may be caused by both interference and development. Special errors are other kinds of errors except the above error types.

Later, in 1982, Dulay, Burt and Krashen worked together to sum up four classification methods:

(1) Classify according to language categories, such as pronunciation, vocabulary, morphology, syntax, etc.

(2) Classify according to the surface strategy taxonomy. Dulay and Kiparsky (1972) classified the errors from the perspective of construction strategy, omissions, additions, misformations and misorderings.

(3) Classify through comparison. To classify errors in this way is to compare mistakes made in the process by foreign language learners and native language learners. For example, when classifying learning errors of a certain group of people in China, the errors made by native speakers in learning English should be collected first, and then we can find out the differences by comparing the two languages. After classification and comparison, errors can be divided into six categories: omission of grammatical morphemes, double marking of semantic features, use of irregular rules, use of wrong word forms, alternating use of two or more forms, and misordering. In order to classify all errors effectively into various types, Dulay et al. (1982) proposed creatively the conception of other errors that are called storage boxes. All errors that do not belong to the first three types can be put into this scope. No clear classification can include all types of errors, but it can ensure that all errors can be classified into their own types completely.

(4) Classify according to the impact of errors on communication. In language communication, wrong language use will affect communication. Therefore, there are two classifications based on this. One is global errors, that is, the listener can't understand the speaker at all or listeners misunderstand a completely different meaning; The other is

local errors, which means speakers associate the meaning of the speaker from his words.

In the late 1990s, James (1998) proposed five categories of errors which include grammatical errors (adjectives, adverbs, articles, nouns, possession, pronouns, prepositions and verbs), substance errors (capitalization, punctuation and spelling), lexical errors (word formation and word selection), syntactic errors (coordination/subordination, sentence structure and ordering), and semantic errors (ambiguous communication and miscommunication). This kind of classification consists of five main categories and 18 sub-categories, which can meet the needs of teachers and researchers in their error-checking and study. Particularly, this kind of classification fits to the grammar teaching in Chinese context, for in the middle school, Chinese students have the similar grammar structure with the above one. This is also the reason why the author chooses this classification as the framework in the later practice part.

In another study, Hengwichitkul (2006) analyzed errors at the sentential level. All the errors were classified as subject-verb agreement, tenses, parts of speech, participial phrases, relative clauses, passive voice, parallel structure, punctuation, run-ons and fragments. Compared with the classification of James (1998), this categorization tends to analyze errors less at single grammatical level, but analyzes more at the sentence structure level. This kind of classification just mentions several aspects of language errors, which might not meet the needs of teachers and researchers, because the classification just focuses on part of the language phenomenon.

There are some other classifications. According to the differences between native language grammar and target language grammar, Chomsky (1965) divided the relationship between the two languages into strong and weak. If the grammatical structures of the target language and the mother tongue are basically the same, but other aspects are different, then the two languages belong to the weak equal relation. If the grammatical structure and meaning expression are basically the same, then the two languages belong to strong equality. However, the simple expression of the relationship as strong equal and weak equal has a certain one-sided nature, but on this basis we can expand the relations of strong inequality and weak inequality, in which strong inequality refers to errors caused by completely different grammatical results and meaning expressions that is also called explicit error. Meanwhile, weak inequality refers to errors that are basically consistent in grammatical form and have certain meaningful relevance which are known as overt errors. To sum up, explicit errors refer to learners' linguistic expressions and meanings expressed in the target language, which is a significant difference between them. Implicit errors refer to that learners use expressions which are similar to the target language and think that they have conveyed what they want to express. But in fact, the form and meaning of expression are biased. For example, learners express *One man is walking along the road*, where "one man" means someone, not "one person".

Lennon (1991) believed that two aspects should be considered when classifying errors, domain and extent. Domain refers to the fact that when making a wrong interpretation, and it is necessary to analyze the language from the perspective of context for a better explanation. All layers of grammar or words used in speech expression should be considered. Extent refers to that when correcting syntactic errors, all the layers of the sentences should be modified by means of deletion, supplement and change.

2.1.5 Contrastive Analysis and Error Analysis

According to Lado (1957), the main function of contrastive analysis is to examine the challenging aspects of any L1 in L2 learning by comparing their structures and cultures. Therefore, the more similarities between the two languages, the easier it becomes to learn the target language, and vice versa. Although CA suggests that errors committed in L2 are caused by the interference of L1, EA studies indicate that learners of different L1 made particular errors in L2. In fact, intralingual and interlingual factors could form major sources of errors (Lennon, 2008). The next section will explain in detail about CA and EA with the critique of them.

In the middle of the twentieth century, CA emerged as a new language discipline, when Fries (1945) emphasized that CA plays a very important role in SLA. According to Fisiak (1981), great efforts and massive funds were spared to establish effective teaching methods in the US during the Second World War. These efforts resulted in the recognition of CA as an essential method of learning an L2. The term CA is defined by Pietro (1968) as "the process of showing how each language interprets universally shared features 33 as unique surface forms" (p. 68). Several educators (e.g., Benathy, Trager & Waddle, 1966; Fries, 1945; Jakobvits, 1970; Lado, 1957) defined CA as a description and comparison between one's native language and the target language including the similarities and differences between them. Fries (1945) was the first linguist to highlight the importance of CA in L2 teaching. He stated that: "The most effective materials are those that are based upon a scientific description of the language to be learned, carefully compared with a parallel description of the native language of the learner". (p. 9)

Another definition was proposed by Fisiak (1981). He viewed CA as a discipline of linguistics that focuses on comparing and contrasting two linguistic systems of two languages for the purpose of deciding their similarities and differences. This definition was based on the hypothesis that the challenges in acquiring a new language emerge from the interference of the L1 features. CA is able to predict those challenges, and the curriculum could make use of CA to minimize the effect of such interference. Furthermore, Selinker (1989) stated that CA provides the most important ways to investigate language transfer by gathering data from participants and analyzing them. Nickel (1971), pointed out that "Both teacher and the author require a knowledge of contrastive grammar in order to predict, explain, correct and eliminate errors due to interference between source and target language" (p. 15). Although CA was regarded as an important aspect of SLA, it was criticized by several educators who raised questions about its theoretical and empirical validity. According to Gradman (1971), CA is not a robust approach since it does not predict all possible errors that the participants made. Gradman also pointed out that the challenges in L2 learning should not be limited to interference, and curriculum and poor teaching methodology should also be taken into account. Another criticism was proposed by Sciarone (1970), who stated that "the idea that difficulties of a foreign language can be predicted implies the supposition that corresponding structures are easy, and structures that differ, difficult. This supposition should be rejected on the ground of being too simplistic" (p. 117). Furthermore, Dulay and Burt (1974) claimed that a great number of errors of L2 students were attributed to developmental issues. They concluded that only 4.7 percent of the total number of students' errors identified in their empirical study was caused by L1 interference. Further, Dulay, Burt and Krashen (1982) stated that they only observed a minor effect of L1 interference in learning a new language. It is noteworthy here to distinguish an error and a mistake before experimenting error analysis. According to James (1998), a mistake could be identified and corrected by the learner whereas an error is likely to occur without being identified by the learner. Moreover, Gass and Selinker (1994) stated that the repetition of the same mistake is considered an error and needs to be treated.

The emergence of EA as a new approach aims to respond to the claim that CA is able to predict the challenges and mistakes in L2 learning process and to attribute them to interference between L1 and L2. Corder (1967) was one of the first educators to address the value of EA. He stated that the learning strategies utilized in L1 could be used in L2. In fact, he believes they are the same and are likely to transfer from L1 to L2 when learning a new language. Richards (1971) defined EA as "The field of error analysis may be defined as dealing with the differences between the way people learning a language speak, and the way adult native speakers of the language use the language" (p. 12). Another definition for EA was suggested by Brown (1994), who viewed it as "the significance of errors in learners' interlanguage system" (p. 204). Richards (1971) suggested that EA to be categorized into two types: Interlingual errors which are caused by the interference of L1 and intralingual or developmental errors which are resulted from lack of knowledge of the L2 structural system. In fact, a review of the literature on EA indicates that the majority of previous studies have classified the errors that L2 learners make into interlingual and intralingual errors (Azzouz, 2013).

According to Corder (1974a), the importance of errors in learning a language stems from the fact that it could be "evidence that the learner is in the process of acquiring language" (p. 93). More importantly, Coder argues that EA is important for teachers, researchers and learners. It is also noteworthy that Corder (1967/1974) proposed a three-stage model of EA: Data collection, Description, and Explanation. The model was then expanded by several researchers such as Brown (1994) and Ellis (1995).

According to Gass and Selinker (1994), there are several procedures to follow when conducting EA, which are "collecting data, identifying errors, classifying errors, quantifying errors, analyzing source of error, and remediating for errors" (p. 67). Although the use of the EA was a significant element in SLA, several aspects were criticized by researchers such as Chau (1975), Dulay, Burt and Krashen (1982) Ellis (1985) and Larsen-Freeman and Long (1991). The criticism mainly revolved around the confusion between the description and explanation of errors and the limited understanding of the definitions and categorizations of errors.

In addition, EA was limited to the final product of written and spoken languages, and it was observed that EA did not adequately classify and justify the sources of errors. To conclude, regardless of the weaknesses of EA, it was a useful approach in SLA as it has enabled educators and curriculum designers to better understand the psycholinguistic processes involved in SLA. This has helped to produce a better syllabus and to improve the L2 teaching methods. This has eventually facilitated the effective acquisition of the L2 (Senders & Moray, 1991).

EA was established by Stephen Corder in the 1970s and has become one of the popular approaches in analyzing errors in second language learning. As one of the most critical theories of L2 acquisition, EA deals with the problems in analyzing the errors which are made by L2 learners through comparing the learners' acquired knowledge with the target language, and explaining the identified errors (James, 1998). In addition, error analysis is the process of determining the incidence, nature, causes, and consequences of unsuccessful language (James, 1998). Prominent scholars in second language teaching and learning have several definitions of error analysis. Taylor (1997) states that "error analysis is the study and evaluation of uncertainty in measurement" (p. 3). It implies that error has a positive role in language learning since it is the sign that a language learner does not learn the rules of the target language effectively. According to Crystal (1999), EA is "the study of the unacceptable forms produced by someone learning a language, especially a foreign language" (p. 108). Meanwhile, James (2001) defines EA as the study of linguistic ignorance, the investigation of what people do not know and how they attempt to cope with their ignorance (p. 62). Erdogan (2005) also emphasizes that "error analysis deals with the learners" performance in terms of the cognitive processes they make use of recognizing or coding the input they receive from the target language. Therefore, a primary focus of error analysis is on the evidence that learners' errors provide with an understanding of the underlying process of second language acquisition (p. 263). From the definitions above, it can be clarified that error analysis is an activity to identify, classify and describe the errors made by learners in speaking or in writing and it is carried out to obtain information on common difficulties faced by someone in speaking or writing English sentences.

EA is developed after contrastive analysis, which is also different from contrastive analysis. The theory of error analysis is developed on the basis of contrastive analysis theory. In the theory of contrastive analysis, all errors are caused by the differences of mother tongue and the target language. However, according to the error analysis theory, the differences between the mother tongue and the target language cannot cause all language errors. Some errors are not related to the influence of mother tongue. In other words, contrastive analysis only explains the causes of some errors, and there was no reasonable explanation for the causes of other errors. Therefore, when scholars found the drawbacks of the contrastive analysis theory, they started to study the deeper causes of errors, and error analysis theory came out.

The data study shows that error analysis is more predictive and explanatory than contrastive analysis. Linguists found that, first of all, there are some differences and similarities between mother tongue and target language in terms of language structure, which are different in the research process. For learners, the probability of making mistakes is much smaller, but it is easier to make errors in the same or similar aspects of the language. However, similar errors predicted by contrastive analysis are not obvious in this respect. This has aroused the concern of linguists, through analysis and research, it is shown that the theoretical methods of error analysis can solve the limitations of contrastive analysis. Besides, error analysis can also provide more scientific learning methods on the basis of analyzing the causes of errors. Of course, it is inevitable to make errors in the learning process, but error analysis describes objectively the logical relationship between the mother tongue and the target language.

In order to consolidate further the theoretical foundation, and at the same time, to explore the practical application of error analysis, researchers have studied the errors made in the learning process and explored the reasons and properties of the cross language behaviors of the mother tongue and the target language, which hopes to reduce the probability of making errors.

The famous scholar Corder (1967) ever pointed out that the error itself is of great significance, and it cannot be simply regarded as a bad phenomenon that should be destroyed. By studying the causes and inherent nature of errors, it can help teachers effectively understand students' learning, help researchers explore language learning strategies, help students correct the rooted causes of the problem, and judge the correctness of the hypothesis of the target language. Therefore, it is of great significance to make a thorough and detailed study of learners' linguistic problems and errors in the learning process.

At the same time, Corder (1974) divided error analysis into the following five steps: first, select the target language, and choose the object of study and relevant language materials. In a certain stage and period, basic information of learners in the process of foreign language can be collected and sorted out purposefully and methodically. Second, through collecting and sorting the basic information, we can judge whether learners are up to the standard through intonation, grammar, context, communication methods and other aspects. Error analysis is used to classify the types and conceptions of errors. In this regard, Corder (1981) divided errors into two categories: systematic errors and non-systematic errors. Systematic errors are caused by insufficient knowledge reserved and learning methods. They are not caused by learners' own abilities in the learning process. While non-systematic errors can be realized obviously through their own capabilities, which is often caused by the physical, emotional, mental and other factors that have nothing to do with learning ability. Third, different error types should be distinguished. There are many kinds of errors for learners in the learning process. James (2001) thinks that these errors are very simple. It is better to analyze with the other levels of errors. But Dulay and Krashen (1982) divided such errors into global and local ones through data evaluation. However, Corder (1967) divided these errors into obvious and potential errors. Fourth, In this regard, Richard (2000) studied the causes of errors in depth and divided the errors into three aspects: interlingual errors, intralingual errors and developmental errors. First of all, interlingual errors, as the name suggests, mean that the learners unconsciously added the original language and culture into the second language learning. It is also called the transfer error. Second, the intralingual error refers to learners' wrong understanding of the wrong rule division in the process of learning the second language. This is the root cause of errors. Finally, compared with the first two errors, the third type, developmental error, is caused by mental fatigue, amnesia or emotional fluctuation during the learning process. Fifth, it is of great significance to evaluate errors in error analysis. First of all, when evaluating errors, we should consider them comprehensively, and combine errors with non-errors together, we should not just study error analysis. The second reason for this is that it is difficult for analysts to determine where and at what stage did these problems occur in the learning process. Of course, error analysis is not comprehensive. In particular, when such phenomena as "error avoidance" occur, we can not give a good explanation, but overemphasize errors, because this is not objective and comprehensive enough.

2.2 Error Analysis and Second Language Acquisition

2.2.1 Error Analysis and Second Language Learning

Error analysis is an important topic in second language (L2) acquisition and a hot research issue in recent years (Wedell & Liu, 2012). It is generally agreed that the development period of the error analysis is not long, but its growth rate is fast with increasing research teams and tools constantly being updated, so the outcomes of error analysis have begun to mushroom and sprout in various fields (Widdowson, 2013). L2 acquisition is the process of improving learners' L2 or foreign language proficiency, which is different from first language acquisition (Hu, 1998). Language acquisition is a psychological, cognitive, and linguistic skill development process (Lightbown, 1983). It should be said that the study of L2 acquisition process is aimed at expecting to obtain something beneficial to language teaching and acquisition in order to enhance the effectiveness of L2 acquisition (Ellis, 2012). As such, most L2 acquisition researchers tend to view error analysis as an entry point and a breakthrough in the study of L2 acquisition (Ellis, 2012).

The notion of error analysis was first raised by the scholar Corder (1967) to analyze the errors in learners' L1. However, it became popular in analyzing errors in second language learning gradually. When we talk about the difficulties and obstacles of acquiring the second language, inevitably, error analysis is the main branch we should consider a lot. Lots of areas in second language acquisition can be illustrated by the theory of error analysis, such as corrective feedback, writing strategies, and individual differences. Gass and Selinker (2008) add that, "focusing on errors is the beginning of the field of Second Language Acquisition, which at this point is the beginning to emerge as a field of interest not only for the pedagogical implications that may result from knowing about second language learning, but also because of the theoretical implication for fields such as psychology (in particular learning theory) and linguistics" (p. 102). Therefore, it can be concluded that study on error analysis is one of interesting topics in Second Language Acquisition study.

2.2.2 FL/L2 Writing Research in China and Abroad

In Chinese context, the empirical study of English writing can fall into the following five aspects, psychology and strategies of students' writing, teachers' factors, linguistic factors, writing environment, and reflection of second language writing. In the next section, we would like to explain them with concrete examples.

The first is about the research on students' writing psychology and strategies. From the year 2009 to 2019, an empirical study was conducted on the topic of English writing strategies, during which students were regarded as the main body, as well as the domestic scholars. For example, Wu (2009) made a prospective analysis of the research that aims to analyze the contents and achievements on metacognition and college English teaching. These papers have been published in 18 Chinese core journals in the past 12 years. Through such research, the limitations in metacognition can be traced and even the trend in this direction is also looked forward to. The other researcher Xiao (2011) introduced an empirical study on the application of metacognitive strategy training in writing teaching in a university. The experimental results showed that metacognitive strategy is closely related to writing performance, and writing metacognitive strategy training can effectively improve students' English writing performance. Liu (2013) summarized the empirical research on college English learners' metacognitive ability in English writing in China, and on this basis the study explored the strategies and contents of how students improve and correct errors in English writing. In addition, many scholars have also paid attention to the issue of writing strategies. At the same time, even some papers did not discuss directly the effect of mother language on students' ways of thinking in their writing, they talked it more or less indirectly.

The second aspect is related to teachers as the factor. In this phase, the interior factor relating to second language teaching focuses on writing teaching method and the development of assessing feedback system. Among these, 12 papers discussed the factor of teachers in English writing. During this stage, the research goes into deeper and broader vision, along with which what appears are experimental and creative. Guo et al. (2010) conducted a teaching experiment in their classroom under the guidance of error analysis theory step-by-step, and tested the students' writing teaching survey in an empirical way. Meanwhile, it analyzes the error types, examines the severity of errors in major English texts and their impact on English writing to explore students' ability to perceive errors and think, and verifies the effectiveness of college students' English writing teaching under the guidance of error analysis theory. The results show that writing teaching based on error analysis theory can reduce the anxiety of students with low self-consciousness, make them afraid of making mistakes in writing, and stimulate their learning interest and enthusiasm.

The third aspect is the study on linguistic factors. The results of the statistics from the year 2009 to 2019 show that domestic researchers pay less attention to the empirical research at the micro level of English writing. Zhu (2011) mentioned that since 2011, the biggest feature of the study of English writing vocabulary is that most studies are based on the comparative analysis of corpus data. In this survey, Wu (2017), based on empirical analysis, applied multi-modal metaphor in college English writing teaching, and explored the impact of multi-modal metaphor on students' metaphorical ability and writing ability in college English writing teaching. The results show that the adoption of multimodal can promote the improvement in metaphorical ability significantly, and thus enhancing students' writing ability.

The fourth aspect is related to the study the factors of writing environment. In recent years, the widespread use of computers and the internet has led to an increase in internal research on the second language writing environment and media (especially online writing resources, writing platform software, etc.). Xue (2010) conducted an experiment to explore the help of Chinese and American college students in their English writing ability through two semesters of online communication and tutoring. The results show that online tutoring and communication between Chinese and American college students is of great help to the improvement of Chinese college students' writing ability. Mou et al. (2013) took the example of the teaching of English writing for freshmen of non-foreign language majors in Lanzhou Jiaotong University, and carried out comparative teaching research on the experimental group and the control group by adopting cross-cultural e-mail communication and traditional paper-and-pencil writing teaching methods respectively. The results showed that cross-cultural e-mail communication improved students' writing skills significantly, especially the fluency and accuracy of writing. It also strengthens students' internal learning motivation. Feng (2012) et al., based on the formative assessment tool Writing Roadmap, analyzed the impact of the mixed method and the simple holistic method in the formative assessment process. This analysis can check on the improvement of learners' writing proficiency in the light of the scoring methods used to evaluate students' writing. The research shows that in the formative assessment process of college English writing, the adoption of the mixed scoring method combining itemized and overall scoring is more helpful to improve learners' writing level. Yu (2010) carried out writing teaching by creating a Wiki writing system for college English writing teaching. The results show that the Wiki writing system can promote the development of collaborative learning ability.

Fifthly, the reflection on the teaching of second language writing. Through the analysis of the current situation of English writing research in China since 1993, Huang et al. (2009) pointed out that the quality of empirical research needs to be further improved, the subject of writing needs to be comprehensive, the use of statistical methods needs to be improved, and the research object writing itself needs to be specific and contextualized. At last, the study called on domestic researchers to attach importance to the study of writing textbooks. Gao (2010) analyzed the basic laws of research trend, research content, research methods and research objects of second language writing evaluation at home and abroad for more than ten years, and put forward the common issues in the field of second language writing evaluation at present, namely, the uncertainty of scoring methods, the relatively lagging evaluation software, the insufficient research on the elements of raters, the lack of empirical research, and the imbalance of research objects. The paper also put forward relevant suggestions, looking forward to pointing out the direction for further research in the future. Li (2014) CSSCI (2014—2015) has published a journal on foreign language teaching methods and content research in the past ten years. The results show that in the past ten years, domestic research on college English teaching methods and contents has been very important. In particular, writing skills and vocabulary teaching methods, especially the research of writing skills, vocabulary teaching methods and writing models, are regarded as the crucial part, but the research of teaching methods such as listening and speaking skills, grammar, culture and general education is not enough. Xiang (2012) found that Chinese college students often use words with broad or similar meanings and relevant sentence patterns to avoid some words and sentences that cannot be understood precisely, so as to minimize errors in the article. Due to the influence of cross-cultural factors and insufficient understanding of language skills, the process of avoiding errors will reduce the quality of English writing and affect the improvement of English writing. It is necessary to solve and analyze the existing problems and causes for college students, concentrate on developing and improving their cross-cultural thinking ability, implement the dichotomy teaching method, build a six-step independent classroom, and change the "avoidance" phenomenon that easily occurs in college students' English writing.

This section mainly reviews the literature on the empirical research of college students' English writing in the past ten years from 2009 to 2019. It is found that the research features of the literature in this period mainly focused on the research of teachers' teaching factors, such as the application of writing teaching methods and the development of evaluation and feedback systems. On the other hand, many domestic researchers have also begun to pay less attention to the empirical research on the micro level of language in writing. The overall situation of the other three aspects is similar, that is, the research on students' writing psychology and strategies, writing environment factors and second language writing teaching reflection shows a balanced development trend.

This section uses the collection of journals of Web of Science core collection database, Z-library, and Google scholar to demonstrate the main development in English writing in the past 10 years. Because of limited space in this book, several representative papers will be discussed here. Each paper represents one aspect of issues which is related to English writing research. The following paragraphs will see the research content and results of these studies.

Mehmet and Serhat (2020) proposed that second language writing is a complex phenomenon in which emotional factors play an important role. Among them, the level of enthusiasm determines whether students can organize the complex writing process successfully and the quality of their second language writing. Their research is divided into two stages, aiming at establishing and verifying the writing motivation scale. A total of 551 EFL students participated in the development phase, and a total of 367 EFL students were recruited to the validation phase of the study. The results reveal a five-element solution that includes self-conscious second language writing ability, teacher practice, attitude, writing materials and methods, and teaching environment. The analysis results show that the model is in good agreement with the actual data. In general, the English Writing Motivation Scale (EWMS) is a reliable and effective tool in psychometrics that can be used to study second language writing motivation.

Kellera et al. (2020) investigated English writing ability of high school students in Germany and Switzerland two years and one year before graduation. It focuses on the level and development of English writing, as well as the differences between groups (country, gender, language background). The researchers conducted a repeated measurement study on 2,847 students, involving two different writing tasks from the TOEFL online test (TOEFLBT). The results show that in these two countries, more than 70% of the tested students have reached the B2 level of the European Common Language Reference Framework (CEFR), thus mastering the target standard one year before graduation. In the whole academic year, the development of writing skills has been little affected, which is similar to the study of reception skills in scale. Swiss students perform better than German students, but gender and language background have no significant impact. These findings are about the application of English writing courses and teacher education in the international context.

Ulicheva et al. (2020) proposed a computational analysis of English writing. They developed a new structure to describe the relationship between spelling and sound. Diagnostics captures the amount of meaningful information in a given spelling, while specificity estimates the dispersion of meaning in different spellings of a specific sound sequence. By using these two structures, it is proved that specific suffix spelling is often reserved for specific meaningful functions. Then three examples (non-verbal classification, spelling and eye movement tracking in sentence reading) are shown. The regularity between spelling and meaning in this form affects the behavior of skilled readers. Finally, they believe that English spelling may have been subdivided, so that the high degree of inconsistency of the dry spelling sounds can transfer meaningful information maximally.

Xu and Mauranen (2020) complement the previous study on the linguistic characteristics of English as a universal language from the perspective of legal complexity. Specifically, the study attempts to find out how ELF users use different syntactic structures to express meaning relationships in research articles. The same syntactic phenomenon is also analyzed in the contrastive text of American English (AmE) writing to understand how ELF writing shapes English research writing. The results show that the values of the nine indicators of the four syntactic complexity dimensions in ELF research papers are significantly different from those in the same AE research papers. ELF writers use longer sentences to improve communication efficiency, and use more coordinate phrases and complex nouns to enhance clarity. In addition, considering the complexity of phrases, ELF research articles rely more on nominal phrases than AmE articles. In other words, in academic writing discourse, the convention of nominal style is valued. These features of syntactic complexity illustrate the author's handling of two opposing goals in academic writing, namely, clarity and conciseness. The significance of this study is that it provides insights for the ELF in the descriptive writing discourse.

Miller (2020) identified all traditional and textbook idioms in the English for Academic English (basic corpus), checked the text range of their occurrence, and then compared their frequency with the same idioms used in the Oxford Corpus of Academic English (OCAE). There are 545 idioms, of which 6 appear in four or more basic texts and 43 appear in OCAE at least 100 times. These idioms can be used confidently by authors and teachers to enrich their own and students' English academic speeches and writing.

Chen et al. (2019) proposed that corpora be widely used in language learning and the creation of teaching materials, such as dictionaries, grammar books, textbooks and glossaries. However, few people pay attention to how to introduce DDL successfully into teacher training programs. This paper introduces the background, implementation process and results of a teacher's writing training teaching model focusing on DDL, aiming to introduce a corpus-assisted writing teaching method for in-service English teachers in Hong Kong. In order to evaluate the success of the seminar and understand further the factors that may lead teachers to accept or reject the method, they conducted a questionnaire survey on participants after the seminar and made a statistical analysis of the responses. The results show that participants usually have a positive willingness to train. In addition, teachers' use of corpus tools and the tendency to integrate data-driven learning in future teaching are related significantly to teachers' experience, professional development motivation, teaching experience and other factors. These findings may be related to the research on teachers' attitudes towards wider use of information technology in the classroom.

Milin and Millin (2018) discussed the main findings of a study that tried to evaluate the impact of reading learning (RL) literacy intervention on individual student performance and applied it to high school students in two schools in the Western Cape of South Africa. In the context of the implementation of RtL intervention, the literacy development of schools in South Africa, especially non-native English students from communities with low socio-economic level and students from immigrant communities, has received more attention. By evaluating and sorting out the written assignments submitted by each student at different stages of the whole school year, descriptive statistics and inferential statistics can be used to conduct a detailed examination of various models. The most significant finding is that students with poor academic performance before the intervention have significantly improved their English writing skills in the whole intervention process. Therefore, if appropriate targeted interventions (such as RL) are taken, there may be a convergence or "catch-up" effect, that is, there are a large number of non-native English students in the class who are immersed in English teaching schools.

In order to conduct a comparative study of abstracts written by native English authors and native Chinese authors, Zhou (2018) constructed a corpus containing 200 abstracts. These abstracts are journal abstracts published from 2012 to 2015, which were published in four applied linguistics journals: two international journals: Applied Linguistics (AL) and TESOL Quarterly (TQ), and Chinese Journal of Applied Linguistics (CJAL) and Foreign Language Teaching and Research (FLTR) are two Chinese journals. The purpose of this study is to fill the gap in the study of grammatical features of compressed discourse style in native and non-native academic writing in applied linguistics. This study reveals the different language strategies used by the two groups of authors in implementing structure compression. These findings provide new ideas for academic writers to use complex noun phrases to complete the challenging task of writing compact abstract texts.

McIntosh and Connor (2017) proposed that in the past few decades, academic English writing (EAP) and professional English writing (ESP), two recognized writing norms, have been affected by the language in a series of fields and environments. As writers and readers become more and more diverse in language and culture, the composition of English at the linguistic, rhetorical and textual levels has also changed, Therefore, people have been looking for an appropriate theoretical framework to describe the reality of academic and professional writing practice. Two related frameworks, namely, English as a lingua franca (ELF) and trans-lingualism, propose a more flexible communication model between users of different English variants. In the paper, they believe that efforts to promote translatualism can make EAP and ESP contexts benefit from cross-cultural rhetoric (IR), or "research between written discourse and individuals from different cultural backgrounds" (Corder, 2011). Finally, they suggested to carry out research and teaching application from IR, ELF and translation linguistics to promote the development of EAP/ESP in the changing global world.

Wu and Lawrence Zhang (2017) reported the results of the study on the impact of language environment on the perception and performance of English writing of Chinese second-year postgraduates. In order to observe the influence of language environment on English writing, they divided 94 students into three groups. One group is a group of 31 non-English majors who came to the United States to study for graduate degree. The other two groups are studying for postgraduate in Chinese universities. In order to understand the impact of language environment on students' English writing perception and performance, they adopted 80 self-designed questionnaires and two writing tests (one is the writing task, the other is the argumentative writing task). The results show that compared with the domestic group, the ESL language environment has a significant impact on the perception and performance of overseas students' English writing. Compared with the other two groups, the international student group is obviously more able to write letters in English. Statistics show that international students also perform better in argumentative writing than non-English majors, although they do not exceed English majors.

Hwang and Lee (2017) aim to develop and validate an English Writing Strategy Scale (EWSI), which measures English writing strategy in college. In order to achieve this goal, their analysis mainly focused on the structure and the response validity, and at the same time adopted a mixed method, like statistical technology, qualitative study, and think-aloud negotiation analysis. They constructed a questionnaire based on the investigation and analysis of English writing experiences of 18 college students and postgraduates and conducted it to 271 Korean students who use English as a foreign language. After exploratory factor analysis of participants' responses, it was found that there were eight factors, including metacognition, memory, cognition, mother tongue use, review, second language use, social strategy and compensatory strategy, each of which showed a high degree of internal consistency. The analysis of voice thinking protocol involving four students identified three main types of questions—writing context, writing task and phrasing questions—which may make respondents uncertain about how to answer, thus affecting the validity and reliability of the questionnaire. The study puts forward possible solutions to these problems, and puts forward suggestions on the practical use of EWSI to minimize the adverse effects of these error sources in the investigation management.

Naghdipour (2016) investigated the teaching of English writing at different educational levels in Iran and the main factors affecting English writing. The data collected from semi-structured interviews and classroom observations between teachers and students shows that although students need to improve their English writing skills, their writing skills are not satisfactory, which is mainly due to the lack of English writing courses and teaching methods. In this context, exploring the dynamics of English writing can provide some enlightenment for similar English writing contexts. In this context, the role of writing as a means to enrich the personal and future professional life of a new generation of students and language learners has not been recognized.

Lee (2016) explored the learner's behavior, strategy and contribution to language learning in teacher-led writing through various qualitative data sources such as the recording of teacher-learner interviews and dialogues. More importantly, it reveals the relationship between self-perception and learning behavior through learning strategies. Nine native and non-native English writing instructors and 23 second language learners from different disciplines participated in the study. Three types of second language learners and 11 learning strategies were identified and analyzed according to the dialogue between data and transcription. The analysis shows that these strategies reflect the learners' learning behavior and their readiness to participate actively in learning to different degrees. learners obtain the language input of the tutor through some active behaviors, indicate their problems, and establish a harmonious relationship with the tutor to complete the learning task. The research also discussed the significance of teaching and future research.

Kaufhold (2015) believes that the writing of graduate thesis in the field of social science is increasingly challenging the traditional model in the field of natural science. In addition, graduate students majoring in second language usually bring their previous academic writing experience, which affects their writing development. This paper uses a case study to investigate how master's degree students in Europe use their previous academic writing experience when they finish their papers in British universities. The detailed analysis of three cases shows that students' initial understanding of academic English conventions as autonomous rules increasingly depends on their subject knowledge and the epistemological method of the thesis. The research results further emphasize that the way students use their previous academic English experience is related to their goals. Based on their experience, students can challenge and maintain actively the formal practice of academic English.

Wilcox and Jeffery (2015) investigated the writing experience of young English learners (ELLs) in English language art, social research, science and mathematics classroom. Based on the writing concept of social constructivism, writing emphasizes the relationship between individual initiative, participation and subject discourse. The research uses the micro-level discourse analysis method to analyze the interviews of 26 English teachers in different schools and core disciplines with different writing priorities. The analysis shows that even if students think that goal-based writing tasks are challenging, they usually hold a positive attitude. However, they hold a negative attitude towards writing tasks that are provided with source materials from the literature.

This section mainly focuses on the literature on foreign English writing in the past decade. It is found that the researchers' study content on English writing is relatively scattered. The research focuses on the following aspects: providing empirical basis for future English writing research, self-made questionnaires, etc. In addition, many researchers have also focused on the study of students' English writing from different language backgrounds. The main research contents include: investigating the teaching of English writing at different levels of education and the main factors affecting English writing factor, exploring the effects of language environment on students' perception and performance of English writing, and studying the English writing skills of children who participate in immersion teaching. At the same time, research on the combination of corpus and English writing is also under way. Chen et al. (2019) proposed that corpus be widely used in language learning and the creation of teaching materials. The research content of other aspects is less found in this study, which is the limitation of foreign research on English writing in recent years.

2.2.3 Error Analysis and Second Language Writing

As we have previously mentioned, error analysis is closely related to many branches of SLA. Meanwhile, it is also related to some other skills in English learning. Some scholars (Honrado & Biray, 2022; Kafifah & Aini, 2019; Liu & Tian, 2021; Zheng & Park, 2013) did the research between error analysis and English spoken English while some others (Corder, 1975; Lan, 2019; Lennon, 2008; Paspita, 2019; Yan & Kang, 2021) pay attention to the correlation between error analysis and interlanguage, or error analysis and English writing. However, most error analysis research focused on the L2 writing. Scholars in China and abroad took different experiments to analyze errors in students' compositions.

Mubarok (2022) conducted an experiment to analyze the grammatical errors in students' writing based on the theory of EA. Focusing on one aspect of errors can dig deeper the causes of such errors. The paper also provides lots of examples towards these errors and its correction, which can give a concrete explanation of each type of error and help teachers or educators to be aware of such errors. The key part in this study is the exploration for the causes behind those errors, because only teachers are conscious of the reasons, they can figure out the targeted implications to such problems.

Monica and Elena (2015) conducted an experiment in Spanish students of 1st and 2nd year students in ESL compositions. The study examined the errors in four categories, spelling, vocabulary, grammar-syntax and punctuation. The results show that the spelling is the most frequent errors students made, which is consistent with the results of this book (Detailed discussion in section 5.1). Then the following errors are the incorrect use of commas, the use of prepositions, the articles, the number of nouns, subject-verb agreement, the use of adverbs, word order and the use of verb senses. This paper compared the compositions in two grades, which can provide the examples in students' different development stages. Besides, this paper can alert teachers be aware of the most typical errors and assist them to master concepts in English.

In Chinese context, lots of researchers (Guo & Ou'yang, 2010; He, 2009; Jia & Qiao, 2014; Jiang & Xie, 2007; Li, 2005; Liu, 2008; Zhan, 2015) studied error analysis from the perspective of college English writing. They all claimed that error analysis was quite important to correct students' writing errors and implicate the teaching methods in writing. Jiang and Wang (2008) conducted an experiment with a theoretical framework of error analysis to analyze the argumentative compositions of English majors. The research method is tracing way, which means they trace the errors committed by the same group of students in three different grades. This methodology is quite different with many other previous studies because previous articles focus on the synchronic research rather than diachronic research. This kind of research can easily see the change and improvement of the participants. After statistical collection, comparing and analyzing, it can investigate what kind of errors can decrease with their grading or what kind of errors are still existing, or even increasing. The conclusion indicates that lexical errors are the most percentage of errors, especially in the aspect of spelling. The paper pointed out the ignorance of spelling is the key to these errors, which probably means college students and teachers don't regard the spelling as the critical part when they compose and teach writing. This conclusion is consist of with the result in this dissertation. This paper also lacks of a solid foundation in literature, and all the literature are all from Chinese scholar, which will decrease the authority of the review and provide weak theoretical framework for the research.

Guo and Ou'yang (2010) studied English majors' compositions with the guidance of error analysis in Chinese writing context. The study analyzed the error types of students' compositions, the frequencies of writing errors and the implications for that. The teaching experiment is conducted with qualitative and qualitative study, which can explore the research topic deeper. The experiment collects students' compositions with a pre-test and post-test, through which the effect of strategies guided by error analysis can be revealed. Through the results it can be seen that the effect of strategies is not obvious, which probably attributes to the short time of teaching experiment. The paper provides a teaching experiment to investigate writing errors and the strategies to lessen those errors, but the literature part is quite weak to shed a theoretical framework for the later research. The implication part is very useful for contemporary English teaching.

Another scholar (He, 2019) examined lexical errors of Chinese non-English majors, but with corpus as the method to get the data. The research only focuses on one aspect of English language, which can examine fully and deeper on writing errors. On the other hand, the research is demonstrated with quantitative and qualitative analysis of the data, which can provide comparatively more angles to investigate writing errors and its causes. In the quantitative research, this study adopted ANOVA to compare the differences of lexical errors in CET – 4 and CET – 6 while the Spearsman is employed to investigate the Correlation of composition score and each kind of error. With the data results, the differences and the correlations can be detected clearly. However, in the qualitative method, the paper did not provide concrete description of the research. Furthermore, the participants were divided into high score group and low score group, which also can examine the differences committing lexical errors between different writing proficiency groups. Even though the paper is concluded with concrete data to answer the questions, the theoretical framework seems not solid because the author only introduces the recent research paper in China and abroad.

Second language writing is recognized as a cognitive process which involves lots of factors and elements. Some elements are related to linguistic factors, such as interlanguage, while some others relating to non-linguistic factors, such as their writing attitudes, motivation, etc. Understanding the theoretical and empirical connections among them provides the global vision in the language learning landscape. The importance of English writing in the lives of students and teachers has been raised substantially in non-English speaking countries over the last two decades. Chinese university students spare no efforts to improve their writing skills before and during entering universities, which pose challenges not for the theories of linguistic factors but for the theories of non-linguistic factors and the development of writing competence. Meanwhile, such requirement also pose challenges to university policy makers in implementing the effective methods and practice in English teaching and learning. Wang and Wen (2002) emphasized that when composing in a second language (L2), writers have two languages (L1 and L2), and they can either switch between them or use both of them. However, some researchers argue that due to the lack of attention to the differences between these two languages, and errors might happen because of a limited understanding of the characteristics of L2 writing.

Meanwhile, abundant time and energy was spared in acquiring English language but with limited expected effect. There is a phenomenon in Chinese L2 learners, which is, even though English learners has acquired the basic grammar and vocabulary, it seems still a little difficult for them to write the qualified composition. On the one hand, they can combine the sentences but neglecting the content, cohesion and the logic among sentences or even paragraphs. On the other hand, learners accomplish their compositions through utilizing grammar and vocabulary, even with some complicated sentences. The lack of logic in the sentences makes it hard to understand and accept.

Corder (1971) pointed out that making errors or mistakes are inevitable in studying whichever stage it is. Therefore, making errors is the necessary process of studying, the point is that how to get the lessons from these errors. Corder claimed that the process of making errors can get clear of the difficulties in study and make the appropriate studying plan and objectives. Secondly, through the analysis of error content, learners can know the direction to improve, thus, they can have the deep understanding about the target language. In conclusion, learning from analysis of error can form the learning habit of the learners, which might lay a foundation in the future.

Mubarok and Budiono (2022) conducted an experiment to analyze the grammatical errors in students' writing based on the theory of EA. Focusing on one aspect of errors can dig deeper into the causes of such errors. The paper also provides lots of examples of these errors and their correction, which can give a concrete explanation of each type of error and help teachers or educators to be aware of such errors. The crucial part in this study is the exploration of the causes behind those errors, because only teachers are conscious of the reasons, they can figure out the targeted implications of such problems.

2.3 Interlanguage

Interlanguage was established as learners' independent system of the language, which is neither the native language nor the second language, but a continuum or approximation from one extreme of his native language to the other of the second language.

The learners' language produced somewhere in-between the native and target language was termed "interlanguage" by Selinker in 1969. This theory originated from a conception of "contrastive analysis". Lado (1957) claimed that a careful analysis of learners' errors shows patterns of similarities between both learners' target language and mother tongue. Stetsenko (2010) claims that defining knowledge as "the ways through which we know the world, including concepts, conceptual understanding, and thinking" (p. 69) is a rather challenging task. This kind of knowledge that underlies a learner's ability to understand the rules and structures of a foreign language, and judge the grammar of any sentences is known as linguistic knowledge. learner's second language knowledge was first said to be only influenced by their native language. Lots of researchers have demonstrated their points of view through their findings. Richards (1974) raised a different point of view from Lado's (1957) contrastive analysis by providing a variety of errors observed in learners' language, which could not have resulted from a native language transfer, such as a "faulty generalization" or an "incomplete application of rules" (p. 174).

2.3.1 Interlanguage Hypothesis

Selinker (1969) initially raised the concept of interlanguage to refer to Isreali students' attempts of producing English, which says, "An Interlanguage may be linguistically described using as data the observable output resulting from a speaker's attempt to produce a foreign norm, i.e., both his 'errors' and 'non-errors'. It is assumed that such behavior is highly structured. In comprehensive language transfer work, it seems that recognition of the existence of an interlanguage cannot be avoided and that it must be dealt with as a system, not as an isolated collection of errors" (p. 117).

Selinker (1974) claimed that interlanguage is defined as a "separate linguistic system" (p. 35). A linguistic system is "a grammar, which underlies the use of language, including comprehension and production." Native-speaker grammars are constrained by built-in universal linguistic principles, known as "Universal Grammar" (Chomsky, 1965), and "non-native grammars are referred to as interlanguage grammars" (White, 2003. p. 1 emphasis in original).

Selinker's (1972) interlanguage hypothesis suggests that the language produced by foreign or second language learners is "an independent interim linguistic system" with its own set of rules. The underlying grammar not only includes the features of the learners' native language and also the language to be learned, but also contains the elements which probably occur in interlanguage (Selinker, 1972), whose origin is neither the native nor the target language (Gass & Selinker, 2008).

In addition to the concept of interlanguage, the learner language is also called "approximative system" (Nemser, 1974) or "transitional competence" (Corder, 1967). However, Corder (1981) argued that each of these alternatives "draws attention to different aspects of the phenomenon" (pp. 66-67). For example, Nemser's (1974) approximate system is directional in the sense that the learner approximates the target language in stages that are separate and distinct. Corder (1981) borrows the notion of competence from Chomsky (1965) to put stress on the idea that language knowledge is "constantly developing" (Corder, 1981, p. 67). The notion of transitional competence represents what is required by the learners, that is "the underlying knowledge of the language to date" (Corder, 1981, p. 10). Neither Corder's transitional hypothesis nor Nemser's approximate system hypothesis considers the existence of fossilized linguistic features (Selinker, 1992, p. 225). The term fossilization is also understood as an incomplete or faulty language learning process, "a permanent cessation of ... learning before the learner attains the target norms at all levels of linguistic structure" (Selinker & Lamendella, 1981, p. 217). Selinker (1972) suggests that IL, as the transitional process between L1 and L2, is observable in a learner's language and can be explored. He considers IL as "a dialect whose rules share characteristics of two social dialects of languages, whether these languages themselves share rules or not" (Selinker, 1972 cited in Corder, 1981, p. 17). According to the above statement, the notion of IL is illustrated in Figure 2 – 1.

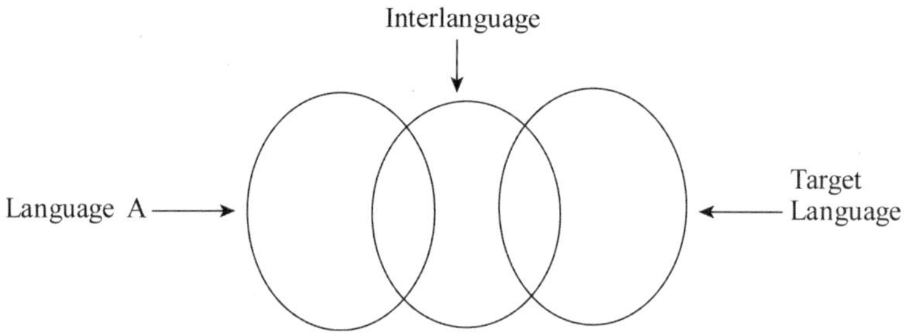

Figure 2 – 1 The Notion of the IL

Note: adopted from Corder, 1981. In this figure, Language A represents the learner's L1.

Corder (1981) states that the learner's language can be considered as a dialect in the linguistic sense, meaning that the two languages sharing some grammar rules can become dialects. Based on this claim, he states that language A and B as illustrated in Figure 2 – 2 are in a dialect relation leading to IL.

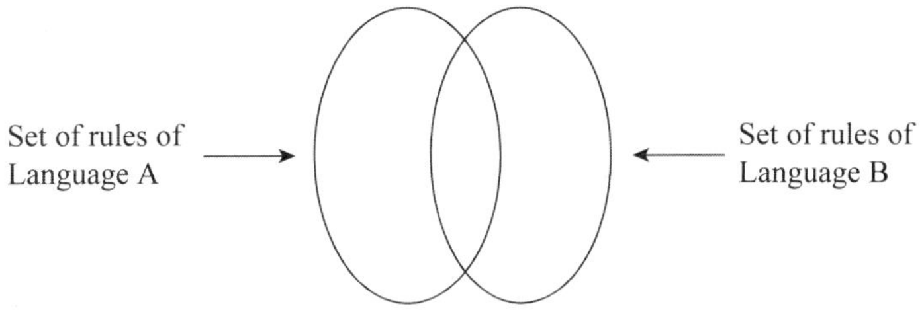

Figure 2 – 2 The Notion of Dialect Relation

Note: adopted from Corder, 1981.

Besides the hypothesis of Selinker, another theoretical assumption of IL theory is that when an FL/L2 learner is trying to communicate in the TL, a new language system different from the NL and the TL will be used. Selinker (1974) states that IL can be "a separate linguistic system based on the observable output which results from learners' attempted production of a TL norm" (p. 35). He also stated that whenever an L2/FL learner attempts to create a sentence, he or she activates "the latent psychological structures". Some other assumptions given by Mitchell and Myles (1998) and Larsen-Freeman (2003) are summarized as follows:

(1) SLA is a "process of increasing conformity to a uniform TL" (590 – 591).

(2) L2 learning is a gradual development from MT toward the TL.

(3) A system of specific rules which is neither the system of NL or MT nor the system of FL or TL can be developed by the learner at every stage of the language learning process.

(4) L2 learners' errors are natural.

(5) Many language learners do not achieve TL competence.

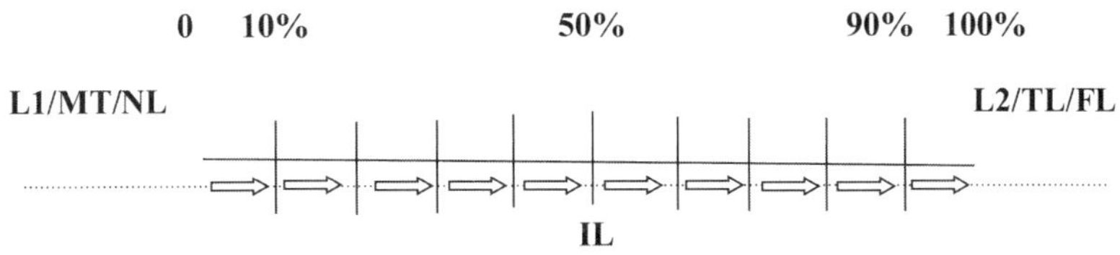

Figure 2 – 3 The IL Continuum

Note: adopted from Tanvir Shameem, 1992.

2.3.2 Interlingual Transfer

According to the different types of reasons which caused the errors in the target language, the components of interlanguage mainly consist of two kinds of transfer, interlingual transfer and intralingual transfer (also called development transfer) (Richard, 1974). These two types of transfer focus on the different aspects of interlanguage.

Richards (1971) defined interlingual transfer of errors as the errors that are caused by the interference of the native language. These errors result from the learners' application of their native language elements in their performances of the target language. When acquiring a new language, people would like to draw a connection between what they have known and what they haven't consciously or unconsciously. learners carry over the existing knowledge of their native language to the performance of the target language (Ellis, 1997). For most cases, it is inevitable to learn a foreign language solely without depending on some linguistic features of the language which has already been acquired. At any rate, interference can occur in various linguistic components, including phonology, morphology, grammar, syntax, semantics, and lexis (Ellis, 1997). Furthermore, the influence presents the differences and similarities between the native language and the target language. The bigger the differences between both languages, the stronger their influences (Odlin, 1989). Krashen (1981) also mentioned that when the linguistic principles of a native language are very different from that of the target language, it makes the learners challenging to comprehend, and then they would like to apply the rules and structures of the native language in their learning process.

According to Allen and Corder (1974), interlingual errors are caused by interlingual interference. Touchie (1986) suggested that interlingual errors are caused mainly by mother tongue interference. Al-Khresheh (2010) suggested that interlingual errors are committed by a literal translation. From the following:

(1) Transfer error: error caused by interference from the mother tongue. The learner who has not known the rules of the target language will use the same rules in his native language.

(2) Mother tongue interference: errors are produced in the learners' attempt to discover the target language's structure rather than transferring models of their first language.

(3) Literal translation: errors happen when a student translates his first language sentence into the target language word by word.

2.3.3 Intralingual Transfer

Richard (1974) states that intralingual interference refers to items that learners produce, and it reflects not the structure of the mother tongue but generalization based on the partial exposure of the target language. Brown (1980) stated that "the early stages of language learning are featured with a predominance of interlingual transfer, but once the learners have begun to obtain the parts of the new system", "more and more transfer generalization within the target language will be manifested" (p. 126).

Richard (1974) classifies intralingual errors into four categories, including over generalization, ignorance of rule restrictions, incomplete application of the rules, and false concept hypothesized or semantic errors.

(1) Overgeneralization: this phenomenon will happen when a learner creates a deviant structure based on his experience of other structures in the target language. According to Richards (1974), "overgeneralization means learners often deduce their own rules from what they have learned before". It also refers to a process.

(2) Ignorance of rule restriction: James (1998) stated that "ignorance is specific in the sense that one is normally said to be ignorant of structure; second language learner does not obey the structure of the target language. In this type of error, the learners fail to observe the restrictions of existing structures" (p. 63).

(3) Incomplete application of the rules: this error may occur when the learner fails to apply the rules entirely due to the stimulus sentence.

(4) False concept hypothesized: learners' faulty understanding of distinctions of target language items leads to false conceptualization. learners' faulty understanding of distinctions of target language items leads to false concept hypothesized.

2.3.4 Applications to Teaching

One important implication of the Interlanguage hypothesis is the fact that errors can be accepted as inevitable. Such attitude actually shows the results in the work of researchers in teaching second language, meanwhile, the results also benefit the language teaching profession. For example, Burt and Kisparsky (1972/1974) wrote the paper *The Gooficon-A Repair Manual for English and Global and Local Mistakes*, which deals comprehensively with error analysis in ESL class room. The authors report that errors within a constituent or a clause affect the comprehension of a sentence far less than errors which are made in a major constituent or across clause boundaries. In other words, errors appearing in pluralization and tense and the omission of function words, such as articles, prepositions and auxiliaries, are less important to the comprehensibility of a sentence than errors in word order or the choice and position of appropriate connectors (Burt & Kisparsky, 1972). For instance, the major signal used in English to express relations among major constituents is word order. In English expression, we expect to see a subject followed by a verb then an object, that is, SVO word order. After that, we can add various adverbial phrases to the main structure. One of the most various ways in which the intended relations in a sentence can be confused is the reversed order of subject and object. For example, Burt and Kiparsky cite the following examples from their data:

(1) *English language use much people.*

Correcting each constituent locally gives:

(2) *The English language uses many people.*

But this improvement is negligible compared with the global correction of word order:

(3) *Much people use English language.*

Since teachers do not have enough time to deal with all the errors committed by their students, the developing stage developed by Burt and Kiparsky serves as a guide to those errors, and students spent most of time. Teachers should provide students with the greatest possible mileage in their efforts to communicate in the TL. The authors' emphasis on rule acquisition rather than on habit formation is an essential part because the audio-lingual method is the opposite of the "Cognitive code" approach to learning.

Holley and King (1974) also suggest some effective ways to deal with errors. Within the interlanguage framework, the two authors present a classroom method to teach German, which can incorporate ideas that are derived from research. They proposed that error should be seen as a necessary feature of experimentation with the language. However, we should bear in mind that the demands for grammatical accuracy, especially at the early stages of SL learning, are contradictory to the free use of the TL. This contradictory can be solved by placing stringent conditions on the kind of correction and the situations under which correction is done, particularly during free conversation. Some correctable errors are common to the group and may include material being currently taught. Errors committed during free conversation without blocking communication should be noted by the teacher and dealt with in the latter lessons, which means activities and drills in dealing with the problems should be presented for extensive practice.

In the next part, I will describe briefly the analysis types for teachers in the high school to do in the classroom. Firstly, not every drill activity, such as multiple-choice response, can give us much information about any creative use of the TL. Meanwhile, there is a difference between choosing from alternatives strictly limited and choosing from several alternatives which have been existing in one's mind during a meaningful exchange. Therefore, the language adopted in this analysis should be the production in a communication or in a communication-like situation. But in real communication, the participants can rarely predict the question and answers that will appear.

The following steps are the process conducted in the classroom of analyzing errors. First, record a conversation or use written material in which the students are concentrating more on message than on the form. Second, the small group can be organized to discuss general topics. Give directions to the participants to share all the information they know. Third, free compositions can be collected to build a corpus for analysis of written forms. Fourth, a language sample should be large enough, which probably means that, each student must provide more than one instance of a particular error, or enough students must be involved to produce one occurrence of an error. Lastly, once the data have been collected, all the information should be compiled. With a frequency count, it should try to discover the structures that can produce the greatest number of errors, the specific errors which occur most frequently, and the structures that are used correctly most frequently.

With the above methods, some incorrect assumptions that are shared by a relatively large number of students can be detected. Consequently, techniques should be developed or explored to help in the form of correct assumptions. Areas where correct hypotheses are evident should be focused on for praise and encouragement.

Teachers could try experimenting with some groups on some expected difficulties or needs, that is, their "build-in syllabus", and compare their progress with other groups following the traditional teacher-directed syllabus of the course book. The results might indicate a shift of emphasis, that is, from dependent on the book to students' perceived needs in the course.

The materials discussed above provide some useful techniques for dealing with errors, but they do not offer a set of dogmatic principles that will answer all the questions. The evaluation of the relevance of a theory must certainly include a consideration of its application to the form of instructional material. The resources adopted in the experiment in the part of case study are good examples of the kind of practical results of error analysis and interlanguage, which are easy to reach for second language teacher.

Table 2 – 1 Examples in Interlingual and Intralingual Transfer

Types	Causes of Writing Errors	Brief Explanations	Examples	Correct Forms
Interlingual Transfer	L1 interference	Caused by the learner's first language.	The teacher want to tell us there have a problem.	The teacher wants to tell us (that) there is a problem.
Intralingual Transfer	Overgenerali-zation	Caused by mixing two or more different structures in target language based on the learners' knowledge.	He runs fastly.	He runs fast.
	Ignorance of rule restriction	Caused by ignoring the rule restrictions of existing structures.	The man whom I saw him yesterday.	The man whom I saw yesterday.
	Incomplete application of rules	Caused by applying a rule in the context of a sentence, but the rule is not complete.	He goes to school?	Does he go to school?
	False concepts hypothesized modal verb	Caused by the faulty rule learning at various levels. learners cannot differentiate between go and come, bring and take, too and very, etc.	You can bring away this book. Thank you too much.	You can take away this book. Thank you very much.

2.4 Error Correction

Error correction is often regarded as the most exhausting and time-consuming part of teachers' work (Ferris, 2002; Mantello, 1997). Hairston (1986) warned that writing teachers should not be "composition slaves" (p. 117). Unfortunately, his advice does not seem to have been fully taken. The fact is that many teachers are still "slaving" over students' writing. Therefore, error correction costs a large proportion of their time.

In the previous studies, most research explores this topic, which has aroused lots of controversies. Truscott (1996) and Ferris (1997, 2002) also hold different opinion on whether teachers should correct errors in students' writing. Although some research provide evidence that error correction can help writing accuracy in students' writing, some contrary evidence also supplies the doubt on the effectiveness of error correction (Hillocks, 1986; Knoblauch & Brannon, 1981). Even though there is a controversial issue on error correction, two main factors are clear. Firstly, writing teachers believe that feedback on students' errors is very crucial as an English teacher (Ferris, 1995a). Secondly, students expect much to receive teachers' feedback on their writing and believe they can benefit from it (Leki, 1991; Radecki & Swales, 1988). They appreciate their teachers have pointed out their grammar problems.

One of the purposes of doing EA is to identify the principles that should be followed in the process of effective error correction (EC). The relationship between EC and EA is that the principled EC is applied EA. Regarding this issue, people's ideas about what kinds of errors should be corrected are not always clear. In the act of attempting to correct errors, several more unrelated mistakes get in. The act of correction fails to clarify. In this chapter, we will first try to clarify what is meant by correction, and then answer the question on whether and why it is desirable. The above activities are very meaningful for teachers and educators in Chinese teaching context.

2.4.1 What is "Correction"?

From the perspective of pragmatics of the speech act, the process of correction is complex. It is an obvious reactive second move of an adjacency pair to a first speaker's or writer's utterance by someone who has made the judgment. All or part of the speaker's utterance is wrong linguistically or factually. EA confines its scope to linguistic aspect of course, while the correction is form-focused rather than a reaction to true value.

Correcting is a metalinguistic act, since it is a comment on language. Self-correction of a slip can be achieved without the benefit of feedback from another person, and as we have been suggesting, feedback can be auto-generated. Self-correction is an interesting phenomenon because for some unknown reasons, it seems quite easy to spot other peoples' errors than our own. Lots of students have the same feeling. According to James (2013), "the reason is probably that self-editing a text one has composed oneself calls for an ability to clear one's mind of one's intended meaning at the time of writing and interpret one's own text with just the information actually available in the words."

However, the degree of correction is hard to grasp, which means whether a "correction" that is in fact no more correct or even less "correct" than the original utterance. Regarding Chinese teaching context, English teachers usually comment their students' writing mainly in grammatical aspects which is also followed by the cohesion and fluency of the writing. The second question is whether the corrected utterance follows the incorrect one that was intended counts as a correction. Such corrections could be done by either the first speaker or the second, in which case we could expect a quite satisfactory self-correction.

According to James (2013), the term "correction" has been used in three senses:

(1) The first function of "correction" is to inform the learners that there is an error, which can leave them to discover it and repair it themselves. This kind of intervention is called feedback, which probably refers to the results given by the corrector, telling them whether their utterance or understanding is right or wrong.

(2) The second aspect of "correction" is to provide the treatment or information that leads to the revision and correction of the specific instance of error. It also indicates the present attempt is wrong, while the corrector can specify how and where to suggest an alternative or give a hint.

(3) The third aspect of "correction" is to provide learners with information that allows them to revise or reject the wrong rule. With the rule, they can operate when they produce the wrong token. The result will induce learners to revise their mental representation of the rule, so that this error type does not recur.

One thing should be noticed that error-token and error-type correction are quite different. According to Prabhu (1987), the distinction between them is very crucial because he uses it to distinguish incidental from systematic correction. The former is confined to particular "tokens", for example, the error itself is corrected, but no generalization to this type of error can be summarized and represented. Hammerly

(1991) also has made the same distinction regarding the "surface" and "deep" correction of errors. The "surface" correction just represents editing but does not point out the source of the problem. However, "deep" correction addresses the source of the problem, because it involves the explanation of the reason why some bit of language is the way it is, so it prompts learners to "reorganize their cognitive structures" (Hammerly, 1991: p. 93).

The other that issue should be addressed is that we should make a distinction between feedback, correction and remediation, because it parallels other distinctions in interesting ways. The first thing we have referred to frequently in this book is that the slip versus mistake versus error trichotomy. Corder (1981) talked about mistakes (although I suggest he had slips in mind), "We are normally immediately aware of them when they occur and can correct them with more or less complete assurance" (1981: p. 10). The above quotation means that slips can be corrected by the learners themselves without benefit of feedback from another person. But feedback is the other situation. The feedback comes from one's intuitions: one just feels that what one has said or written is wrong. The mistakes, conversely, are self-correctable only with the benefit of feedback, that is, the comment persons have to tell the learners that they are wrong, but no more. It is not necessary to specify in what respect. In such cases, it should inform the learners that the present form is wrong. Giving feedback will usually be enough to cause the learners to reject their current hypothesis.

The conceptions of feedback and correction are discussed broadly in the contemporary L1 – acquisition and linguistics literature (Chomsky, 1986; Cook, 1988: p. 60; Radford, 1988: p. 44) with the proper evidence. learners can improve their ability in correction through receiving from the information of knowers or the "evidence" about the target language and also with their own attempts to produce it. This evidence comes in four forms: positive or negative, direct or indirect. Positive evidence informs you which forms are used in the target language, while the negative evidence tells you which are not. These two kinds of evidence can be got incidentally, for example, you notice data of what the speakers of a language do and don't say or write. One thing should be noticed is that what they do and don't understand also provides indirect evidence for learners.

2.4.2 Pros and Cons towards Correction

The question whether or not to correct the errors is not as simple as it seems. Two key questions should be figured out before answering them. The first is whether prevention of error is better than cure, while the second question is whether the explicit formal instruction or so-called teaching is effective. How should writing teachers mark errors? Much attention to errors may prove frustrating for students and exhausting for teachers. When teachers comment on students' writing errors comprehensively, they have the responsibility of correcting errors, which makes students reliant on teachers. However, when teachers focus on the errors of students' writing, there is less time to provide feedback on other more important aspects, such as content and coherence. It has also been found that L2 writing teachers tend to pay more attention to formal correctness than to the discourse level of writing (Zamel, 1985). Such action may lead students to believe that accuracy is more important than the transmission of meaning, overall organization, and content development (Hedgcock & Lefkowitz, 1996). If the feedback just focuses on the linguistic aspect, it will discourage writers and prevent them from making needed discourse-level changes, especially for L2 learners. Unlikely, teachers' error feedback proves that it can encourage weak students' motivation in writing. However, there is an argument that selective error correction also pays attention to specific error patterns rather than to all errors. Definitely, any effective feedback should consider carefully student's reaction. In this regard, treating errors selectively is a better option than comprehensive error correction.

Research has found that correcting errors does not necessarily help students avoid making mistakes, whether these errors are treated selectively or comprehensively (Leki, 1991; Takala, 1984). One issue in correction research is to investigate the factors responsible for the effectiveness of error correction. It should be noted that the feedback on intermediate drafts of students' writing is more effective to facilitate their writing development than comments on final drafts (Ferris, 1995a). Error correction is likely more effective if students are required to revise their writing based on their teachers' feedback, otherwise, students would not take it seriously.

Nowadays, research on error correction has focused on teachers, for example, the strategies they use in providing error feedback (Ferris & Robert, 2001) and whether grammar teaching in class helps students improve their writing (Ferris, 1995b; Lalande, 1982). But less research has been done to investigate the beliefs and attitudes of the students on error feedback. Some studies (Cohen, 1987; Ferris, 1995c; Ferris et al., 1997; Leki, 1991; Redecki & Swales, 1998) investigate student preferences about reactions and coping strategies for teacher feedback. The results of these research indicate that students wish teachers correct errors in their writing. For example, in Leki's study, it was found that most ESL students in the study wished their teachers to correct errors for them. Hedgcock and Lefkowitz found that EFL college students prefer teachers' comments and corrections on grammatical, lexical, and mechanical features more than those on content and style. Both EFL and ESL students expressed a moderate preference for the use of correction symbols, and both kinds of students don't like their teachers using the red pen. In Saito's (1994) study, most ESL students considered teacher feedback most useful "when it focused precisely on grammatical errors" (p. 65). Similarly, the other researcher Olajedo (1993) found that students regarded error correction as the primary responsibility of their teachers.

Prevent the occurrence of errors, because they think prevention is better than cure. Our focus should be on teaching, not correcting (James, 2013). George (1972) makes a strong case and support for this idea with practical guidelines for preventing errors. However, he suggests that turning a blind eye to errors prevents them for the learners will be less inclined to focus on them if they are ignored. The second method is to ensure the input, that is, the teacher should make sure that newly-taught knowledge is repeated a lot, and different from other similar TL forms, while it might compete with the item being taught by association. Another method to teach calls for a request to reduce the syllabus, that is, to teach a "little language". In a sense, it refers to the mini-version of the native speakers' target language.

The main argument supporting the idea of prevention was that if erroneous forms are learnt, these will first have to be unlearnt before the correct ones can be learnt (James, 2013). Gatbonton (1983) shows that right and wrong forms can coexist side by side in interlanguage that is described as variability. This item is not the case that the learners use either the right or the wrong form. At the same time, one is exclusive of the other. It is more than a case to help the learners to retain the right while it can reject the co-occurring wrong form.

Ehri, Gibbs and Underwood (1988) set up a series of learning experiments. In these learning experiments the groups of ELI children and adults were required to "invent" spellings before being given a chance to study the correct spellings, while a matched control group was allowed to study correct spellings before being tested. A comparison of the test results showed that "making spelling errors neither hindered nor helped subjects learn correct spellings" (Ehri et al., 1988: p. 240). From this experiment, it can be concluded that the prevention is not better than cure. However, cure is not necessarily better than prevention. But when prevention does not work, or is not attempted, and errors have happened, then there must be the cure in the form of correction. The other result concluded from this experiment is that delaying correction of misspelling words allows these "inventions" to take a foothold in the learners' minds. One idea about error mentioned in this paper is noteworthy, that is, learners resorted to misspelling "only when they could not remember correct spellings" (Ehri et al., 1988: p. 244). The suggestion that we learn by making errors is the basis for the second study. Tomasello and Herron (1988, 1989) reported the idea in their two papers that the idea is explored if we were to induce error-making by leading learners astray or "up the garden path" into committing errors, we would be doing them a favour. These two papers report the experiments in which L1 English learners were encouraged to make certain common types of French FL error. In such situation, the errors could be "systematically" corrected by the teacher who can supply the correct form immediately after hearing the error. Actually, the experimental condition was contrasted with a control condition which involved the teacher trying to forestall the students' error-making. The experiments were conducted, among which, the first one involving intralingual overgeneralization errors within French, while the second one involving L1 transfer (interlingual overgeneralization) errors into the L2 French.

For some years, it seemed very fashionable to reject grammar teaching. It is also called Explicit Formal Instruction (EFI). It was regarded as being the best ineffectual and at worst an obstacle to L2 learning (Krashen, 1982; Prabhu, 1987). In fact, most of the researches on the effectiveness of instruction makes reference to the relative error-making in learners' production. Researchers like Dulay, Burt and Krashen (1982) subscribe to the universal order of acquisition theory. They claimed that teacher cannot alter the order of acquisition of TL items, and so is a waste of effort. However, Pavesi's (1986) research has shown that even though the order of acquisition is not altered by teaching, the rate of learning is. Additionally, the learners who have been instructed demonstrate the higher ultimate achievement. These differences are surely desirable, and correction is part of teaching then correction is effective (James, 2013). The other scholar Pica (1984) compared the errors of learners who had or had not received instruction. The result showed that the taught learners likely produced the errors of redundancy, which is, they oversupply grammatical morphology. The other positive effect of correction is that it brings defossilization. Now fossilization is likely to happen when it is TL features. Unfortunately, erroneous forms fossilize too. Thus, the improvement would be blocked. According to Harley (1993: p. 245), "a code-focused L2 instruction" must imply correction of error that is called defossilization. He emphasizes the importance of teaching that addresses seriously the "barrier-breaking principle". Magnan (1979) describes her Focus Approach to FL teaching. This is an approach that is closely linked correction with "receptive" noticing. And finally, Ellis (1995a) has suggested that it is wrong to associate grammar teaching exclusively with the improvement of active production in the L2. He advocates the idea of "interpretation-based grammar teaching". He backs his idea with the argument that in the first instance on the success recorded in receptive learning.

2.4.3 Rules and Principles in Error Correction

According to James (2013), there are some rules and principles during error correction, for example, correct effectively, correction should be sensitive, match correction to student preferences, two-stage correction, and noticing errors.

The first rule is to correct effectively, which means two things. The first is that using correction techniques can bring about improvements in accuracy and using efficient techniques can carry out the least effort by the teacher and register by the learners. Robb, Ross and Shortreed (1986) ever conducted a research to compare four types of feedback on the EL2 writing of 134 Japanese students. The four types were controlled with a scale of salience, which corresponds both to "explicit" (as in explicit formal instruction) and to "form-focus". The formal errors of Group A were corrected in their compositions but not the errors of fact or content: this was the most "salient" feedback. Group B received coded feedback that indicated what needed to be corrected but not how. Group C was marked with uncoded feedback, that is, a marker pen indicated where there was an error but without any indication of its nature. Group D had "marginal" feedback that shows only how many errors there were on any line, but indicating neither their precise location nor their nature. The effects of these four types of feedback on the students' writing over a two-year treatment period were not differentiated by their relative "salience". It must be concluded that making feedback more overt, direct, salient, or explicit is not worth the effort and "time may be more profitably spent responding to more important aspects of student writing" (Robb et al., 1986: p. 91). However, this statement is too general, and the relative effectiveness of different feedback types will depend on individual differences and the learners' level of attainment in the FL. This means correction must be subject-sensitive.

The second rule to correct errors is that the correction should be sensitive. Sensitive in this aspect means when correcting learners' errors, the correcter should pay attention to the situation of the learners, not causing embarrassment. Day, Chenoweth, Chun and Luppescu (1983) studied in their research that little correcting done by NS friends seems to be effective. Two kinds of correction dominate, one is focused correction and the other is conformation checks. Form this study, of all the 189 corrections, 125 were focused corrections. The following is an example of a focused correction:

Learner: *Then you say what* × *number it is.*

NS friend: *Then you say what* √ *letter it is.*

Regarding the confirmation check, the NS produces a corrected version of the learner's incorrect utterance with question (rising) intonation:

Learner: × *How do you do on weekends?*

NS friend: √ *What do you do on weekends?*

The above two examples on error corrections are form-focused, but the important point is that they don't embarrass the learner. These errors are treated as slips, indicating that the native speaker believe that the learner knows these forms but confuses momentarily. One crucial point should be noted is that correction should be "non-threatening" (James, 2013). Non-threatening correction means self-correction or any sort of correction that appears to be self-initiated. Wlaz (1982) concludes form his study that learners can self-correct between 50 percent and 90 percent of their own errors with given time and encouragement. Extending wait-time is advocated to spare to students, because for most students they need wait-time to the self-correction.

Another way for non-threatening correction can be achieved in class, and such correction should be aimed at the whole class rather than the individuals. When individuals can make an example of correction, it is likely that they will benefit less than other students in the class, who hear the correction only incidentally. As for the correction of spoken errors, the more sensitive the learner, the more gentle should be the correction. But the gentleness might cause a price, which means the relatively insensitive risk-taker is the better FL learner, because they can accept correction.

However, there is a common but unwarranted assumption that feedback on writing must be written and the correction for spoken errors should be oral form. It has been suggested that if one wishes to avoid oral feedback on oral error, one should resort to finger indications of error (Rixon, 1993). However, one can also give spoken feedback on written errors. Written feedback on written work is less traumatic (James, 2013), but many students ignore it anyway.

A fast-developing computer technology offers a further way to make correction less traumatic, that is, delivering it in a private context, not a social context, which is called the text editor. Nowadays, there are some standard software appendages on PCs, in the form of grammar-checkers, spell-checkers, and style-checks. In the part of case study, writing errors of college students in the experiment were mainly checked by the software Grammarly. Grammarly is a cloud-based writing assistant that reviews spelling, grammar, punctuation, clarity, engagement, and delivery mistakes (Grammarly). It uses AI to identify and search for an appropriate replacement for the mistakes it locates. It also allows users to customize their style, tone, and context-specific language (Lardinois, 2016). I adopted the premium version of the software, compared to the free one which paid attention only on spelling, grammar, punctuation and conciseness, this version could examine the compositions from the following aspects: clarity-focused sentence rewrites, tone adjustment, plagiarism detection, word choice, formality level, and fluency (https://www. grammarly. com/premium). With the assistance of this software, a precise assessment was expected to achieve. Some scholars (Granger & Meunier, 1994) assess these facilities according to ESL/EFL users' needs. They usually take text editors like *Correct Grammar* and *Grammatik* 5 as their primary choices. The limitation of such text editors is that they are designed to correct native speakers' errors, and the errors are very different. Those errors are often passed over by the editor. Sometimes, in the corpora of learner English, the grammar checkers ignore some details and simply detect only about half the errors committed. Therefore, the two scholars conclude that a good EFL text editor must be based on authentic learner errors, which is itself sufficient justification for anyone who does EA.

The third point that should be cleared out is that when given corrections, it must match correction to student preferences. Some study exists on students' preferences among the various feedback options on their writing. Leki (1991b) ever conducted an experiment to explore ESL students' preferences for different feedback forms in this modality. The result showed that, rightly or wrongly, these students expect their teachers to mark their errors in grammar, spelling, vocabulary and punctuation. Meanwhile, 70% of the total students expected all their errors to be corrected. Regarding the question on how they wanted to be corrected, they reported that they "wanted their teachers to show where the error was and to give a clue how to correct it" (1991b: p. 207). Students in this experiment claimed that they did not want the teacher to write in the correction, but preferred to solve the correction problem themselves, which means, they were not looking for easy way out, but expected to have to work in order to improve.

Another study on learners' preferences is from Hedgcock and Lefkowitz (1994), which examined any differences in preferred feedback between ESL and EFL writers simultaneously. The assumption is that composition is a form of language practice for EFL students, so they will expect or even welcome teachers' feedback on written accuracy. On the other hand, ESL writers regard writing as a means of communication, so they value most on the aspects of function and content of the language. Kaufmann (1993) investigated students' preferences for feedback on their spoken errors. A questionnaire was administered to teachers and students of EL2 in Puerto Rico and Turkey of descriptions and examples of 12 types of feedback on spoken errors ranging on a scale from explicit to implicit. Explicit correction refers to "those where the teacher directly informs the student that he has made an error" (1993: p. 2). Implicit correction took on forms such as accepting as in "Really? Did you make a deposit?". The two kinds of errors that have been investigated were grammar errors such as wrong tense, and pronunciation errors. One interesting finding is that teachers tended to give implicit corrections while students preferred to receive explicit ones. Another enquiring was conducted following the previous questionnaire to investigate how learners feel that non-teacher interlocutors (friends, colleagues, employers) should respond to their EL2 spoken errors. The above finding indicates it is acceptable for erroneous forms among friends, but not acceptable for teachers. Teachers usually like to correct them.

During the correction process, there is a two-stage correction. The previous research literature forms the impression that teachers must choose between formal and functional focus. For example, Prabhu (1987) investigated the Bangalore ELT project and insisted that correction must be content-focused "taking care to exclude any sustained attention to language itself, which would have resulted in a reduction in the focus on meaning" (Prabhu, 1987: p. 63). In another study, Beretta (1989) analyzed transcripts of 21 lessons taught in the Bangalore Project, quite a large percentage of form errors (65%) were corrected by key teachers, and 88% of content errors were corrected. These findings reflect the parallel one for teaching, that is, the discrediting of the form-focused audiolingual approach in favor of the function-focused communicative approach. During the teaching, form-focus was the first step (at the practice phase), which was followed by the function-focus in the production phase. Therefore, we call this two-stage approach to initial teaching. Here comes the question: during error correction, could we take two-stage approach?

The scholar Levenston (1978) proposes that students' composition errors are two removes from the native speakers' version. Thus, he challenges Corder's (1981) claim that the data of EA are "two sentences", one is the idiosyncratic sentence (produced by the learner) and a well-formed sentence (that which the native would have produced) (Corder, 1981: p. 22). Actually, the data of EA comprise not two but three sentences, they are, ① what the learners said; ② what they were attempting to say; and ③ what the NSs would have said (or written). Levenston claims that these three sentences must also figure in error correction. When learners compose their writing, what they tried to say is its reconstruction. Reconstruction involves putting the grammar right. Reconstruction also involves what James (2013) calls the naturalization, involving the introduction of nonnative elements into an originally native text. Levenston sees naturalization as something that happens when we "rationalize the paragraphing, remove obscurity and ambiguity, iron out infelicities, and generally try to turn it into a reasonable essay" (1978: p. 5). It should be noticed that naturalization involves just the sorts of improvement that native-speaking writers, who are ideally at least knowers of their language, find difficult but have to edit-in to their compositions (Davies, 1991a). Regarding the case of FL/SL writers, many of these improvements will involve the removal of L1 features that have been called negative transfer.

The fourth aspect of these rules and principles in error-correction is that learners can notice their errors. Ellis (1992) pointed out that grammar teaching should be less immediately concerned with accurate production, and more with helping learners to notice TL forms receptively. Once the learner starts noticing, learning starts to take off. Language test designers know that noticing enhances performance on tests. The distinction drawn between production and noticing is to be found in the options of practice and consciousness raising (CR). Ellis (1992) sees CR as being a straight alternative to practice: "Whereas practice is primarily behavioral, consciousness raising is essentially concept-forming." (1992: p. 234) In other words, practice is for improving performance, while CR is for teaching repeatedly on cognitive structure or competence. In a sense, CR can mediate direct positive evidence by saying to the learners "*Look, this is how it is in the TL!*". Practice and CR have different purposes: practice is supposed to improve performance, which mainly enhances implicit knowledge, while CR is supposed to improve L2's explicit knowledge. Practice is usually adopted in initial teaching, while CR is used in correcting. Fotos (1993) ever conducted an experiment involved in noticing. The research's assumption is that noticing could be commented by two sorts of teaching: teacher-fronted formal instruction, and doing grammar tasks in groups. So she gave two matched groups of learners grammar-noticing opportunities under these two conditions in order to find out which way is more effective. The grammar points raised in the research question were indirect object position, adverb placement, and relative clause position. In the experiment, students were given texts and asked to underline "anything which they considered special or noteworthy" (Fotos, 1993: p. 400). The results showed that both types of instruction improved noticing by the learners when compared with a control group that had not been encouraged to notice. The study also had the findings that there were no significant differences in the noticing degree of the two experimental groups. In other words, traditional teacher-centered grammar work is effective as the teaching form in setting group tasks to promote noticing.

The above section describes four rules and principles that are related to error correction. These principles reflect the steps in the process of correcting errors. This issue aroused interest of teachers and educators, and some researchers conducted lots of experiments to explore the scientific ways in error correction. This theme still needs time and methods to investigate into a broad sense.

In this part, we examined the key questions relating to error analysis, such as the definition of correction, pros and cons of correction, and principles of error correction. Actually, error correction is undoubtedly important in EFL/ESL learning, but it suggests that how to correct the errors and to what extent the errors should be corrected do not reach into agreement. It seems that different teachers have different opinions, and the results of experiments also vary from one to another. Therefore, as a hot issue in SLA, error correction is still worthy of being explored in FL teaching context.

2.5 Previous Studies on Error Analysis from the Perspective of Interlanguage

China is a country where English is taught as a foreign language. As a result, the learners commit errors due to the interference of L1 into the negative transfer within the target language. Lots of studies and researches were conducted to investigate the relationship between error analysis and interlanguage from the perspective of theories or applications (Al-Khresheh, 2010/2011; Brudhiprabha, 1972; Chelli, 2013; Corder, 1975; Gai, 2022; George, 1972; Guo, Yang, Wang et al., 2022; James, 1998; Richards, 1971; Selinker, 1974; Solano, 2014; Yang, 2018), and also conducted experiments and got the results that only one-third of the second language learners' errors can be attributed to native language transfer. Deductive (explicit) teaching of interlingual and inductive (implicit) teaching of intralingual erroneous points decreased the error frequency of students. Moreover, interlingual errors were more affected than that of intralingual in the case of error reduction. It states that interlingual errors are committed by the result of word-for-word (literal translation) from Arabic. It meant that interlingual interference might be the leading cause of committing this massive number of errors.

Lots of books and articles (Corder, 1975; Bose, 2005; Gai, 2022; Guo, Yang, Wang et al., 2022; James, 1998; Selinker, 1974; Solano, 2014; Yang, 2018) demonstrated the investigation in the relationship between error analysis and interlanguage. Among these research products, Corder (1975), James (1998) and Selinker (1974) are the three scholars who explored this relationship early. In their works, they explored error analysis and interlanguage from different perspectives. For example, James (1998) paid more attention to the scope of errors, including the definition of errors, description of errors, and levels of errors, only one chapter left to discuss the cause of errors: Interlingual and intralingual transfer. The author pointed out different sources of errors, such as mother-tongue influence, target language sources, communication strategy-based errors, induced errors, and compound and ambiguous errors. The framework of sources to make errors provided in the book was quite different from other scholars because it investigated errors from many different angles, which explored deeper language errors and supplied effective methods to deal with these errors. And to illustrate the theoretical frameworks mentioned in the previous chapters, the book provided a case study in the last chapter, which gives a detailed explanation of how to identify errors, categorize errors and diagnose errors. The book provides theories and applications, which can help the beginner in the research to follow this research method.

The research article written by Corder (1975) mainly talked about error analysis and interlanguage in second language acquisition. The article briefly introduced the definition of error analysis, the overview of lapses and mistakes, the methods in error analysis, the classification of errors, the evaluation of errors and the simplified linguistic systems (interlanguage system). The whole passage provided a general introduction for each part in the process of error analysis, from which the learners or researchers can understand them very quickly, but on the other hand, it might indicate the article could only be regarded as the lead-in function in familiar with such topic. Furthermore, the article has no application examples to provide, which can be understood when combining with the other scholars' works.

In a research study, Chelli (2013) found that the students' errors in the use of prepositions and articles can be identified as interlingual and intralingual errors. The result showed that 79. 15% of the errors made in prepositions and 72. 85% in articles are caused by a negative transfer of the Arabic language. 20. 85% in the use of prepositions and 27. 15% in the use of articles due to overgeneralization and false concepts hypothesized are mainly caused by the lack of practice. In a study conducted by Solano (2014), he found that the most common Spanish interference errors were misuse of verbs, omission of personal and object pronouns, misuse of the preposition, overuse of articles, and inappropriate/unnatural word order. It shows that L1 caused interference in EFL learners when writing in English, which is often due to the fact that there is a linguistic transference from the native language to the target language. In conclusion, this study differs from previous studies as it aims to describe interlingual and intralingual errors and their implementation.

The researcher Bose (2005) also mentioned that one of the reasons for learner errors is the interference of his mother tongue, which is described as the negative and positive transfer between the mother tongue and the target language. The negative transfer happens when the forms of the target language and those of the learner's mother tongue are different from each other. Meanwhile, the positive transfer occurs when the mother tongue and the target language are similar. He added that a teacher could make a teaching plan to remedy after he corrects the written compositions of his learners and collects their common errors in a notebook.

2. 6 The Development of Learner Language and Error Analysis Research

As a research tool for investigating L2 learner language, EA has a short history dating from the 1960s, when it was introduced as a superior, alternative approach to contrastive analysis (CA). However, CA itself was not a method for examining learners' language, rather it involved comparing the system of the learner's L1 with that of the target language (TL). It was believed that errors were the product of a negative transfer, and CA was concerned with the identification of the mismatches between the L1 and the TL in order to predict what errors learners would make. Proponents of CA claimed that the differences in linguistic features between the mother tongue and the TL could be utilized in designing language teaching materials according to the CA hypothesis: "Where two languages were similar, positive transfer would occur; where they were different, negative transfer, or interference, would result." (Larsen-Freeman & Long, 1991, p. 53) Most of all, CA did not involve identifying and describing performance errors in learners' production, which was what language practitioners were concerned with, rather it focused on predicting error occurrence based on the differences between the linguistic systems of the L1 and the L2. Following this development, EA was the method that researchers turned to. EA is associated with nativist theories of language learning which attribute the process of learning a language to the mental processes that occur in the mind. Furthermore, EA is also closely linked to the interlanguage theory.

According to Corder (1974), EA consists of the following stages: ①collection of a sample of learner language; ② identification of errors; ③ description of errors; ④explanation of errors; and ⑤ error evaluation. These procedures are not straightforward and there are different problems associated with some of the stages. In particular, of direct relevance to the purposes of the present study, some problems are related to stages ② and ③.

Some researchers consider EA to be theoretically flawed because it considers a certain target language variety as its reference point. This is considered a problem because "it is not always clear what the learners' reference group is and that, in some cases (for example, a Hispanic living in an African American area of New York), they may be targeted on some non-standard variety" (p. 61). However, studies in EA continued and responses to the criticism appeared in a number of studies (Abbott, 1980; Corder, 1971; Faerch, 1978; Zydatiss, 1974). Today, it seems that EA has had a rebirth following significant research in the past three decades, such as James (1998/2013), Kellerman (1995), Kellerman and Smith (1986), and Odlin (1989) and the availability and advancement of tools for computer-based analyses of learner language (Ellis, 2008).

2.7 Error Analysis and Corpus Linguistics

Nowadays, error analysis is frequently adopted in learner corpus research based on the form of a computer-aided error analysis which is concerned with an error annotation of learner corpora.

2.7.1 Learner Corpora

Learner corpora is a sub-field of acquisition corpora which are electronic databases that contain continuous written data or spoken data produced by native speakers, second language learners, and learners of a foreign language (Granger, 2013). They contain attested language which, as Thomas (2017) explains, means that the language has not been "created for the purpose of exemplifying language" (p. 9) and can thus function as an authentic source of data for the study of the first and second language, which is the primary function of acquisition corpora.

There exist both learner corpora that contain written and learner corpora that contain spoken data. The majority of the corpora, though, consists of texts, such as essays written during language examinations or at school. The most common target language of learners is English and there are far more monolingual than translational corpora. Also the synchronic type of corpora, which captures learner use at one particular time, at one particular level of proficiency, is more common than quasi-longitudinal corpora that gathers "data from a homogeneous group of learners at different levels of proficiency" (Granger, 2013, p. 8), and even more common than the longitudinal corpora which cover the language development of particular students.

Analyzing learner corpora is said to provide researchers with a great insight into the learner language. These corpora become especially useful for the SLA researchers when they contain meta data about the collected sample and when some kind of linguistic annotation is carried out. Linguistic annotation includes for instance, part-of-speech tagging, lemmatization, or parsing, which is the process of making a syntactic analysis (Granger, 2013). What proved to be of the most fruitful nature, however, is a procedure that is central to the method of the computer-aided error analysis. Error annotation of corpora is based on the process of error tagging (Granger, 2013) —i. e., the insertion of standardized error tags into the corpora system in order to classify the errors. The error tags represent the individual error types that are distinguished by the error classification designed for the corpora/research; classification that usually has its foundation in one of the two error descriptive typologies.

2.7.2 Strengths of the Computer-aided Error Analysis of Learner Corpora

One of the biggest strengths of using corpora for conducting error analysis is that the data is digitalized, or as Granger (2013) calls it "computerized" (p. 10). As Granger (2013) highlights, digitalization makes the whole long process of error annotation more manageable by enabling researchers to efficiently manipulate the data and also by allowing researchers to easily supplement the "raw data" with linguistic or extralinguistic information.

The second strength of using corpora for the error analyses is that they contain big volumes of data. Through corpora, analysts can access much larger collections of data than they did in the "pre-electronic era" of error analysis, which is something that is especially suitable for conducting quantitative analyses (Gráf, 2015; Granger, 2013).

Another advantage of corpora is that the errors in them are contextualized. The corpora provide context, co-text and present errors not in isolation but alongside correct language usage which, as Negrillo and Domínguez (2006) point out, better reflects "learner's total interlanguage" and thus allows for a more precise analysis.

This chapter reviewed the literature in many aspects: first, the factors affecting the writing of L2 learners in China and other international settings. Linguistic factors are the main factors that influence the writing of the present research sample in line with some relevant studies from the literature. Besides these, this part also discussed CA and EA and highlighted their importance in L2 writing. The criticism of CA and EA by several scholars was also demonstrated. Then this chapter continually discussed to what extent L1 interference could affect L2 writing. Furthermore, the correlations between error analysis and second language acquisition, error analysis and English writing, error analysis and interlanguage, error analysis and corpus linguistics have also been reviewed with the previous studies and researches. Those of important literature will also guide the discussion in this book and play an important role in providing the theoretical background of this research and prove the scientificity of this research. The following chapter will present the methodology adopted in collecting data and the research instrument and samples. The procedures for collecting and analyzing the data will also be demonstrated.

CHAPTER 3 METHODOLOGY

The previous chapter reviewed error analysis, interlanguage and their relationship in L2 writing. The literature presents the development of error analysis and interlanguage both in China and beyond. Furthermore, this section will display the methodology adopted in this study to gain a comprehensive understanding of not only errors in the L2 written product but also the linguistic and non-linguistic elements that affect such product. To achieve above goals, this research has employed a mixed-method approach, namely, written products, a questionnaire, and semi-structured interviews of students and teachers. The conception and the entire justification adopting such a model will be discussed in detail, along with the strengths and limitations of each one.

This chapter also summarized the pilot study that was conducted before implementing the main study. The data was collected from the same population. The research procedure, results, analysis, and discussion will be presented briefly. Afterwards, the chapter also displayed a comprehensive description, followed by the procedure of selecting and classifying the participants from the whole population. The process was composed of the context of the study, background of the participants, the whole population, instructions, analysis of samplings, questionnaire conduction of the pilot and the main study holistically, trying to establish a theoretical framework for the data analysis, transcription, coding scheme, inter-rater reliability of the compositions and the method in which their frequencies are calculated.

3.1 Research Design

This study sought to investigate the errors committed by Chinese learners in their L2 writing, the linguistic and non-linguistic factors that affected their compositions. At the same time, the possible relationships between errors and their writing scores were also revealed with concrete data and statistics. This research also aimed to examine the differences in these variables in reference to participants' language or writing proficiency. This study adopted a triangulation of qualitative and quantitative tools, namely, a writing proficiency test, a questionnaire, and semi-structured interviews. The quantitative method was employed to count the frequencies and ranks of writing errors and correlations between the frequency of writing errors and their writing proficiency. The reason for adopting all these instruments was to gain strong and sufficient data.

Triangulation of data helps to enhance the validity and reliability of the study by using data from multiple sources. Johnson (1992) ever mentioned that triangulation data could minimize the bias or influence of the researcher. Thus it can enrich the results and compensate for any limitations when the data is collected from one source. It also supplies the researcher with comprehensive data, ultimately helping him/her be close to the topic from different perspectives. Therefore, the triangulated data can make the researcher more confident about his findings (Yeasmin & Rahman, 2012).

Nevertheless, triangulation also has its limitations among which is the need of researchers with good knowledge of both quantitative and qualitative data. Moreover, the research process is usually regarded time-consuming.

However, the advantages of triangulation are more than its shortcomings, so this study adopted a mixed-method approach which involved collecting data (a writing proficiency test, questionnaire and semi-structured interview) and analyzing the data quantitatively and qualitatively.

Concerning the data collection, this research mainly employs quantitative and qualitative methods because of the nature of the study, because it examines human behavior and cognitive activity. As Denzin and Lincoln (2005) pointed out, "Qualitative research is a situated activity that locates the observer in the world. It consists of a set of interpretive, material practices that make the world visible. These practices can transform the world. They turn the world into a series of representations, including field notes, interviews, conversations, photographs, memos, and recordings of the self". (p. 3)

According to the above explanation, the qualitative method is distinctive in its variety of data collection instruments, such as description and interviews. These methods can create a clearer image in the conception of the activities in participants' minds.

Regarding data analysis, the quantitative method was employed in this research to count the frequencies and percentages of the writing errors committed by Chinese L2 learners. In addition, the questionnaire in the main study was conducted on 292 L2 learners to examine the relationship between their writing proficiency and writing attitudes, difficulties, and corrective feedback (one-way within-subjects ANOVA and Spearman's correlation). The questions raised in the first chapter can utilize these statistical methods to explore the relationship with different writing variables.

3.2 Participants

All the participants in this study are from a national normal university in South China. This university belongs to the second-class university in terms of the scores which are used as the admission line in their national entrance examination. All the subjects are non-English majors of first-year undergraduates who had more than ten years of English learning experience, and Chinese is their mother tongue. They had no overseas study experience. Even though all of these participants are from different disciplines, their majors did not influence their writing performance as they experienced the same English learning syllabus at a national university. For all these subjects, they have three periods of offline college English classes in one week including two integrated courses and one listening and speaking course. Besides this, two periods of online classes weekly are supplied with additional listening and comprehension materials to improve students' autonomous learning abilities.

In the first step, there are totally 320 participants' compositions of eight years selected from the whole population with a stratified random sampling method. This method was adopted according to the purpose of the research questions. Our research questions mainly stated the writing errors among three writing proficiency groups. Therefore, the pure convenience sampling cannot achieve such a goal. Conversely, a stratified random sampling can remedy the limitation. The samplings selected by this method would be representative of the whole population. Regarding our research questions, we would like to examine the differences of writing errors in different language proficiency groups. Therefore, the stratification of each group should be necessary to divide the whole population into three groups according to their final scores (see Appendix 12, the dividing line). The three groups were divided into high, fair, and low proficiency with the percentage of 27%, 46% and 27%. The reason why I chose this ratio was that according to Wiersma and Jurs (1990), they stated that "27% is used in the division of different proficiency groups because it has shown that this value will maximize differences in normal distributions while providing enough cases for analysis" (p. 145). Similarly, Kelly (as cited in Popham, 1981) also asserted that the use of 27% maximizes stability and clarifies discrimination in the sampling. This division method was employed for different proficiency groups in a questionnaire and the interview. After stratifying three groups in one year's population, the convenience sampling method will be employed to select the concrete data of composition in each strata. Convenience sampling is a non-probability sample type that can be employed to select target population members. The condition is that if they are consistent with the specific criteria, such as geographical proximity or easy accessibility (Dornyei & Taguch, 2009). Actually, the convenience sampling method has been criticized for there is a risk of misrepresenting a whole population. The latent problem was estimated in this research. For one thing, the large-scale samplings have been selected from almost 20 different majors, which represents a variety of students types. In addition, participants of the research share some ordinary academic and contextual characteristics. On average, these participants had 11.3 years (see Table 3 – 2) of formal English education at the time of this research. All of these participants were in their second semester of college. Some students planned to take the CET – 4 exam at the end of this semester. But for some others, they would like to take the exam the following semester. Because these compositions were just selected from their final exams, only their majors and classes were available.

Table 3 – 1 An Overview of the Research Design

Research Methods	Research Objectives	Instruments	Participants
Composition	To analyze 320 compositions based on the inter-rater agreement of three raters	320 compositions	320 participants in the compositions analysis
Questionnaire	To conduct the questionnaire	Questionnaire	292 EFL learners in the questionnaire
Interview	To obtain in-depth information about students' awareness of the errors in their compositions and teachers' methods on how to minimize those errors	Interview questions based on the questionnaire	14 students and 9 teachers are required to discuss with the interviewer on 6 questions, respectively

The test paper sheet didn't mention their genders and age, so we would like to skip that factual information. But the detailed personal information of the participants in the questionnaire and interview are all supplied in Table 3 – 2.

There are almost 3,000 undergraduates' compositions in each semester, meaning there are about 810, 1,380 and 810 samples for each group. Convenient sampling was used to select samples in the interior of each group. For each year, 40 compositions were selected among the whole population, and they were 11, 18, and 11, respectively. The reasons for the number of sampling selected each year lie in the following two aspects: first, when conducting a research, it does not mean the more samples you select, the better results you can get. How many samplings were selected largely depending on the research questions? The results of the sample analysis could answer the research questions, which satisfy the research objective; second, the writing of this book is an individual work, so I should take the timeline into account. For the above situations, 320 samples are selected for this study.

3.3 Instruments

The primary purpose of this section is to introduce the instruments adopted to examine L2 learners' writing performance, writing proficiency, the frequencies of writing errors, and the reasons behind these errors. Moreover, it also supplies the underlying philosophy for selecting these measures. The instruments in this study would employ three kinds of methods (see Figure 3 – 1), and each of them was explained and elaborated on in the following picture.

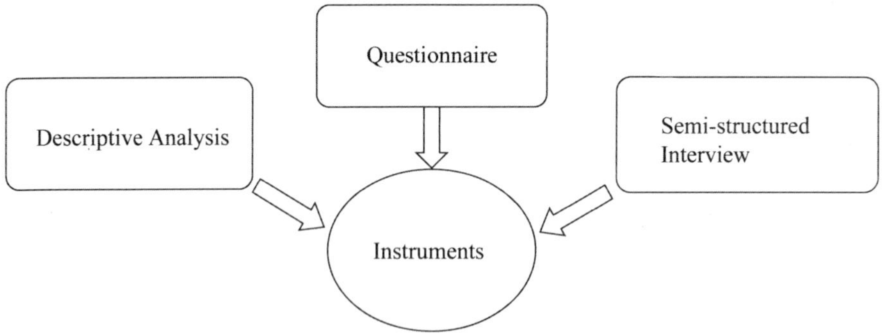

Figure 3 – 1 The Mixed Research Methods in This Study

Table 3 – 2 An Overview of Participants Information

Phases	Objectives	Total	Groups			Age
			High writing proficiency	Fair writing proficiency	Low writing proficiency	
Phase one	To test the inter-rater agreement of the error analysis	40	11	18	11	
Phase two	To conduct a pilot study of the self-administrated questionnaire	140	38	64	38	19.23
Phase three	To investigate students' writing motivation, habits, and difficulties in L2 writing	292	79	134	79	19.35
Phase four	To obtain in-depth information about the elements causing L2 writing errors of Chinese learners	13 students	S5	S8	S5	18
		9 teachers				
Phase five	To calculate the frequencies of writing errors and their ranks	320	86	148	86	

3.3.1 Writing Proficiency Test

According to McNamara (2000), the language proficiency test is employed to examine students' individual differences in a particular area. In this dissertation, based on the making scheme proposed by Jacobs (1981), the writing proficiency test was adopted to divide L2 students' English proficiency into high, fair, and low groups according to their performance in the test. Actually, this procedure was very crucial for the selection of the most suitable participants in terms of their actual proficiency level. Furthermore, this step enhanced the accuracy and reliability of the measurements used to assess the L2 students' writing and to group them accordingly. All the compositions selected from the whole population were from the final exam.

In the examination, students were required to finish their task in 30 minutes without looking up the dictionary or seeking help on the Internet. The words were at least 120 but no more than 180. The requirement of such composition is directed by the principles and criteria of CET Band 4 or 6 issued by the Chinese Ministry of Education (see Appendix 2). The writing part was based on the corpus of college English in which there were about 20 topics (see Appendix 1) for each semester. All the writing requirements are quite similar, and the validity and reliability of the topics have been tested. The hardness of these different topics is quite the same, for these topics are pretty familiar to college students. Based on the above assumptions, the writing proficiency test can meet the requirements of examining L2 learners' writing ability.

3.3.2 Error Analysis Categorization

The categorization of the error analysis in this book will adopt the theoretical framework of Carl James (1998). In his theory, James proposed that errors be classified into five categories: substance errors (capitalization, punctuation, and spelling), grammatical errors (adjectives, adverbs, articles, nouns, possession, pronouns, preposition, and verbs), lexical errors (word formation and word selection), syntactic errors (coordination/subordination, sentence structure and ordering), and semantic errors (ambiguous communication and miscommunication). The reason for choosing this theory is that this theoretical framework analyzes the errors, firstly, from the perspective of different aspects of texts or passages. And the order of the analysis is from superficial to deep level, from substance to semantic errors. Besides the five main categories of errors, the subcategories are also offered under each category, which can explain the error types in detail and elaborate each main category very clearly. The procedure of collecting and analyzing errors were adopted from Ellis (1994), which provided an obvious and comprehensive way to error analysis (see Figure 3 – 2). All the errors existing in the compositions will be recognized and categorized one by one according to the theoretical framework of James. After categorizing all these errors, the frequencies and the ranks of each error type in the total samplings will be displayed with different tables or figures. The concrete examples of error type and categorization will be exhibited and explained in 4. 2. 2.

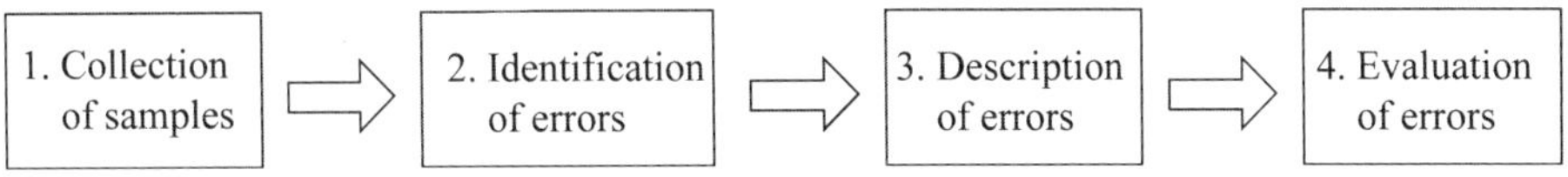

Figure 3 – 2 Theoretical Framework of EA Cited from Ellis (1994)

3. 3. 3 Questionnaire

Oxford (2011) ever proposed that "self-reporting is one of the very few ways that researchers can gain access to learners' thoughts, attitudes, feelings, and strategies" (p. 142). The other famous scholar Dörnyei (2010) further explained that the questionnaire is one of the most influential and versatile instruments for gathering factual, attitudinal, and behavioral data. The objective of the questionnaire was to explore in-depth information about students' writing habits, writing difficulties, corrective feedback, and investigate the relationships among different writing variables in three groups. The researcher took five dimensions of writing elements. However, after the pilot study, we keep three of them. The details of this part will be reported in the pilot study. Comprehension is another reason for researchers to use a questionnaire. Undoubtedly, the researcher wanted the participants to understand the questions. That is why we conducted a pilot study before the main study. Because after the pilot stage, a final decision on many variables and items adopted in the main study was made.

The questionnaire adopted in this study is designed under the guidance of the theories (Alivernini & Lucid, 2008; Payne, 2012; You, Dörnyei & Csizér, 2016). These theories focus on different aspects of writing motivation, writing attitudes, writing difficulty, writing habits and feedback. I just selected some items from each theory for each dimension of the questionnaire regarding my research questions. In the pilot study, there were totally 28 items in the questionnaire, and participants had to indicate on a 5-

point scale from 1 (strongly disagree) to 5 (strongly agree) to what extent they agreed or disagreed with statements.

The questionnaire included two parts. The first part was composed of 15 items on three variables, while the second part required personal and demographic information, including students' ID, age, grade, major, whether being abroad and the length of learning English. The questionnaire of this study was highly structured because, firstly, reference questionnaires were developed in general learning contexts. Secondly, we constructed this questionnaire cautiously and creatively to motivate participants to supply truthful and thoughtful reflections. Lastly, the word choice is carefully considered for each selected item, and at the same time, the selected items were checked (by students and teachers), changed, and fully considered to fit the Chinese learning context. The procedure of checking will be addressed in the section on a pilot study.

3.3.4 Semi-structured Interview

The semi-structured interview consists of two sections, one for students and the other for teachers, which could explore the same research theme from two different angles. These two different aspects could display an all-around overview of the reasons of making errors. A qualitative method was employed in collecting, analyzing, and summarizing the data. The concrete procedure can be seen in Figure 3-3.

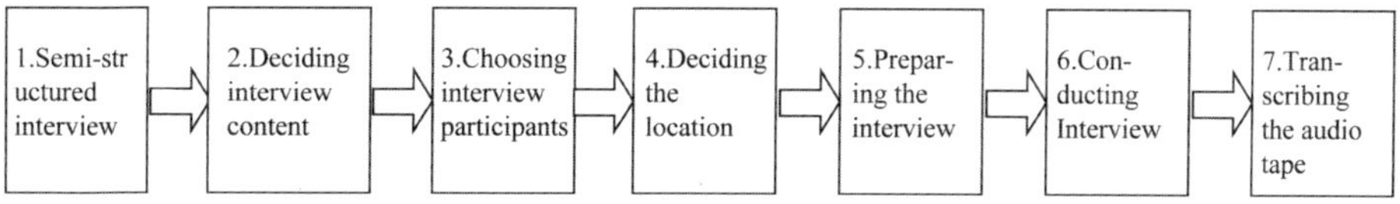

Figure 3-3 The Procedure of Conducting the Interview

Semi-structured interviews are widely used in qualitative research (Edwards & Janet, 2013). Qualitative methods, such as interviews, are believed to provide a 'deeper' understanding of social phenomena than would be obtained from purely quantitative methods, such as questionnaires (Silverman, 2020). In a semi-structured interview, the interviewee can express their ideas or opinions, and ask questions to the interviewer during the interview. They could more easily supply the reasons for their answers during the interview (Keller & Katharina, 2020). The flexibility in semi-structured interviews makes it possible to cross-check and validate the information from previous interviews (Bryman & Bell, 2015). Compared with a questionnaire, in a word, semi-structured interviews can directly know clearly about the thoughts and feelings of the participants in each question and sometimes can explore more profound reflections on their inner side.

An explanatory semi-structured interview was adopted in the present study, because it could supplement the questionnaire stage of the research design. What's more, the comprehensive nature of the questionnaire and the large sample in the research need further interpretation and explanation. Furthermore, the interview can give an additional opportunity to explore deeply on other related questions and compensate for the imperfections of the questionnaire. Additionally, the interviews in this study would explore the reflections of both teachers and students, which helped to seek the deeper reasons behind these writing errors.

The semi-structured interviews were carried out one participant by another. Choosing such a method was time-consuming, but we paid more attention to its advantages. One-on-one interview was not interrupted by others, and the interviewees would not dare to express their own opinions if other interviewers were present. Furthermore, they could discuss deeper related questions with no limited time string. The process of the interview was under control. In this study one interview took about 20 minutes on average and the audio tapes were recorded and transcribed. The personal information of participants and interview schedules (see Appendix 8 and 9) were attached in the appendix. Actually, there were two interviews, one for students and one for teachers. The questions for students (see Appendix 8) mainly focused on the possible reasons they thought for making writing errors. The questions for teachers (see Appendix 9) focused on the error types of students' making, the possible reasons and effective ways to induce fewer errors in students' L2 writing. Through these two parts of the interview, further details and deeper reasons on error analysis could be revealed, which laid a foundation for the later exploration of the possible reasons for students' errors.

3.4 The Pilot Study

Before the main study, a pilot study was conducted to examine the inter-rater agreement of analyzing errors, the validity, and the reliability of the questionnaire. Conducting a pilot study did a favor for the research in two ways. First, the hypothesis of the study was confirmed that Chinese college students encounter difficulties in L2 writing. More specifically, the results showed the types of errors and their frequencies in students' L2 writing. Second, the pilot study supplies the researcher with a rough idea of students' motivation, attitudes, and difficulties in L2 writing, which ultimately helped to decide the final factors of the questionnaire for the main study.

3.4.1 Data Collection Procedures

The data in this part consist of two parts: participants in the samplings and participants involved in the questionnaire. All the participants are junior students from a public normal university. The participants in the composition samplings are totally 40. They are all Chinese college students with Chinese as their first language. The compositions of the final exams of the participants were selected to test the inter-rater agreement, which is critical in analyzing errors and categorizing errors in the main study. The values of inter-rater reliability can be represented by Cohen's Kappa (see Table 3-4): values ≤ 0 indicating no agreement and 0.01 ~ 0.20 as none to slight, 0.21 ~ 0.39 as minimal, 0.41 ~ 0.59 as weak, 0.60 ~ 0.79 as moderate, 0.80 ~ 0.90 as strong agreement, and 0.91 ~ 1.00 as almost perfect agreement. The value in these three raters is about 0.78 (see Table 3-3), which is substantial for analyzing writing errors. The results also proposed that the training be conducted to improve the inter-rater agreement. The participants in the questionnaire were 141, whose ages ranged from 17 to 19, with a mean age of 20 (see Table 3-2), and learning English for more than 12 years. The purpose and requirement for answering the questionnaire were issued to the participants before they took part in. Data collection was conducted through an online questionnaire. The advantage of online working is that it solves the distance problem and saves much time in inputting the data into SPSS.

Table 3-3 Inter-rater Reliability of the Three Raters

Var#	Rater 1	Rater 2	Rater 3	Agreement/%
1				
2				
3				
…	…	…	…	…
Inter-rater reliability				0.90

Table 3 – 4 Interpretation of Cohen's Kappa

Value of Kappa	Level of Agreement/%	Of Data That Are Reliable
0 ~ .20	None	0 ~ 4%
.21 ~ .39	Minimal	4% ~ 15%
.40 ~ .59	Weak	15% ~ 35%
.60 ~ .79	Moderate	35% ~ 63%
.80 ~ .90	Strong	64% ~ 81%
Above .90	Almost perfect	82% ~ 100%

The questionnaire participants consisted of 141 junior students in a public normal university in the South of China (see Table 3 – 10). They were all Chinese college students with Chinese as their first language. The aim of the questionnaire was explained very clearly before they took part in the survey, and at the same time, the consent form was distributed to them online (see Appendix 11) and gained their agreement. Most participants can honestly contribute their thoughts and ideas on the initial 28 items. However, after implementing the data into the software, some items did not combine into a particular fact. Therefore, in the main study, only three factors were mentioned and distributed to the participants in the main study.

3.4.2 Data Analysis

Manual analysis and coding of errors in the compositions of final exams were undertaken to identify different error types the students committed to their English writing. The findings revealed that there were total of 987 errors, with the highest frequency errors in grammatical errors, quite high frequent errors in substance errors, and lexical errors, then syntax errors and semantic errors. The following tables (Tables 3 – 5, 3 – 6, 3 – 7, 3 – 8, and 3 – 9) present the error types and examples of these errors from the students' writing.

Table 3 – 5 Grammatical Errors That Chinese Students Are Faced with

Sub-category	Examples from the Students' Compositions
subject-verb agreement	e. g. *She come back home at six.*
Verb tense	e. g. *Christmas coming soon.*

(To be continued)

Sub-category		Examples from the Students' Compositions
Link verb		e. g. *She a student.*
Auxiliary verb		e. g. *What not you like?*
Adjectives		e. g. *I have not many time to spend at home.*
Preposition		e. g. *We did not use to sit on tables when eating.*
Adverbs		e. g. *She was disappointed so much.*
Modal verb		e. g. *I will must to study Norwegian.*
Pronouns		e. g. *John decided to return the book to he friend.*
Conjunction		e. g. *When I was a millionaire, I could ask for anything not in the air.*
Determiners	Articles	e. g. "*a*", "*an*", and "*the*"
	Demonstratives	e. g. "*this*", "*that*", "*these*", and "*those*"
	Quantifiers	e. g. "*few*" and "*many*"
	Possessives	e. g. "*my*", "*your*", "*his*", "*her*", "*its*", "*our*", and "*their*"
Plural forms		e. g. *Every coins has two sides.*
Other grammatical errors		

Table 3 - 6 Substance Errors That Chinese Students Are Faced with

Sub-category	Examples from the Students' Compositions
Capitalization	e. g. *I will buy benze.*
Punctuation	e. g. *I liked them, they were so nice to me.*
Spelling	e. g. *I want to go some intesting places to visit.*

Table 3 - 7 Lexical Errors That Chinese Students Are Faced with

Sub-category	Examples from the Students' Compositions
Word form	e. g. *Young people can be independence in the United States.*
Word deficiency	e. g. *She is a beautiful.*

(To be continued)

Sub-category	Examples from the Students' Compositions
Word abundance	e. g. *I have many lots of books.*
Word selection	e. g. *Both sicks are kids.*

Table 3 – 8 Syntactic Errors That Chinese Students Are Faced with

Sub-category	Examples from the Students' Compositions.
Coordination/ subordination	e. g. *Jasmine is afraid of dogs, she was bitten by a dog when she was young.*
Sentence structure	e. g. *I dinner like to eat spaghetti.*
Ordering	e. g. *The ball dropped the boy.*

Table 3 – 9 Semantic Errors That Chinese Students Are Faced with

Sub-category	Examples from the Students' Compositions
Ambiguity	e. g. *I saw the bank this morning.*
Miscommunication	e. g. *He should love his work who is belong to his job.*

As stated above, the most frequent errors that Chinese college students made were substance errors, followed by grammatical, lexical, semantic, and syntactic errors. Interestingly, the findings in the preliminary stage have much in common with previous research on writing errors committed by L2 writer in general, particularly Chinese learners in composing their essays. There are many examples of error analysis in L2 writing in the categories of grammatical, substance, syntactic, semantic, and lexical errors.

Previous studies have shown that the most difficulty learners experience with L2 vocabulary, grammar, and syntax could be attributed to the negative interference of L1 features (Beardsmore, 1982). More specifically, the use of L1 elements in L2 production is regarded as a major cause of errors, particularly when the two languages have different structures. Dechert (1983) ever stated that the negative transfer of L1 components happens when the learner assumes that in L2, they have similar forms and functions. Therefore, we might explain some error types which are linked to L1. In the main study, the negative interference was re-considered with further and detailed data, and the interviews provided additional insights into the fundamental fact of influence of the L1 (Chinese) on L2 (English) writing.

3.4.3 Piloting the Questionnaire

The questionnaire data collection was from Oct. 22 to 27, 2021, while the analysis of the data was from Oct. 28 to Nov. 5, 2021. The questionnaire was composed of two parts. The first part (see Table 3 – 10) was about the demographic information of the participants: their age, gender, grade, time to start to learn English, whether they have been abroad, etc. The second part included 5 dimensions with a total of 28 items: writing motivation, writing attitudes, writing difficulties, writing behavior, and corrective feedback. The questionnaire was conducted to investigate the correlation between EFL writing proficiency and these five aspects of the learners.

Before the questionnaire was conducted in the pilot study, two professors in College English teaching checked it. They provided much feedback, and during this process, they asked lots of questions to make sure the compatibility between the research questions and the five dimensions in the questionnaire. More importantly, I have required ten students to read the items and give their reactions to the questionnaire. They read very carefully and supplied much feedback. Student A thought that "*good writer*" in the third item hasn't been translated correctly because the Chinese version only focuses on the writer's writing proficiency.

Table 3 – 10 Background Information of Questionnaire Participants

Group	Mean Age (*SD*)	Mean Score (*SD*)	Gender (*N*)	Years of Learning English		Whether Being Abroad
				M	*SD*	*N*
High proficiency	19.3 (.704)	87.132 (4.3038)	Male (=2) Female (=36)	11.29	1.592	Yes (=0) No (=38)
Fair proficiency	19.22 (.696)	68.977 (7.8142)	Male(=11) Female(=54)	11.25	2.829	Yes (=3) No (=62)
Low proficiency	19.18 (.652)	46.171 (9.2395)	Male(=16) Female(=22)	10.87	1.862	Yes (=1) No (=37)

Note: high proficiency group ($N = 38$), fair proficiency group ($N = 65$), and low proficiency group ($N = 38$).

The other suggestion he talked about was that he could not understand the Chinese version “用英语写句子结构” which means *compose the sentence structure in Chinese*. I think the misunderstanding was aroused because the English version of the items was translated literally. Therefore, I revised the Chinese version of Item No. 3 and English expression in Item No. 23. Student B said in the Chinese version of all those items, sometimes it was called “英文写作” and sometimes it was called “英语写作”, even though they are both translated into *English writing*. The suggestion provides that the Chinese version should be unified in form even though they expressed the same meaning. Otherwise, it would ruin the uniformity of the questionnaire. Student C argued that all items of the Chinese version should be in brackets to make a clear line from the English version. Students D said that the Chinese version of “*only necessary*” in Item No. 25 was difficult to answer. Therefore, a clear expression should be provided.

The pilot study was implemented to examine the quality, genre, time scale, and procedure for conducting the study. The aim of the questionnaire was explained to the participants, and at the same time, they were told they had the right to give up filling in the answers at anytime.

The questionnaire was extracted as an excel file, which was then input into the software SPSS 26.0 to investigate the number of constructs and structure of this measure. A pilot study in a questionnaire is significant because it can measure the reliability and validity of it and then test the factors involved in the questionnaire. The piloting also can investigate the value of each item to see if each item is reliable to be conducted or employed in the main study. According to Bartlett's test ($p < .001$) (see Table 3 - 11), the correlation matrix is not an identified matrix. An examination of the Kaiser-Meyer Olkin (KMO) measure of sampling adequacy suggests the sample was factor-able (KMO = .838). The presented coefficients were grouped by size and small efficient with an absolute value < .60 were excluded from the items in the main study.

Table 3 - 11 KMO and Bartlett's Test

KMO measure of sampling adequacy		.838
Bartlett's test of sphericity	Approx. Chi-Square	1, 904.450
	df	378
	Sig.	<.001

Table 3 – 12 Results of Factor Analysis of Piloting Questionnaire

Component	Items	Initial	Extraction
Factor 1	Q1 English writing can be important to me because I think it will be someday be useful in getting a good job.	1.000	.456
	Q2 English writing can be important to me because I think I'll need it for further studies.	1.000	.687
	Q3 I study English writing in order to get others' recognition as a good writer.	1.000	.707
	Q4 I study English writing to prove I can write as well as other students.	1.000	.763
	Q5 I study English writing because I need to learn it for examination, such as final exam, CET 4 or 6, and entrance examination for postgraduates.	1.000	.580
	Q6 I study English writing because I experience pleasure and satisfaction while learning it.	1.000	.673
	Q7 English writing is necessary for me because I don't want to get a poor score or a fail mark in English proficiency tests.	1.000	.593
Factor 2	Q8 When asked to write a piece of work in English, I feel comfortable and confident.	1.000	.638
	Q9 I find it interesting to express my ideas in English writing.	1.000	.739
	Q10 In English, writing is the most difficult of all learning skills.	1.000	.662
	Q11 It is not easy to find the ideas that help me to write in English.	1.000	.838

(To be continued)

Component	Items	Initial	Extraction
Factor 3	Q12 When writing in English, I feel I am lack of vocabulary.	1.000	.640
	Q13 When writing in English, the problem lies in making grammatical errors.	1.000	.704
	Q14 When writing in English, I face problems on how to combine words in sentences.	1.000	.759
	Q15 I feel I have a lot to say, but I don't know to deliver it in English in my composition.	1.000	.651
	Q16 When writing in English, I usually use Chinese English in the composition.	1.000	.678
	Q17 After writing in English, I face the problem in modifying the composition.	1.000	.517
Factor 4	Q18 When writing in English, first I think in Chinese, and then I write in English.	1.000	.503
	Q19 I use an English/Chinese, Chinese/English dictionary when writing in English.	1.000	.563
	Q20 I check my compositions for some errors before I submit them.	1.000	.851
	Q21 When writing in English, I write the structure of the sentence in Chinese, and then I translate it into English.	1.000	.579
Factor 5	Q22 I would like to get the direct feedback with corrections on my composition from my English teacher.	1.000	.674
	Q23 Indirect feedback with some indications from English teacher can inspire me in improving the language accuracy in composition.	1.000	.732
	Q24 If my teacher can give me feedback in time, I can perform well in English writing.	1.000	.724
	Q25 I would like my English teacher to underline all the errors in my composition.	1.000	.692

3.4.4 Piloting the Category of Error Types

The pilot of the categorization of error types was conducted by the researcher and the other two university teachers who have been teaching college English in a public university in South China. The two inter-raters, an associated professor and a professor, have abundant teaching experience in college English writing and reading. The quantity of samplings employed in the pilot study is 40 pieces, which covers the high, fair, and low writing proficiency groups. Firstly, the researcher presented the framework of error analysis and informed the two raters how to categorize and record the errors. Secondly, the other two raters and the researcher worked on the project respectively while implementing the error analysis knowledge into practice. Thirdly, the results of each rater will be calculated according to Scholfield's (2005) formula, although this formula is related to the writing strategies identification, as the following figure shows.

$$\frac{\text{Number of strategies the researcher coded similarly in the 1st and 2nd coding sessions}}{\text{Number of strategies the researcher coded in the 1st session}} \times 100\%$$

Inspired by the above formula, the similar formula on error analysis can be formed.

$$\frac{\text{Number of errors the researcher coded similarly in the 1st and 2nd coding sessions}}{\text{Number of errors the researcher coded in the 1st session}} \times 100\%$$

The following table (see Table 3 – 13) shows that inter-rater reliability was calculated according to the above formula:

Table 3 – 13 Inter-rater Reliability for the Errors Identified by All Three Raters

Participants	Errors Coded by the Researcher	Errors Coded by the Second Rater	Errors Coded by the Third Rater	Errors Agreed on
SP1	6	5	6	4
SP2	5	6	6	4
SP3	2	3	3	2
SP4	2	2	2	2

(To be continued)

Participants	Errors Coded by the Researcher	Errors Coded by the Second Rater	Errors Coded by the Third Rater	Errors Agreed on
SP5	3	5	4	3
SP6	1	2	2	1
SP7	8	8	9	7
SP8	3	5	5	3
SP9	10	11	10	9
SP10	8	9	8	7
SP11	14	12	13	10
SP12	19	18	21	15
SP13	6	6	7	4
SP14	11	12	12	10
SP15	11	10	12	8
SP16	13	12	11	9
SP17	10	8	9	7
SP18	16	15	18	13
SP19	12	12	10	9
SP20	11	10	11	9
SP21	7	9	7	6
SP22	26	23	25	20
SP23	12	13	12	9
SP24	12	12	11	9
SP25	17	16	17	12
SP26	20	21	22	18
SP27	14	15	16	12
SP28	15	14	15	12
SP29	15	13	14	11

(To be continued)

Participants	Errors Coded by the Researcher	Errors Coded by the Second Rater	Errors Coded by the Third Rater	Errors Agreed on
SP30	2	2	3	2
SP31	16	15	13	12
SP32	11	10	9	8
SP33	4	4	4	3
SP34	15	16	17	12
SP35	22	20	21	18
SP36	23	22	21	17
SP37	7	5	8	4
SP38	12	13	12	9
SP39	7	5	7	4
SP40	15	15	18	13
Total	443	434	451	347

Number of errors coded similarly by all raters = 347 / 443 × 100% = 78.33% agreement.

One aspect that should be noticed is that three raters identified the number of errors, and then the agreed errors are calculated and recorded. The inter-rater reliability can be concluded with the formula.

The values of inter-rater reliability can be represented by Cohen's Kappa: values ≤ 0 as indicating no agreement and 0.01 ~ 0.20 as none to slight, 0.21 ~ 0.40 as minimal, 0.41 ~ 0.60 as weak, 0.61 ~ 0.79 as moderate, 0.81 ~ 0.90 as strong agreement, and 0.91 ~ 1.00 as almost perfect agreement. The frequency and the category of errors were counted according to the whole errors and the data was input into the software SPSS 26. The results showed that the value in these three raters is about 0.78 (see Table 3 – 12), which is substantial in the reliability of categorizing and analyzing writing errors. The results also proposed that the training be conducted to improve the inter-rater agreement.

3.5 The Main Study

3.5.1 The Sampling Method and Description of the Samples

This study was carried out among non-English majors in a public normal university in southern China. The reasons for selecting this college were the convenient consideration. On the one hand, I worked there as a lecturer for more than ten years, so I have a good working relationship with the related staff. On the other hand, the English final exams for non-English majors were implemented in a computer for about ten years, which supplied the direct doc. form compositions for my sampling selection. Therefore, the preliminary and the main studies were all conducted in this university. The age of participants is from 17 to 19 who are all junior college students with Chinese as their first language. They have learned English language in school for at least nine years. All participants have no experience living abroad.

The whole population of the data was collected during the summer holiday of 2021, and the staff administrating computer-assisted final exams packaged the file with my concrete request and sent them to my email box. The population of each year is 40 participants who will be divided into three groups with the criteria of Wiersma and Jurs (1990). Because of the different numbers of admitted college students, the yearly population is not identical. For the composition samplings, the students' personal information is presented in their test papers. Therefore, when selecting the samplings, all the information will be included to investigate deeply in the later questionnaire and interviews.

3.5.2 Data Collection Procedures

The main study for the questionnaire took place from Nov. 11 to Dec. 15 in 2021, with interviews from Dec. 23 to Dec. 31, 2021, while error analysis happened during January, 2022. All the data was collected from non-English majors of a public normal university in southern China. The other two colleagues agreed to work as raters or coders in my research, and I discussed the procedure of error analysis and the criteria for categorizing those errors under the guidance of theories of second language learning. The meeting among the three raters was fundamental, because the timetable for every stage of analyzing writing errors was set. It presents accurate coordination in arranging every step of the data collection. This study adopted a mixed method approach, so more time and a detailed timeline was needed. The original number of participants in the questionnaire was 292 students, while the participants in interviews for students were 14 and teachers 9. The samples selected from the whole population were totally of 320 in 8 years, with 40 pieces each year.

3.5.2.1 Administering the Writing Proficiency Test

With the agreement from the head of College English Department, I can adopt the writing materials in the final exam for I just use them for academic purpose. And simultaneously, all of these data should be prohibited from being revealed to the third party no matter its purpose. The consent form was assigned to ensure the confidentiality of all those final exam papers. The writing proficiency test was included as part of the English final exam in each semester of the first two years of non-English majors in the selected university. In the writing section, the students are required to type a short essay on their computers on a given topic within 30 minutes with more than 120 words but no more than 180 words. And in the process, it is prohibited to look up a dictionary or turn to the Internet, which can ensure the authenticity of students' writing proficiency. The topic for each student was not the same for the writing part was composed as a small corpus that includes a great number of topics. At the beginning of corpus building, the depth of difficulty and the reliability has been investigated to ensure the uniformity of different topics. Furthermore, different topics were randomly distributed to students when they entered the exam software. Different topics can be seen from Appendix 1. At the same time, the participant information sheet was also composed of the names, majors, students' ID, final examination score, and their writing scores.

3.5.2.2 Categorizing Error Types and Analyzing

After calculating the inter-rater agreement of three raters, proper training was provided to enhance the reliability of the agreement. Then the three raters would analyze the writing errors respectively according to the rules which were agreed together. The theoretical framework adopted in the error analysis was from James (1998), which first identified error types from the first level of passage, like substance errors, grammatical errors, lexical errors, syntactic errors, and semantic errors. For each type of level errors, there are some sub-categories under it, which elaborates in depth in the L2 writing errors, such as substance errors (capitalization, punctuation, and spelling), grammatical errors (adjectives, adverbs, determiners, link verb, auxiliary verb, nouns, possession, pronouns, preposition, and verbs), lexical errors (word formation, word deficiency, word abundance and word selection), syntactic errors (coordination/subordination, sentence structure and ordering), and semantic errors (ambiguity and miscommunication). The reason why I employed this theoretical framework was explained in Section 3.2.1. With this relatively comprehensive framework, different errors could be categorized. The more attention in error analysis was paid to the frequencies and rank order of each error in the total calculation. Each rater has distributed the templates which recorded each concrete type of error and the times it appears in one composition (see Appendix 13).

Table 3 - 14 Steps to Analyze Writing Errors

Corder's Steps	Researcher's Steps
1. Collect data	Collect 320 writing samples from English final exams
2. Identify errors	A. Subject-verb agreement, verb tense, link verb, auxiliary verb, model verb, adjective, adverb, preposition, pronoun, plural forms, conjunction, determiners B. Word selection, word abundance, word deficiency C. Capitalization, punctuation, spelling D. Subordinate, sentence structure, ordering E. Ambiguity, miscommunication
3. Classify errors	A. Grammatical errors B. Substance errors C. Lexical errors D. Syntax errors E. Semantic errors
4. Qualify errors	How many types of each error occur? What are the differences in errors in the past eight years? What percentage of each error type is in the overall error types?
5. Analyze source	Intralingual transfer Interlingual transfer

Each composition was recorded into a template which includes each type of error mentioned above. After all the samples were analyzed, the frequencies and the rank order were presented in one template, and at the same time, those numbers would be input into the software SPSS 26.0, as well as the final exam score and their writing score. The purpose of such action was to investigate the correlation between their writing proficiency and the frequencies of writing errors. Ultimately, when all the errors were recorded and calculated, the final inter-rater agreement would be checked.

Table 3 – 15 Background Information of Questionnaire Participants in the Main Study

Group	Mean Age (*SD*)	Gender (*N*)	Years of Learning English		Whether Being Abroad
			M	*SD*	*N*
High proficiency	18.6 (.827)	Male (=9) Female (=70)	10.83	2.041	Yes (=2) No (=77)
Fair proficiency	18.69 (.825)	Male (=11) Female (=123)	10.41	2.598	Yes (=10) No (=124)
Low proficiency	18.79 (.873)	Male (=35) Female (=44)	10.24	2.234	Yes (=2) No (=77)

Note: high proficiency group (*N* = 79), fair proficiency group (*N* = 134), and poor proficiency group (*N* = 79).

3.5.2.3 Operating the Questionnaire

The participants in the questionnaire in this stage were 292, and the essential information was provided in Table 3 – 15. All the participants signed the consent form text to participant in the experiment. The questionnaire instructions were explained very clearly (see Appendix 13) before they took the items. And at the same time, the consent forms were distributed to the participants and assigned by each participant. With all of these instructions, the participants were aware the participation in the study was voluntary and they could drop from the data collection procedure at any stage without offering any reasons and without any consequences (see Appendix 11 and 12 about the Informed Consent Form).

The above assurance was confirmed by their English teachers (my colleagues) so that the students would ensure the participation in this research would not have any consequences and there were no effect on their marks in English subject. Rather, the items in the questionnaire could help them face their problems and difficulties in English writing.

The data was collected through online questionnaire, which can solve the distance problem. The date I decided to distribute the questionnaire was Oct. 27, during which I was in Busan, South Korea. It was impossible to go back to China to do the questionnaire survey because of pandemic. Initially, an online questionnaire was created with many kinds of buttons existing in the website (add, delete, multiple choice, Q&A, etc.) and then an online questionnaire link was generated, which can be transferred to others through WeChat or QQ (two kinds of social media which are popular among Chinese). When receiving the link, the online questionnaire would exhibit out while clicking it. Of course, before conducting in the mass students, those students who have read the items would be excluded from participants and provide feedback, which was explained in detail in the pilot study (see Section 3. 5. 3). The online questionnaire format was suitable to read on the cellphone, which enhances the readability of the online questionnaire. When the participants complete it, the online questionnaire answers could be selected together and combined into one excel form, which is very convenient to input into the software SPSS.

3. 5. 2. 4 Conducting Interviews

The interview parts are composed of two sections, one for students and one for teachers. 14 students and 9 teachers will be involved into the interviews (see Table 3 – 16 and 3 – 17). 14 student participants are collected according to their writing proficiency, while 9 teachers are my colleagues who have been teaching college English for more than 10 years. I met the participants through the Internet video (the same reason with the questionnaire), introduced myself to them and also explained the aim of the study, the procedure and the duration of the interview. The instructions were also explained directly, while the consent forms were sent to clarify the requirement in detail.

Table 3 – 16 Interview Schedule for Students

Group	Number of Participants	Time	Interview Method Nover net
High proficiency	4	From Nov. 25 to Nov. 30	4
Fair proficiency	6	From Dec. 1 to Dec. 5	6
Low proficiency	4	From Dec. 6 to Dec. 10	4

The criteria were quite similar to the questionnaire, that was, everyone was voluntary to participate and could withdraw without any reasons and any consequences. Hearing all the instructions, some students showed a certain degree of concern over audio taping. To solve these problems, firstly, I tried to convince them that their identity would be confidential without names needed. They were only requested to tell the researcher their student's ID number; secondly, I informed them that their English teachers would never access their audio recordings, and I was the only one who could listen to them. What's more, for each student's ID number, there would be a random code which nobody can identify except the researcher. Ultimately, student participants were all willing to take part in the interview and authorize the researcher to record and transcribe what they said and discussed in the interview. Interviews for teachers were quite easy because they are my long-term colleagues, teachers or researchers, so they cooperated very well in every step of the interview. Certainly, before the interview, the instructions which were similar to students were all informed to teacher interviewees. They showed high cooperation and high efficiency in answering questions and discussions, furthermore, they provided much feedback on the interview topics, which were really gained beyond expectation.

There are six questions for the student interview (see Appendix 8) which started with an easy and straightforward question. The purpose of such a design could draw the distance close between students and the interviewer, and easy questions can make interviewees relaxed when they face the researcher for the first time. The total time for each student was about 20 minutes. However, the entire procedure took about 300 minutes, as I spent 25 minutes preparing, explaining the procedure and answering the students' questions. The audio tape was recorded through WeChat audio software and then saved into one file with similar to the their code number in the computer. For the teacher interview, the procedure was the following part, six interview questions, with an average of 30 minutes of talking. The significant differences between these two sections lie in that teacher interviewees had much to discuss with the researcher for they also had lots of puzzles and confusions when they taught English writing. However, they had little time to think carefully about the possible reasons which caused these errors.

Table 3 – 17 Interview Schedule for Teachers

	Professional Title	Length of Teaching (Year)	Time	Gender (*N*)	Interview Method Nover net
Huang	Associated Professor	15	Nov. 25	Male	Yes
Yuan	Lecturer	13	Nov. 25	Female	Yes
Zhuang	Lecturer	12	Nov. 26	Female	Yes
Yang	Associated Professor	16	Nov. 26	Female	Yes
Tang	Professor	30	Nov. 27	Female	Yes
Lu	Lecturer	15	Nov. 27	Female	Yes
Liu	Lecturer	15	Nov. 28	Female	Yes
Huang	Associated Professor	23	Nov. 28	Female	Yes
Yan	Lecturer	30	Nov. 29	Female	Yes

3.6 Data Analysis

3.6.1 Scoring the Writing Proficiency Test

The total number of participants in the selected compositions was 320, 40 pieces each year, lasting 8 years. The samples were selected, first, by stratified sampling method because this research would like to examine the differences among different writing proficiency groups, that is, high, fair and low three groups. The cutting point is presented in Appendix 12. After stratifying the different proficiency groups, convenience sampling was adopted to select compositions in each stratification. During the random selection process, I discarded some samples for validity reasons because some compositions were too short or had digressed from the topic. All of these compositions were scored because they were generated as part of the English final exam. The scoring criteria followed the CET – 4 principles (see Appendix 2). Therefore, a final list of 320 compositions were selected, including 86 high proficiency writers, 148 fair proficiency writers and 86 low proficiency writers.

3.6.2 Calculating Frequencies of Writing Errors

After collecting the samplings by the stratified random method, three raters categorized different errors of three different writing proficiency groups into the template for each participant (see Appendix 4). Besides three raters, a well-known software *Grammarly* was also employed together to assist in examining the error types. *Grammarly* is a cloud-based writing assistant which reviews spelling, grammar, punctuation, clarity, engagement, and delivery mistakes. It uses AI to identify and search for an appropriate replacement for the mistakes it locates. It also allows users to customize their style, tone, and context-specific language (Lardinois, 2016). I adopted the premium version of the software, compared to the free one which paid attention only on spelling, grammar, punctuation and conciseness, this version could examine the compositions from the following aspects: clarity-focused sentence rewrites, tone adjustment, plagiarism detection, word choice, formality level, and fluency (https://www.grammarly.com/premium). With the assistance of this software, a precise assessment was expected to achieve. After assessing the errors, the total numbers of the error types were input in the excel format, which was very convenient for calculating the frequencies and rank order of each error type. This step was the descriptive analysis of the error analysis, which laid a foundation for further investigation on the correlation between students' writing proficiency and their errors. This further operation was conducted in the SPSS 26.0, which could supply intuitionistic numbers with statistical results.

3.6.3 Implementing the Questionnaire

The data obtained from the questionnaire was computer-coded with the statistical software SPSS 26.0. Data was cleaned and imputed before the data analysis. Even though we have checked the validity and reliability of the questionnaire in the pilot study, some items whose values were below 0.60 would be excluded from the questionnaire. The revised questionnaire was conducted with a total of 292 participants, and 15 were eliminated for invalid answers, such as choosing the same degree for all the items (e.g., circled 1 for the first 5 items, 2 for the next items, etc.). The principal statistical methods adopted for the data analysis were factor analysis, Pearson correlation analysis, One-way ANOVA (analysis of variance), independent T-test, and multiple regression analysis. At the same time, the effect size (see Table 3 – 15) was reported when Pearson correlation analysis and multiple regressions were conducted and used to evaluate how the independent variables influenced the dependent variables.

3.6.4 Transcribing and Analyzing Interviews

The recordings of students' interviews and teachers' interviews were transcribed by the researcher. A copy of the transcription would be given to the interviewees to review and point out the improper meaning of their expressions. After that, the transcriptions of students and teachers were translated into English for further analysis. The method of analyzing the semi-structured interview belongs to the qualitative type, which explains the transcription in its own way. The data processing adopted what the qualitative method suggested. Firstly, the content of the interviews should be recorded, and the transcriptions should be translated into English and read to the interviewees. Secondly, the researcher extracted significant statements from each interviewee's transcription, and then input them in the templates for each interviewee. The selected parts of the transcription were related to the research questions. Following the above approach, interview data could be interpreted and categorized in depth. The transcription and categorization were examined by two Chinese experts who were experienced in English writing to evaluate the coding and categorization to increase the trustworthiness and reliability of the data analysis. Any questions and doubts proposed by the two experts were presented in the procedure. The researcher processed the interview data through detailed content analysis. In order to explain the data clearly and reasonably, different writing proficiency groups were categorized into different templates. Ultimately, the researcher selected the significant findings to report.

In this chapter, I have presented and discussed the methodology which was adopted to investigate writing errors and the possible reasons behind these errors. Mixed research methods and instruments have been employed to achieve the goals of this research: writing proficiency tests, a questionnaire, and interviews. These methods and instruments could investigate different angles of the research questions, which provided clues for further analysis. The procedure for data collection and analysis during the pilot study and the main study has also been addressed and justified. In the next section, Chapter 4 will provide a comprehensive analysis of, first, writing errors, their frequencies and rank orders; second, linguistic and non-linguistic reasons affecting participants' writing proficiency. With these results, the concrete numbers could solve the problems we raised in the first chapter.

CHAPTER 4
RESULTS AND DATA ANALYSIS

This chapter first presents the data obtained from the descriptive analysis of writing errors in 320 students' compositions to answer the first two research questions posed in this study. The trend of writing errors in the past eight years was revealed through the frequencies and percentages of the occurring of those errors. With all of those descriptive analyses, the correlation between writing proficiency and error types and the possible reasons behind writing errors were also investigated and presented with statistical analysis of the software SPSS 26.0 to answer questions 3 and 4. The following part focuses on the non-linguistic variables which affect students' writing performance. The results of this part come from questionnaire outcomes described in detail in Chapter 3. The data of this section are mainly responsible for Research Question 4, which presents the correlation and ANOVA of different variables. The last part of this chapter demonstrates the qualitative data of the interviews, which aims to explore in depth the possible reasons causing students writing errors. This whole chapter exhibits different tables and figures with descriptions of different data, which lays a foundation for the later discussion of these data and answers the related research questions in Chapter 5.

4.1 Descriptive Statistics in Chinese L2 Students' Writing Error Patterns

In order to obtain an overview of the linguistic errors that Chinese writers encountered when writing in English, Figure 4 – 1 below exhibits the types of errors they made and the frequency of commission of these errors in the last eight years.

From Figure 4 – 1 we can see that the overall trend of making errors from the year 2013 (633 errors) to the year 2020 (458 errors) is decreasing even though the change from the year 2014 (441 errors) to the year 2020 (458 errors) is not apparent. This could indicate that in the last eight years, students' writing proficiency has been improved a little bit but not noticeable. For most college students, writing error is still a problem that cannot avoid in their writing.

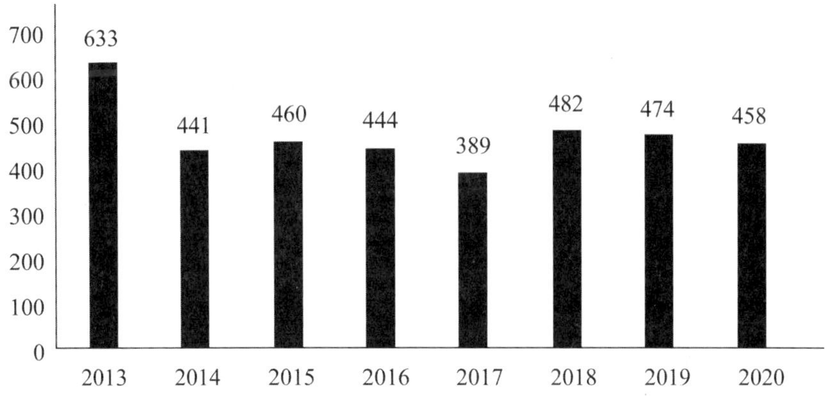

Figure 4 – 1 The Frequencies of the Linguistic Errors Made from the Year 2013 to 2020

According to Figure 4 – 2, the overall trend in three groups is decreasing even though the degrees vary. The amplitude scope of the high proficiency level is the smallest, from about 60 to 100. Whereas, the other two groups obtained quite similar trend lines, which crossed three regions of the figure. At the same time, the degree of fair and low proficiency groups shakes to a large extent, meanwhile the two lines are quite the same except for the year 2016 for it ranks the second highest in making errors of FPG except the year 2013.

The last trend in this part is the changes of errors in terms of each category in the past eight years. The chart depicts very clearly of these five main error categories. Among these, the highest line indicates the most errors committed by students, while the middle line represents the medium, and the lowest represents the least errors. Obviously, semantic errors are the least one in them. The second biggest problem for L2 learners is grammatical errors, which includes lots of items under this category, like subject-verb agreement, verb tense, adjective, adverb, preposition, plural form, modal verb, link verb, etc. These grammars are the obstacles to acquiring L2 because the differences in such grammars are significant between Chinese and English. Even though teaching English grammar is the most important part of school education, students still have many confusions and difficulties. The results can provide some implications for grammar teaching, which will be discussed later in Chapter 6.

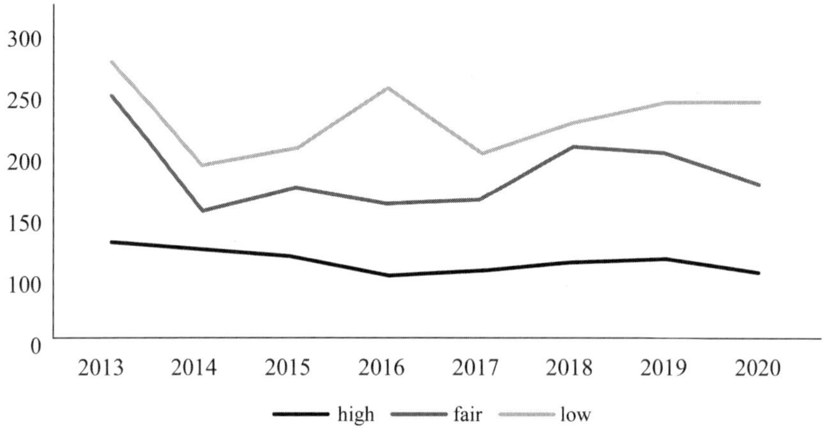

Figure 4 – 2 The Changes in Total Error Numbers of Each Year in Terms of Proficiency Levels

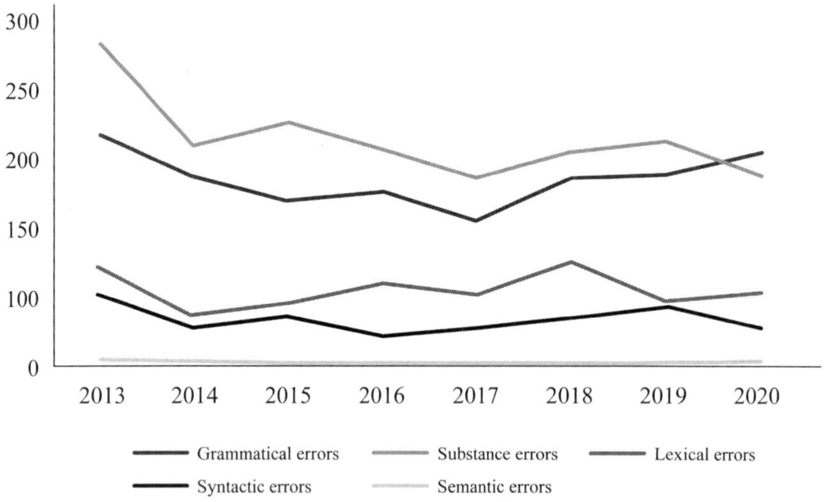

Figure 4 – 3 The Changes in Errors in Terms of Each Category from the Year 2013 to 2020

4.1.1 Frequencies and Percentages of Writing Errors

The bar chart presents that substance errors were the most problematic category to the participants in this research (1,585). The rest challenging types were grammatical errors (1,306), lexical errors (532), syntactic errors (337), and semantic errors (21). Among these, the frequencies of each category are different even though the frequencies between substance and grammatical errors are similar. In the category of substance errors, three sub-type errors, like errors in capitalization, punctuation, and spelling, are included, which exhibit the percentage respectively 14% (224), 7% (111), and 79% (1,250) of the total substance errors.

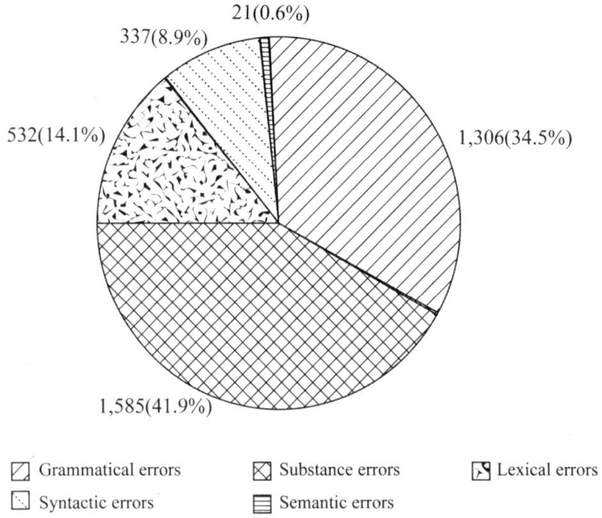

Figure 4 – 4 The Types and Frequencies of Linguistic Errors

Regarding the frequencies of each sub-type of errors, it can be seen clearly from Figure 4 – 5 that spelling is the most frequent error with a total of 1,250 errors, which is followed by word form, subject-verb agreement, verb tense, capitalization and sentence structure.

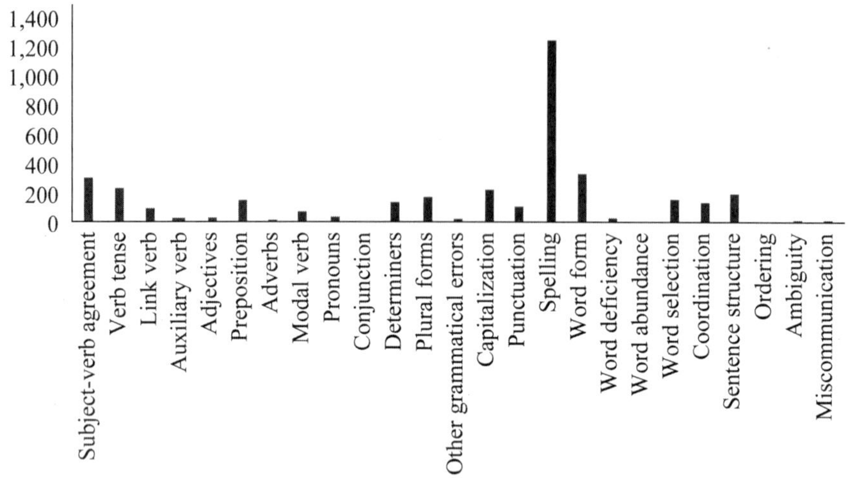

Figure 4 – 5 Frequencies of Each Type of Errors

In order to show the characteristics of different proficiency groups, a statistical analysis is conducted to show the difference between them. The statistics showed that the average error number of each composition in the high, fair and low proficiency group is 7.18, 12.78, and 15.81, respectively, which means that the average errors in the low proficiency level double that of the high proficiency group. The ANOVA shows that it is significantly different between high and low proficiency levels, the same as fair and low proficiency levels. Regarding different error types, the average number of errors in the low proficiency group is higher than that of the high proficiency group, and the ANOVA presents that it is a significant difference between high, fair and low proficiency groups ($p < 0.05$) except the type of semantic errors (see Table 4 – 1).

Table 4 – 1 The Differences among Three Proficiency Groups in Different Types of Errors

Error Types	Samples	*N*	*M*	*SD*	*F* (ANOVA)	*Sig.*
Grammatical errors	HPG	88	2.77	1.981	9.652	.000**
	FPG	144	4.40	2.136		
	LPG	88	4.73	2.382		
Substance errors	HPG	88	2.66	2.034	35.797	.000**
	FPG	144	5.42	4.164		
	LPG	88	6.48	4.229		

(To be continued)

Error Types	Samples	*N*	*M*	*SD*	*F* (ANOVA)	*Sig.*
Lexical errors	HPG	88	1.19	1.202	5.007	.000 **
	FPG	144	1.81	1.640		
	LPG	88	1.88	1.453		
Syntactic errors	HPG	88	.53	.772	4.184	.000 **
	FPG	144	1.10	1.541		
	LPG	88	1.81	1.618		
Semantic errors	HPG	88	.03	.183	1.543	.043
	FPG	144	.05	.216		
	LPG	88	.91	5.392		
Total	HPG	88	7.18			.000 **
	FPG	144	12.78			
	LPG	88	15.81			

Notes: HPG = high proficiency group; FPG = fair proficiency group; LPG = low proficiency group (** : $p < .01$)

Of course, besides these five categories of errors, the participants in this study also found other errors, like structure errors. Since this research mainly examined the linguistic errors that the writers made, structure errors were not included in the scope of this research. In the following section, I will discuss each main category and its sub-category errors mentioned in the previous part, and attempt to locate the findings of this study within the broader literature.

In the following part, we would like to explain each category and its sub-category errors which will be illustrated with the concrete examples found in Chinese L2 writings. These examples and explanations will depict a clear picture of the category.

Table 4 – 2 Frequency and Percentage of Errors

Types	Sub-category		Examples	Frequency	Percentage	Rank Order
Grammatical errors	Subject-verb agreement		e. g. *She come back home at six.*	302	7. 99%	3
	Verb tense		e. g. *Christmas coming soon.*	233	6. 16%	4
	Linking verbs		e. g. *She a student.*	98	2. 59%	13
	Auxiliary verbs		e. g. *What not you like?*	16	0. 42%	19
	Adjectives		e. g. *I have not many time to spend at home.*	32	0. 85%	15
	Prepositions		e. g. *We did not use to sit on tables when eating.*	152	4%	9
	Adverbs		e. g. *She was disappointed so much.*	14	0. 37%	21
	Modal verbs		e. g. *I will must to study Norwegian.*	75	1. 98%	14
	Pronouns		e. g. *John decided to return the book to he friend.*	37	0. 98%	15
	Conjunctions			11	0. 29%	22
	Deter-miners	articles	e. g. "*a*", "*an*", and "*the*"	140	3. 70%	10
		demons-tratives	e. g. "*this*", "*that*", "*these*", and "*those*"			
		quanti-fiers	e. g. "*few*" and "*many*"			
		posse-ssives	e. g. , "*my*", "*your*", "*his*", "*her*", "*its*", "*our*", and "*their*"			
	Plural forms		e. g. *Every coins has two sides.*	174	4. 60%	7
	Other gramma-tical errors			22	0. 58%	17

(To be continued)

Types	Sub-category	Examples	Frequency	Percentage	Rank Order
Substance errors	Capitalization	e. g. *I will buy benze.*	224	5.92%	5
	Punctuation	e. g. *I liked them. they were so nice to me.*	111	2.94%	12
	Spelling	e. g. *I want to go some intesting places to visit.*	1250	33.06%	1
Lexical errors	Word form	e. g. *Young people can be independence in the United States.*	336	8.90%	2
	Word deficiency	e. g. *She is a beautiful.*	26	0.69%	17
	Word abundance	e. g. *I have many lots of books.*	8	0.22%	23
	Word selection	e. g. *Both sicks are kids.*	162	4.29%	8
Syntactic errors	Coordination/ subordination/ correlative	e. g. *Jasmine is afraid of dogs, she was bitten by a dog when she was young.*	141	3.73%	10
	Sentence structure	e. g. *I dinner like to eat spaghetti.*	193	5.11%	6
	Ordering	e. g. *The ball dropped the boy.*	3	0.08%	25
Semantic errors	Ambiguity	e. g. *I saw the bank this morning.*	5	0.13%	24
	Miscommunication	e. g. *He should love his work who is belong to his job.*	16	0.42%	19

4.1.2 Levels of Error

In the previous chapter, we looked at ways to describe errors. In this chapter, we would like to focus on the classification of those errors. According to James (1998), the classification of errors takes reference to three criteria: modality, medium and level.

Modality refers to whether the learners' behaviour was receptive or productive. The author uses the word "receptive" instead of "passive" because language processing is never passive. Instead, "passive" processing involves mental and interpretive activity on the receiver's part. Medium indicates whether the language produced or received was spoken or written. Taking modality and medium together, we can identify "four skills" that learner was operating at the time of the error: speaking, writing, listening or reading. Besides what we have specified on what level of language the learner was operating at the time of making errors. In this regard, there are five levels of language: grammatical levels, substance levels, lexical levels, syntactic levels and semantic levels. In each type of levels, there are some sub-categorizations to explain each type of errors in detail. The following part will illustrate each type of error with concrete examples that are quoted from a self-build file. Those examples are all from the compositions of final exam papers of non-English majors in a normal university in southern China. The compositions are all data that will be adopted to the last chapter of the case study. The code number attached to the end of each example is the index in this self-build file. In addition to the levels of each type of error, the linguistic differences between Chinese and English are also mentioned to lay a foundation for the later exploration on writing errors.

Grammatical Errors

Errors in these levels mainly include subject-verb agreement, verb tense, preposition, determiners, plural form, modal verb, link verb, auxiliary verb, pronouns and so on, which cover most of types of errors committed by the participants, respectively are 7.99%, 6.16%, 4%, 3.70%, 4.60%, 1.98%, 2.59%, 0.42%, 0.98%, of the total errors. In the following part, we would like to explain each type of error with concrete examples.

a. Subject-verb agreement

In English, verbs should agree with their subjects in number and in person. A singular subject matches a singular verb while a plural subject matches a plural verb. However, Chinese verbs are not inflected for person or number, and hence, a great number of errors occur in the writers' essays. For example, Participant 13FM_024 wrote:

1. *He hope I can study hard.*

Another example from Participant 15FM_026's essay was:

2. *Someone think the money is the source of happiness.*

Also other participants overgeneralized the rule and made sentences like:

3. *The learning methods I used at high school is quite different from what I used at college* (17FM_004).
4. *Digital products has been widly (wildly) used in modern life* (20FM_011).

The possible reason for this error type is that in Chinese, there are no requirements in agreement both in person and in number, which means that the verb is always the same no matter the person is singular or plural form. The differences lying behind Chinese and English in this aspect puzzled Chinese students since the beginning of their learning English. For example:

5. 他每天骑自行车去学校。
6. 他们每天都骑自行车去学校。

The subjects "他" and "他们" are respectively singular and plural form, however, the verb "骑 (qi)" in both sentences are quite the same. Whereas, in English the verb in both sentences are different because the singular subject takes "rides" as its predicate while the plural subject takes "ride" as its predicate.

One note should be pointed out that "there be +" structure is also included in this scope for some students are puzzled when dealing with this structure. Particularly, principle of proximity in "there be +" structure puzzled Chinese L2 students a lot for there are no such sentence patterns in Chinese expression. For most of time, they cannot figure out clearly the difference between "there are" and "there is". On the other hand, because this sentence structure also focuses on the number and its person agreement, it also belongs to this scope.

Subject-verb agreement errors were also reported by previous studies on Chinese EFL writers, such as Xu (2005), Lu (2018) and so on. Those researchers found that subject-verb agreement was challenging to the participants particularly. Wen's (2005) study, for example, categories this kind of error made by the writers into two types.

b. Verb tense

Thomas (1993) ever explained that there are two tenses in English: present and past tenses. Future tense does not exist in English, but it can deliver the future situation by using auxiliary verbs. In Chinese, there is no verb tense like English. The past tense or present tense of the verbs is demonstrated with the auxiliary verbs or time adverbial modifiers. Therefore, the verb tense of English is also one of the problematic part to the participants when they are written in English. Among the main difficulties, employing the correct sequences of tenses is one of them when combining the complex sentences, which affects the understanding of their essays negatively. For example, Participant 14FM_009 wrote:

1. *And he will work happily because he loved it.*

In the example, we can see that the writer failed to maintain the tense sequence which could increase the comprehensibility of the text. He started the sentence with a future tense (he will...) but a past tense follows (he loved...).

Other participants combine the sentences with more than one tense in it. Such as the example in 14FM_023:

2. ..., *that will benefits for us.*

In this sentence, it combines two kinds of tense into one sentence, the future tense and the present tense. In English, one sentence has only one tense. The example will arouse the confusion of understanding the text. Those errors are usually called intralingual errors, which will be explained in Chapter 5.

In Chinese, the verb tense is not obvious like in English. The past or present situation of Chinese is usually demonstrated with auxiliary verbs or time adverbial modifiers. Such as:

3. 我昨天去了学校。(*I went to school yesterday.*)
4. 我明天将要去学校。(*I will go to school tomorrow.*)
5. 我每天都去公园。(*I go to park every day.*)

These three examples represent the past and present tense very clearly in English with the change of verb form. However, in Chinese the verb itself has no change, while the different situations of past and present are demonstrated with different expressions from English. Specifically, in Example 3, the word "了" usually follows the verb to represent the past tense. In Example 4, the future situation is delivered by the auxiliary verb "将要 (will)" and time adverbial "tomorrow". While in Example 5, the present tense is represented with the time adverbial "每天 (every day)" without form change in the verb.

When the participants were interviewed about such challenge, a few of them reported that the difficulties were aroused because of the tense systems in Chinese and English. Other participants mentioned that they were probably lack of practices with the use of different tenses in different context at the beginning of the acquisition (e. g. Participants SI4 and SI5). These statements are consistent with those of previous researches, such as Xu (2015) and Qafishen's (1997), all of whom stated that verb tense was one of the most difficult grammatical aspects in English writing.

c. Plural forms

One of the distinct features of the structure of Chinese is that there are no plural forms of nouns in Chinese. The meaning of plural nouns attaches the number adverbials before the nouns. Therefore, using plural forms of nouns, particularly irregular ones, was found to be problematic to the fair and low proficiency participants in the present research. The following are a few examples in which the errors in plural form were used by the students:

1. ... *different people have different point* (Participant 17FM_020).
2. ... *if we meet some problem, such as...* (Participant 19FM_019)
3. *There are forty childs in my class.* (Participant 19FM_020).

More students are not aware of the suffix after the noun to express its plural forms, such as:

4. *We can plant more tree.* (Participant 18FM_024).
5. *It will produce more opportunity.* (Participant 19FM_017)

The reasons attributed to such errors are probably that in Chinese there are no suffixes adding to the nouns. To express the plural form of the nouns in Chinese, they usually modify the nouns with adjectives, such as "many trees" in English, which can be literally expressed as "xu duo shu (many trees)", not to mention some irregular form of nouns. Those kinds of errors made by Chinese writers are caused by negative interference of L1, which coincide with the research results of Azzou (2013). Azzou's (2013) study also reported that his participants made errors in the use of the plural form, and he attributed these errors to the negative interference of L1.

Some researchers state that the problems in plural form that Chinese learners experience in English writing are due to the fact that it is a little difficult to decide whether irregular words in English are singular or plural (El-Aswad, 2002). In English some words end with letter (s) as if they were plural but the participants treat them as singular forms. The researcher Xu (2019) attributes some of these errors to the negative interference of L1. But the interviewers attributed these errors as the confusion of irregular plural forms.

Thus, it can be concluded that the confusion between singular and plural forms among Chinese students when writing in English could be challenging to them. Importantly, similar conclusion were reached by the current experiment research in the last chapter.

d. Prepositions

Prepositions made a great challenge for Chinese-speaking participants when writing in English. In the category of grammatical errors, this type of error raises the fourth frequent errors. Compared with Chinese, English has a complexity of the prepositional system and each preposition can indicate several different relations. For example, the preposition *at* is adopted in English when referring to time, place, distance, speed, and so on. Therefore, the low proficiency writers are not certain about what prepositions should be used to express their thinking, because in Chinese there are no equivalent prepositions. Consequently, errors occur when Chinese learners of English try to use their linguistic language of their L1 in English writing. The observation of the essays of the participates can show the problem, such as the following examples:

1. *When I was (in) high school, I...* (Participant 18FM_033)

(The preposition *in* is omitted in the writing because of nonequivalent preposition in Chinese)

2. *I go (went) to a university for studying in last summer.* (Participant 16FM_027)

(The preposition *in* is overused in the writing because of nonequivalent preposition in Chinese)

In Chinese, "在 (zai)" is usually regarded as the most frequent preposition in referring the place, time and location without any form change. Compared with the various prepositions in English, Chinese has only a few of them, which caused the confusion when students adopt them in writing English.

3. 我在五点钟回到了家。(*I went home <u>at</u> five o'clock.*)
4. 在这个城市里，有我的家人。(*<u>In</u> this city, there are my family members.*)

According to AL-Sindy's (1994) study, preposition errors found in his students' writing were caused by improper use, dropping, omission, and insertion of prepositions. He stated that the students appeared to misuse prepositions such as the use of (in) instead of (on), the use of (in) instead of (at), the use of (in) instead of (by) and (of), the use of (with) instead of (by) and (to), the use of (by) instead of (with) and (of), the use of (to) instead of (in) and (at), the use of (for) instead of (to), the use of (from) instead of (of), (about) and (from). In his study, the data indicated that some students were thinking in L1 while engaging in L2 writing. Similarly, the scholars Li (2000) and James (2012) also reported that the challenges in the use of prepositions faced by Chinese writers when writing English could be attributed to the complex nature of the English preposition system, and all of those errors made by Chinese L2 learners are caused by the negative interference of L1.

e. Articles

Definite and indefinite articles are commonly adopted in Noun Phrase (NPs). A definite article is defined as "a determiner that introduces a noun phrase and implies that the thing mentioned has either already been mentioned, or is common knowledge, or is about to be defined" (*Oxforddictionaries. com*, 2017). This could be another problematic aspect for Chinese L2 writers when writing in English, especially for fair and low proficiency ones. Because in Chinese, as the scholar Xu (2009) puts it, Chinese and English belong to different two systems, and the writers might apply their previous knowledge [of Chinese] when they began to learn English. Particularly, Chinese learners cannot identify the differences between the definite article and the indefinite article for there is no such conception in Chinese. In these writings of this dissertation, the errors fall into the following four categories:

Dropping a definite article:

1. *For (the) student of (the) college, they often play Internet game (s).* (Participant 14FM_036)

Dropping an indefinite article:

2. *We should realize computer have (has) both (a) good side and (a) bad side.* (Participant 17FM_034)

Using an unnecessary article:

3. *It is no doubt that the Spring *Festival has (a) long *history in China.* (Participant 18FM_016)

Confusing of the indefinite article "a" and "an":

4. *Spoiling is a (an) unreasonable behavior.* (Participant 19FM_012)

In fact, besides the above four categories of errors, there are still two other kinds of errors in the use of articles which are not mentioned here: one is replacing the definite article by the indefinite article and the other is replacing the indefinite article by the definite article. It seemed that if some students cannot grasp the use of article, they probably omitted articles when referring to the noun. Meanwhile, if Chinese learners have the awareness of articles when describing the irregular noun, they can figure out the differences between the definite article and the indefinite article, but always make confusions between "a" and "an". Among all of those errors, omitting the articles is the most frequent one. The reason for this is the differences of using articles between Chinese and English, because in Chinese there are no definite or indefinite articles. Chinese use quantifiers to define the nouns.

f. Modal verbs

In English, there are several modal verbs: *can*, *could*, *may*, *might*, *must*, *will*, *would*, *shall*, and *should*. There are still some semi-modals like *have to*, *ought to*, *supposed to*, *going to* and *used to* which share the same function. Greenbaum and Quirk (1990) stated that in general, each modal verb has more than one meaning. Therefore, the classification of the modal verb depends on what they classified themselves according to the meaning they convey. They regarded this feature as a significant challenging factor, which was to master modal verbs usage in English.

The use of modal verbs was also found to be challenging to the participants in this study, particularly the forms of words or phrases after the modal verb. In all of these participants, most of them can choose the right modal verb but with wrong words followed, as the following examples show:

1. *People can so happy.* (Participant 19FM_035)

Actually, in Chinese there are also such modal verbs like "can", "may", "must" etc., however, there are no such inflections which are followed by different words with different parts of speech, for example, "people can so happy" should be corrected into "people can be so happy". Chinese writers may not be aware of the word "be" in this sentence, so they omit it. Other participants were found to combine a modal verb with the preposition "to":

2. *I will must to study English.* (Participant 15FM_021)

The other participants overgeneralize the rule of modal verb, combining the modal verb with an auxiliary verb, like the following example:

3. *Many students may don't like study...* (Participant 13FM_022)

The participants who wrote the above examples were not able to apply the rules of English grammar successfully. The finding emphasizes the importance of improving the students' sensitivity of the unique linguistic features of English and also the differences between them and those of Chinese (See Chapter 6 for the implication of the study). The result is consistent with those of some scholars, Xu (2009) and Li (2014), etc.

g. Linking verbs

According to Ellis (2022), linking verbs are verbs that don't show action but rather describe the subject. While verbs like *play* or *walk* represent an action, linking verbs like *seem* or *be* describe more details to the subject, such as "he seems very well" or "he is a professor."

Linking verbs are important part of any language, especially in English. Because the most common verb *be* is a linking verb. As we have mentioned, linking verbs do not show an action, or to be concrete, they only show the existing action. Linking verbs simply explain the state of the subject, such as what it is or how it looks.

1. *She is twelve years old.*
2. *He seems very happy today.*
3. *This place looks like a garden*!

This kind of application is different from other types of verbs' usage, like ditransitive verbs, phrasal verbs, or impersonal verbs, which all describe specific actions. Verbs can be categorized into two groups, action verbs and linking verbs. However, sometimes some verbs can play both roles.

Linking verbs define the subject or add more details about it. That means sensory verbs like *smell*, *sound*, *taste*, *look*, *appear*, or *feel* can act as linking verbs when they describe the subject.

4. *The flower smells sweet.*
5. *This music sounds raspy.*

In the data of the compositions, the following situations are very common, omitting and misusing the linking verb, especially when the linking verb is related to different tenses.

6. *Our earth will more and more beautiful*! (14FM_035)
7. *Before I just afraid of English*… (18FM_026)

In Examples 6 and 7, the student omitted the linking verbs *be* and *is*, which seems the expression was influenced by his L1. Because in Chinese, it always says "我们的地球会越来越漂亮", which is the literal translation of the above example. The same situation appears in Example 7, which is also the direct translation of Chinese expression. The errors in the above two sentences indicate that in Chinese, the linking verb is not necessary in such situations, but in English, it is a necessity. The differences between Chinese and English caused such errors.

8. *We is best friend.* (20FM_037)

Example 8 shows the misuse of the linking verb *is* instead of *are*. Because in Chinese, the linking verbs *am*, *is* and *are* are expressed with the same word "是", without difference in person and number. The discrepancy between Chinese and English also arouses the confusion in application of linking verbs.

h. Pronouns

Pronouns are the words you substitute for other nouns when your reader or listener already knows which nouns you're referring to (Kramer, 2022). They're words like *they*, *I*, *you*, *who*, *themselves*, *each other* and so on.

Pronouns make up a small sub-category of nouns. The distinctive characteristic of pronouns is that they can be substituted for other nouns. For example, if you are telling a story about your brother John, it seems repetitive if you keep repeating "John" over and over again. For instance:

1. *John likes playing football. John says John will become a football player one day.*

You might try to mix it up by sometimes referring to John as "my brother", but then it sounds like you're referring to two different people:

2. *John likes playing football. My brother says John will become a football player one day.*

Instead, pronoun *he* can be adopted to refer to John:

3. *John likes playing football. He says he will become a football player one day.*

Actually, pronouns act in many different situations with different categories. And to make them more complicated, many pronouns change forms when they are used in different positions within a sentence or different tenses (Kramer, 2022). The following table shows the different types of pronouns and their forms.

From Table 4 – 3, we can have a very clear overview about different pronouns with concrete examples. Regarding these pronouns, we would spare much effort to explain them while demonstrating examples of pronoun errors in students' compositions.

Table 4 – 3 Different Types of Pronouns and Their Forms

Type	Pronouns in This Category	Example Sentences
Personal	I/me, they/them, he/him, she/her, it, we/us, you	e. g. *I brought all the snacks.* *We weren't planning on staying over.*
Relative	that, what, which, who, whom	e. g. *My car, which is twenty years old, doesn't connect to Bluetooth.* *The professor who ran the meeting ended it promptly.*
Demonstrative	that, this, these, those	e. g. *You've seen clear quartz and smoky quartz, but have you seen these stones?* *I ordered Hawaiian pizza. I like that a lot.*
Indefinite	one, other, some, none, everybody, anybody, no one, nobody, both	e. g. *We need cashiers up front. Anybody who's available, please report to the front end.* "*Why can't we fix this?*" *I asked nobody in particular.*
Reflexive	myself, yourself/yourselves, themself/themselves, herself, himself, oneself, itself, ourselves	e. g. *The car began to swerve, then corrected itself.* *He made himself a sandwich.*
Intensive	myself, yourself/yourselves, themself/themselves, herself, himself, oneself, itself, ourselves	e. g. *You did all of this yourself?* *She did the entire group project by herself.*
Possessive	my, your, his, her, their, our, its, whose	e. g. *We're lounging out by our pool.* *His car is green.*
Interrogative	who, what, which, whose	e. g. *Whose bike is this?* *What is the answer?*

(To be continued)

Type	Pronouns in This Category	Example Sentences
Reciprocal	each other, one another	e. g. *We ran into each other on the subway.* *They've been fighting with one another for decades.*

4. *I am looking *forwoog to *you reply.* (17FM_024)

In the above example, personal pronoun *you* replaces possessive pronoun *your*. However, the noun *reply* should be modified by the possessive pronoun *your*, not *you*. The personal pronoun *you* can be the subject, while the object should not be the possessive pronoun.

5. *You should give they a chance to do some good things.* (13FM_002)

This example misuses personal pronoun *they* as *them*. Even though both the words are personal pronouns, one is adopted as a subject, and the other is used as an object. The writer confuses the usage of the personal pronouns.

6. *Only myself could help me.* (16FM_013)

This example misuses reflexive pronoun *myself* itself as a subject. Actually, reflexive pronoun itself can be placed in the position of a subject, but should be combined with a personal pronoun. For instance, in this sentence, a personal pronoun *I* should be posed before the reflexive pronoun *myself* to strengthen the subject. The error in this sentence is caused by student's L1 interference, because in Chinese, the reflexive pronoun can act as a subject individually.

7. *Let we *togerher do it*! (18FM_034)

In this example, the writer misuses personal pronoun *we* as the personal pronoun *us*. The error is caused by the student's L1 interference, because in Chinese, the personal pronoun *we* and *us* has the same form "我们" even though it can play both roles. Therefore, Chinese students usually confuse different forms of pronouns.

8. . . . , *but also their can give* **preasure to their parents*. (15FM_023)

This example misuses possessive pronoun *their* as a personal pronoun. Possessive pronouns are usually placed before nouns to show the relationship between them but not acting as a subject. Chinese L2 learners always confuse about the above pronouns, because in Chinese the expression of all of these pronouns are quite simple. Personal pronouns can become possessive pronoun with "的" attached after the personal pronoun. All the other pronouns can originate from the personal pronoun with different words attached. The differences between English and Chinese always confuse Chinese L2 students in their expression.

i. Auxiliary verbs

Auxiliary verbs are a type of verbs that plays a supportive role in a sentence, second to the main verb. They're used mainly to create complex grammatical tenses, like the perfect and continuous tenses, which show different aspects of time, or how long an action takes place (Ellis, 2022). For instance:

Simple present (no auxiliary verbs):

1. *I go to the zoo.*

Present continuous:

2. *I am going to the zoo.*

Future perfect continuous:

3. *In September, I will have been going to the zoo for a year.*

Definitely, besides these auxiliary verbs, there are still lots of others that can support the sentence's main verb, like *do*, *does*, *did*, *have*, *has*, *had* and so on. Of course, the three main auxiliary verbs are *be*, *do* and *have*. One thing should be noted that the word *be* has been discussed in the category of linking verb, so we won't overstate in this part.

The two main auxiliary verbs are *do* and *have*. However, both of them can also be used separately as action verbs. When you see one of these verbs, look for a second verb to determine if it's used as an action verb or an auxiliary verb. There is another auxiliary verb *will* which should be treated differently, because sometimes *will* is adopted as a modal verb when it express the meaning of willingness but an auxiliary verb delivers the meaning of *be going to*, usually adopted in future tense.

4. [action verb] *I did my homework already.*
5. [auxiliary verb] *I did not want to go home.*
6. [action verb] *I have a selfie with Neil deGrasse Tyson.*
7. [auxiliary verb] *I have waited a long time for this.*

In the compositions of Chinese L2 students, the errors in auxiliary verbs also lie in the above aspects.

8. *I will speak with the foreigners when I *will work in the future.* (16FM_028)

In the above example, the writer overuses the auxiliary verb *will* in the relative clause. Because in grammar, when expressing the future tense, the main clause can use the auxiliary verb *will* while the relative clause only can adopt the present tense. Therefore, in this sentence, the *will* should be canceled.

Substance Errors

In this part, the substance errors mainly include errors in capitalization, punctuation and spelling, which represent the percentage of total number respectively of 5.92%, 2.94% and 33.06%. Especially errors in spelling, it is about one third of the total number, which probably showed that Chinese learners were problematic in memorizing English vocabulary, particularly in the aspect of accuracy of the words. The types of spelling errors are various, for most of them were caused by the unstable memorizing of the words. For this error, we will spare no effort to explain them, because there is no solid rules for such errors. In the following part, some examples will be exhibited to show the errors in the capitalization and punctuation.

a. Capitalization

For this part, there are three main kinds of errors here: one is that the initial letter of the word at the beginning of the sentence which was not capitalized, and the other is the proper noun without capitalization. The following examples can represent these two types:

1. *Certainly, In college, our spare time become more and we can arrange it freely.* (Participant 14FM_023)

In the above example, "in" is within the sentence, so it doesn't need to be capitalized. But the following example is the opposite:

2. ... *if you love our "mother"*,... (Participant 14FM_035)

In the example, "if" is located at the initial of the sentence, so the letter "i" should be capitalized.

Among these situations, personal pronoun "i" is a special case, which is always capitalized whether it is located at the beginning of the sentence or not. Such situation also confused lots of Chinese L2 writers. Within the sentence, "i" is always spelled without capitalization.

There are also lots of students who usually omitted the capitalization of "i".

3. *In the future i want to be a teacher.* (Participant 17FM_031)

The last example is about the proper nouns without capitalization, like "Shanghai", "Benze", "China" etc.

4. *I am a college student from china.* (Participant 17FM_031)

The errors in this part are attributed to the differences between Chinese and English, because in Chinese there is no form change when referring proper nouns, personal nouns or common nouns. But the participants who were interviewed didn't think this part was problematic to them, they only thought they were lack of such awareness when writing in English.

b. Punctuation

Actually, punctuation seemed not a big problem for Chinese L2 learners, for there are only 2.9% of the total errors. Here is the case, all of those 2.9% punctuation errors were caused by some students, which means if one student can grasp the usage of the punctuation, it will not be problematic to them. Otherwise, the punctuation in their writing is a barrier to express their ideas. The errors in this part fell into three main types, like the following examples:

1. *On the one hand. It is good for use developing.* (Participant 13FM_038)

This example shows that the full stop after "On the one hand" should be replaced by comma. Simultaneously, the capitalization of "It" should change its form into "it".

2. *This is the *vecture (virtue) life's bad effects Besides, ...* (Participant 17FM_035)

In this sentence, the participant omitted the punctuation, a full stop. It was probably omitted unconsciously because the next word "Besides" was capitalized, which implied that the writer was aware of the ending of the sentence. Therefore, the punctuation in this sentence was skipped without consciousness.

Lexical Errors

In this part, there are four types of errors: word form, word selection, word deficiency and word abundance. The percentages of these four categories are respectively 8.9%, 4.29%, 0.69% and 0.22%. Definitely, the first two kinds of errors, word form and word selection, are the main types of errors in this scope. More details will be demonstrated in these two aspects.

Word form and word selection seemed to be problematic for Chinese L2 learners. In fact, word form is related with the negative influence of their L1 while word selection is to the accuracy of the words. According to the explanation of the category and sub-category, word form usually refers to those words which cannot be identified the part of speech of the words, like the following examples:

1. *..., but only should pay attention to the extra *knowledges about social and nation.* (Participant 17FM_019)

(the adjective "social" should be replaced by the noun "society")

2. *Now dogs are the *turely friends about *human.* (Participant 18FM_027)
[the adverb "tru (e) ly" should be changed into the adjective "true"]

3. *Virtual life can make people feel relax.* (Participant 14FM_019)
(the verb "relax" should be replaced by the adjective "relaxed")

Word selection is closely related to accuracy of the word choice, which probably was caused by the negative interference of their L1, or influenced by the wrong collocations they compiled, like the following examples:

Replacing the words with that who has the same pronunciation:

4. *Therefore many people have many different ideas about weather agree people play computer games.* (Participant 13FM_031)
(The writer misused "weather" as the conjunction "whether")

Replacing the word with its root word:

5. ... *that what makers a good teacher from the angle of a student.* (Participant 14FM_018)
(The same root words "makers" was confused as the word "makes")

Replacing the word with that which has the similar spelling:

6. *People are admitted in the computer games.* (Participant 17FM_035)
(The word "admitted" should be replaced by the word "addicted" according to the context)

The other two types of errors in the lexical levels are word deficiency and word abundance. These two kinds of errors are named by the author according to the errors committed by Chinese L2 writers. Word deficiency refers to the situation the students omit the words which are necessary in the expression, while word abundance refers to overuse of the adjectives or adverbs. The concrete examples will illustrate the above explanations:

7. *I have many lots of books.* (Participant 16FM_034)

In this sentence, the writer overuses adjectives to express the quantity of the books, which caused the word abundance in the lexical level:

8. *She is a beautiful.* (Participant 17FM_025)

From the above examples, it can be concluded that Chinese L2 writers have grasped certain rules of choosing appropriate words, but when referring to some key words, they usually confuse.

Syntactic Errors

Syntactic errors mainly include three kinds of categories, coordination/subordination/correlative, sentence structure and ordering. These three aspects are respectively about 3.1%, 5.7% and 0.07% of the total errors. Coordination/subordination /correlative and sentence structure seemed a big challenge to Chinese L2 students for their mother tongue has quite big differences with English. For this part, we will explain respectively:

a. Coordination/subordination/correlative errors

Lots of Chinese writers, especially fair and low proficiency writers, are unaware of such conjunctions within sentences, which belong to negative interference of their L1 (detailed explanation will be exhibited in Chapter 5).

The following examples can illustrate the above point of view:

1. *Play (ing) computer games *have a lot of *disadvantages, many of people be for in love with computer games.* (Participant 13FM_036)

In Chinese, within sentences, it doesn't need conjunctions to connect the clauses. Therefore, when writing in English, they usually omitted the subordinate words.

2. *I have studied at school for 13 years, there are some *actives by myself.* (Participant 15FM_018)

b. Sentence structure

Sentence structure is another challenging part for Chinese L2 writers for some sentences patterns between English and Chinese are quite different. English sentences usually place subject, predicate and object at the beginning of the sentence while Chinese pay more attention to the meaning of the sentence rather than the pattern of it. The differences between Chinese and English in sentence structure caused many syntactic errors in their structure. The following sentences present such errors caused by the linguistic gap:

1. *They not *understand is dirty of *society.* (Participant 13FM_035)

The student would like to express their meaning with a subject clause sentence like "*What they don't understand is the dirty of the society.*"

The other example shows:

2. *You can by *click the keyboard to *accomplish your aim.* (Participant 15FM_034)

The ordering of the sentence words is strictly following the sentence structure of Chinese, which is also the negative interference of their L1.

4.1.3 The Relationship between Students' Writing Errors and Their Writing Proficiency

In order to examine the relationship between final exam scores and composition scores, the data of eight years have been collected and examined through SPSS. When examining the correlation among two scale variables—the final score—and the composition score, the final score (see Table 4 – 4) is positively related to the composition score (R final score-composition score = .838), which suggests that the correlation between them is significant. The following analysis concludes that the higher the final score, the higher the composition score.

Table 4 – 4 Correlation of Final Exam Score and Composition Score

		Final Score	Score of Compositions
Final score	Pearson Correlation	1	.838**
	Sig. (2-tailed)		.000
	N	320	320
Composition score	Pearson Correlation	.838**	1
	Sig. (2-tailed)	.000	
	N	320	320

Note: ** : Correlation is significant at the 0.01 level (2-tailed).
* : Correlation is significant at the 0.05 level (2-tailed).

As shown in Table 4 – 5, there is a significant negative correlation between the final score and error numbers, which is represented by the coefficient r = –.440**, a quite high correlation.

Table 4 – 5 Correlation of Error Number and Composition Score

		Composition Score	Error Numbers
Composition Score	Pearson Correlation	1	–.440**
	Sig. (2-tailed)		.000
	N	320	320
Error Number	Pearson Correlation	–.440**	1
	Sig. (2-tailed)	.000	
	N	320	320

Note: ** : Correlation is significant at the 0.01 level (2-tailed).
* : Correlation is significant at the 0.05 level (2-tailed).

Table 4 – 6 mainly examined the correlation between error types and composition scores. Errors occurring in the compositions can reflect one's writing proficiency to a large extent, which can decide the scope and ability to express information. The statistics show that all these five types of errors are negatively related to composition scores (grammatical errors = −.283**; substance errors = −.460**; lexical errors = −.216**; syntactic errors = −.324**; semantic errors = −.107. $p = 0.01$), even though the related coefficient is not so high, it reaches the significant level except semantic errors, which has the statistical meaning. These results suggest that the students of low proficiency level are equipped with low capability to apply the above linguistic factors, which affects writing quality.

Table 4 – 6 Correlation of Error Type and Composition Score

	Grammatical Errors	Substance Errors	Lexical Errors	Syntactic Errors	Semantic Errors
Score Spearman's Rho	−.283**	−.460**	−.216**	−.324**	−.107

Note: **: Correlation is significant at the 0.01 level (2-tailed).
*: Correlation is significant at the 0.05 level (2-tailed).

According to Table 4 – 7, it can be seen that there is a significant positive relationship among grammatical errors, substance errors, lexical errors and syntactic errors (R grammatical errors-substance errors = .201, $p < 0.01$; R substance errors-lexical errors = .194, $p < 0.01$; R lexical errors-syntactic errors = .150, $p < 0.01$; R lexical errors-syntactic errors = .140, $p < 0.05$; R substance errors-syntactic errors = .193, $p < 0.01$), but not with semantic errors.

Table 4 – 7 Pearson Correlation of Five Error Types

Grammatical Errors	Pearson Correlation	1	.201**	.140*	.085	.075
	Sig. (2-tailed)		.000	.012	.128	.183
	N	320	320	320	320	320
Substance Errors	Pearson Correlation	.201**	1	.194**	.193**	.054
	Sig. (2-tailed)	.000		.000	.001	.335
	N	320	320	320	320	320
Lexical Errors	Pearson Correlation	.140*	.194**	1	.150**	.015
	Sig. (2-tailed)	.012	.000		.007	.785
	N	320	320	320	320	320

(To be continued)

Syntactic Errors	Pearson Correlation	.085	.193 **	.150 **	1	.017
	Sig. (2-tailed)	.128	.001	.007		.756
	N	320	320	320	320	320
Semantic Errors	Pearson Correlation	.075	.054	.015	.017	1
	Sig. (2-tailed)	.183	.335	.785	.756	
	N	320	320	320	320	320

Note: ** : Correlation is significant at the 0.01 level (2-tailed).
* : Correlation is significant at the 0.05 level (2-tailed)

4.2 Linguistic Factors Causing Writing Errors

In Chapter 3, we have introduced the concept of interlanguage and also know its origin and components. From which two other sub-conceptions were also mentioned and explained, they are interlingual and intralingual transfer. In this part, firstly, we would like to present the results and the percentage of interlingual or intralingual transfers which are caused by three students of different proficiency level. Then, this research will dig deeper into its reasons and illustrate these abstract conceptions with concrete examples which are selected from the compositions of the participants in this research.

4.2.1 The Frequencies of Interlingual and Intralingual Transfer

Before discussing the concrete examples, Table 4 – 8 will exhibit the frequency of interlingual and intralingual transfer made by high, fair and low proficiency level students.

Table 4 – 8 The Frequency of Interlingual and Intralingual Transfer Made by Students of High, Fair and Low Proficiency Level

Types of Errors	High Proficiency		Fair Proficiency		Low Proficiency	
	Cases	Percentage	Cases	Percentage	Cases	Percentage
Interlingual	17	28.8%	37	19.8%	15	17.4%
Intralingual	42	71.2%	149	80.2%	71	82.6%
Total	59	100%	186	100%	86	100%

Table 4 - 9 compares interlingual and interlingual transfer made by students of high, fair and low proficiency level. The data of interlingual errors and intralingual transfer are shown in five categories: grammatical level, lexical level, substance level, syntactic level, and semantic level. However, the percentage of these categories is not the same. The interlingual errors made by high proficiency level students are divided into five categories, and they are ① subject-verb agreements, consisting of 5 cases (8.49%), ② linking verbs, consisting of 1 case (1.69%), ③ capitalizations with 6 cases (10.12%), ④ punctuations, consisting of 1 case (1.69%), ⑤ subordinations with 4 cases (6.79%) and ⑥ sentence structures consisting of 1 case (8.49%). The interlingual transfers made by students of fair proficiency level are divided into seven categories, and they are ① subject-verb agreement, consisting of 8 cases (4.30%), ② linking verbs, consisting of 1 case (0.53%), ③ prepositions with 2 cases (1.08%), ④ capitalization with 10 cases (5.38%), ⑤ punctuationing consist of 2 cases (1.08%), ⑥ subordination with 2 cases (1.08%), and ⑦ sentence structure consisting of 12 cases (6.45%). Finally, the interlingual transfers made by low proficiency level students are divided into six categories, and they are ① conjunction, consisting of 1 case (1.16%), ② plural form, consisting of 2 cases (2.33%), ③ capitalization with 1 case (1.16%), ④ punctuation with 1 case (1.16%), ⑤ subordinations, consisting of 2 cases (2.33%), and ⑥ sentence structure, consisting of 4 cases (4.65%).

Table 4 - 9 The Comparison of Interlingual Transfer and Intralingual Transfer Made by High, Fair and Low Proficiency Levels

No.	Types of Interlingual Transfer and Intralingual Transfer	High Proficiency		Fair Proficiency		Low Proficiency	
		f	%	*f*	%	*f*	%
Interlingual Transfer							
1	Subject-verb agreement	5	8.47	8	4.30		
2	Linking verbs	1	1.69	1	0.54		
3	Prepositions			2	1.08		
4	Capitalization	7	11.86	10	5.38	1	1.15
5	Punctuation			2	1.08	2	2.30

(To be continued)

No.	Types of Interlingual Transfer and Intralingual Transfer	High Proficiency		Fair Proficiency		Low Proficiency	
		f	%	*f*	%	*f*	%
Interlingual Transfer							
6	Coordination/subordination/correlative	4	6.78	2	1.08	2	2.30
7	Sentence structure	1	1.69	12	6.45	5	5.75
Intralingual transfer							
1	Subject-verb agreement	8	13.56	20	10.75	15	17.24
2	Verb tense	3	5.08	11	5.91	6	6.90
3	Auxiliary verbs			1	0.54	3	3.45
4	Linking verbs	1	1.69	8	4.30	1	1.15
5	Adjectives			2	1.08	1	1.15
6	Prepositions	1	1.69	7	3.76	3	3.45
7	Modal verbs			6	3.23	1	1.15
8	Pronouns			4	2.15	1	1.15
9	Determiners	2	3.39	6	3.23	4	4.60
10	Plural forms	3	5.08	14	7.53	6	6.90
11	Capitalization			6	3.23	10	11.49
12	Punctuation			26	13.98	5	5.75
13	Word form	17	28.81	20	10.75	10	11.49
14	Word selection	2	3.39	12	6.45	7	8.05
15	Coordination/subordination/correlative	2	3.39	2	1.08	3	3.45
16	Sentence structure	1	1.69	3	1.61	1	1.15
17	Ambiguity	1	1.69				
18	Miscommunication			1	0.54		
	Total	59	100	186	100	87	100

Note: *f*: number of cases, %: percentage of cases.

Table 4 – 8 and intralingual transfer shows that the most frequent errors of the three groups are on intralingual (71.2%, 80.2% and 82.6%), which is due to overgeneralization, ignorance rule of restrictions, incomplete application of language rules and false concept hypothesis.

From Table 4 – 9, the similarities of writing errors caused by interlingual transfer and intralingual transfer made by high, fair, and low proficiency level students can be identified. The similarities of writing errors caused by interlingual transfer in three groups found by the researchers are capitalization, punctuation, subordinate, and sentence structure. The differences in writing errors caused by interlingual transfer in three groups are subject-verb agreement, verb tense, prepositions, conjunction, and plural forms. Among these, sentence structure and capitalization are the most frequent errors students made by the interlingual transfer. Compared with interlingual transfer, intralingual transfer was distributed more widely at different levels. The similarities of writing errors caused by intralingual transfer in three groups are subject-verb agreement, verb tense, prepositions, determiners, plural forms, word form, word selection, subordinate, and sentence structure. From the data it can be seen that intralingual transfer occurs more frequently than interlingual transfer. And in the perspective of intralingual transfer, ignorance of restrict rules is the most frequent reason (about 91%) for L2 participants in this study.

In this analyzing part, we just selected the compositions of participants of 2016 to analyze the category of these errors, and the reasons are as followed. Firstly, the book is an individual work, so the time should be taken into consideration. The initial analysis of different errors cost too much time. Therefore, I don't have enough time to analyze the whole data at the moment. Secondly, in the past eight years, except the year 2013, the errors in the other seven years are quite similar, so in my mind, the result in the year 2016 would probably represent the whole data.

Table 4 – 8 shows that the percentage of writing errors caused by intralingual transfer (70.7%, 79.7% and 82.6%) is more than that of interlingual transfer (28.8%, 19.8% and 17.4%) in three groups respectively. This result is fit to many previous studies. The table shows that in interlingual transfer, the percentage is from high to low while the intralingual transfer is from low to high. The three groups had not so obvious differences in the interlingual and intralingual aspects. One thing should be noticed that the spelling errors in the study have been excluded from the total errors for these errors are mainly caused by the slip of the pen or the way of test (English test by computers), so it cannot represent the real situation of the intralingual or interlingual errors.

The following part is about each type of writing error caused by interlingual and intralingual transfer in three proficiency groups, and each type of errors will be illustrated with many concrete examples. From Table 4 – 8 we can see that nearly one fifth of errors could be attributed to the negative transfer of some of Chinese linguistic features. Meanwhile, the errors caused by interference of L1 mainly focus on the nine categories of different linguistic levels. These are presented in Table 4 – 10 below.

Table 4 – 10 Examples of Interlingual and Intralingual Transfer

types	Causes of Writing Errors	Brief Explanation	Examples	Correct Forms
Interlingual transfer	L1 interference	Caused by the learner's first language.	e. g. *The teacher want to tell us there have a problem.*	e. g. The teacher wants to tell us (that) there is a problem.
Intralingual transfer	Overgeneralization	Caused by mixing two or more different structures in the target language based on the learner's knowledge.	e. g. *He runs fastly.*	e. g. *He runs fast.*
	Ignorance of rule restriction	Caused by ignoring the rule restrictions of existing structures.	e. g. *The man whom I saw him yesterday.*	e. g. *The man whom I saw yesterday.*
	Incomplete application of rules	Caused by applying a rule in the context of a sentence, but the rule is not complete.	e. g. *He goes to school?*	e. g. *Does he go to school?*
	False concepts hypothesis	Caused by the faulty rule learning at various levels. learners cannot differentiate between go and come, bring and take, too and very, etc.	e. g. *You can bring away this book.* *Thank you too much.*	e. g. *You can take away this book.* *Thank you very much.*

Table 4 – 11 Errors in Three Groups Caused by Interference of L1

Category of the Error	Example	Correct Form	Possible Explanation for the Error
Subject-verb agreement	e. g. *I think whichever job, both have different points.* (16FM_018)	e. g. *I think whichever job has its own different points.*	In Chinese, there is no subject-verb agreement. Whether the subject is singular or plural, the verb is the same.
Verb tense	e. g. *I travel to Beijing last year.* (16FM_015)	e. g. *I traveled to Beijing last year.*	In Chinese, the verb is not inflected for tense, whether it is singular or plural, past or future.
Linking verb	e. g. *Computer games just as an entertainment in our life.* (16FM_003)	e. g. *Computer games are just as an entertainment in our life.*	In Chinese, the linking verb in a sentence is not necessary.
Determiners	e. g. *I think* * *goverment should change this opinion.* (16FM_019)	e. g. *I think the* * *goverment should change this opinion.*	Definite articles such as "the" does not exist in Chinese.
Preposition	e. g. *In the past, I always learned under my teachers and my parents.* (16FM_003)	e. g. *In the past, I always studied with the instruction of my teachers and my parents.*	The participant misused the preposition "under" as "with" because of the literal translation.
Capitalization	e. g. *when I was a child.* ... (16FM_028)	e. g. *When I was a child*, ...	In Chinese, there is no capitalization at the beginning of a sentence.
Word selection	e. g. *In my opinion, the computer games can develop the intelligence.* (16FM_016)	e. g. *In my opinion, the computer games can exercise the intelligence.*	This error is caused by the literal translation from Chinese to English on the key word "exercise". In Chinese, the real meaning of "exercise" means "develop".

(To be continued)

Category of the Error	Example	Correct Form	Possible Explanation for the Error
Coordination/ subordination/ correlative	e. g. *I decided to be alone, no longer depend on others, only myself could help me.* (16FM_003)	e. g. *I decided to be alone, no longer depend on others, and only I myself could help me.*	In Chinese, subordinate words are not necessary between clauses of a sentence.
Sentence structure	e. g. *There is nobody could help me.* (16FM_003)	e. g. *There is nobody who could help me.*	In Chinese, the relatives do not exist in attributive clause.

4. 2. 2 Correlation of Writing Errors with Interlingual and Intralingual Reasons

As we have mentioned in Chapter 2, interlingual and intralingual transfer are the linguistic factors that arouse writing errors in L2 students' learning. The theoretical framework of interlanguage is quoted from the scholar Richard (1974), which provides two sources of the above transfers for writing errors. Whether the writing errors are caused by interlingual or intralingual transfer, they will depend on the deficiency of the sentences. As the interlanguage hypothesis reported that interlingual transfer is mainly caused by the interference of the learner's L1 while intralingual transfer is the generalization based on the partial exposure of the target language (Richard, 1974).

Regarding the differences of percentages between interlingual and intralingual errors, it can be seen that the mean of high, fair, and low proficiency group in interlingual are 1. 55, 1. 36, and 1. 94, while in intralingual 3. 73, 6. 45, and 7. 61. The low proficiency group has almost double errors than the high proficiency group in terms of intralingual errors. The ANOVA analysis showed that in the scope of interlingual errors, the difference is significant ($F = 1.824$, $P = .000$).

Table 4 - 12 Compared Differences in Writing Errors Caused by Interlingual and Intralingual Transfer

Reasons	Samples	*N*	*M*	*SD.*	*F* (ANOVA)	*Sig.*
Interlingual	High	11	1.55	1.128	1.824	.000
	Fair	18	1.36	1.392		
	Low	11	1.94	1.804		
Intralingual	High	11	3.73	2.789	6.655	.098
	Fair	18	6.45	3.560		
	Low	11	7.61	3.901		

4.2.3 Errors Caused by Interlingual Transfer

The interference of their L1 mainly caused the errors in this respect. Even though the three groups perform differently in different categories of these errors, the deeper reasons are the same—their performances. The three reasons are mainly linguistic interference, cultural interference, and mother tongue transfer. In these compositions, most interlingual errors are caused by their L1 interference of linguistic aspect, not relating too much cultural interference.

Table 4 - 13 Errors Caused by L1 Interference

Category	Error	Correct Form	Causes	Possible Explanation
Interlingual Transfer	e. g. *There are so many students are crazy about it.* (16FM_014) *I think is benefits for our normal life.* 16FM_017)	e. g. *Many students are crazy about it.* Or *There are so many students who are crazy about it.* *I think it is benefit for our normal life.*	L1 interference	The participant composed these two sentences directly with Chinese expression, word by word.

4.2.4 Errors Caused by Intralingual Transfer

For this type of error, there are mainly four types of causes: overgeneralization, incomplete application of rules, ignorance rule of restrictions, false concept hypothesis. As we have mentioned, 90% of intralingual errors are caused by their ignorance rule of restrictions, which probably means that the participants have grasped most of the rules in English. This also fits to the real condition that in this study, the participants belong to intermediate level students in China. The following table (see Table 4 – 14) will illustrate each type of cause that arouses the errors in students' compositions.

Table 4 – 14 Errors Caused by Overgeneralization, Incomplete Application of Rules, Ignorance Rule of Restrictions and False Concept Hypothesis

Category of the Error	Error	Correct Form	Causes	Possible Explanation for the Error
Subject-verb agreement	e. g. *Human have known a truth that* ... (16FM_020)	e. g. *Human has known a truth that...*	Ignorance of rule of restrictions	The participant knew the rule of the present perfect to some extent, but made a confusion between singular or plural form of the subject "human".
Verb tense	e. g. *Later, when I was at college, I have to learn all the things by myself.* (16FM_013)	e. g. *Later, when I was at college, I had to learn all the things by myself.*	Ignorance of rule of restriction	The participant has noticed the past tense in the first clause, but ignore the tense in the second clause.
Linking verb	e. g. ..., *the one thing which most * important for us is going ahead.* (16FM_009)	e. g. ..., *the one thing which is most important for us is going ahead.*	Ignorance of rule of restriction	The participant ignored the linking verb "is" between the relative word "which" and "important".

(To be continued)

Category of the Error	Error	Correct Form	Causes	Possible Explanation for the Error
Adjectives	e. g. *Because we have many extra time.* (16FM_027)	e. g. *Because we have much extra time.*	Ignorance of rule of restriction	The object "time" is uncountable noun, so the adjective to modify it should be "much" instead of "many".
Preposition	e. g. *I also study from Monday to Friday, but it only in night.* (16FM_038)	e. g. *I also study from Monday to Friday, but it only at night.*	Ignorance of rule of restrictions	In Chinese, the preposition before the time is the same whether it refers to one day, one month or one year.
Modal verb	e. g. ... *so we shouldn't spent too much time in playing computer games.* (16FM_014)	e. g. ... *so we shouldn't spend too much time in playing computer games.*	Ignorance of rule of restrictions	In English, the modal verb is followed by a verb with its original form instead of the past tense.
Pronoun	e. g. *And we can play the computer games with our friend, that can make our friendship become better and better.* (16FM_021)	e. g. *And we can play the computer games with our friend, which can make our friendship become better and better.*	Ignorance of rule of restrictions	The participant has acquired the structure of non-restrictive attributive clause, but misuse the relative word "that" instead of "which".

(To be continued)

Category of the Error	Error	Correct Form	Causes	Possible Explanation for the Error
Plural forms	e. g. *The teacher is one of the most important player in the society.* (16FM_015)	e. g. *The teacher is one of the most important players in the society.*	Ignorance of rule of restrictions	The participant ignored the rule that there should be a single form in the sentence of superlative degree.
Word forms	e. g. *We will learn to be harmony with others.* (16*FM*_004)	e. g. *We will learn to be harmonious with others.*	Ignorance of rule of restrictions	The participant ignored the rule that there should be an adjective because "*be harmonious with*" is a collocation.
	e. g. *Playing computer games can make friends become more and more closer.* (16FM_014)	e. g. *Playing computer games can make friends become closer and closer.*	Overgenerization	The participant overgenerates the comparative by "*more and more*" and "*closer*".
Word selection	e. g. ..., *they can speak clearly.* (16FM_014)	e. g. ..., *they can speak clearly.*	False concept hypothesis	The participant misused the word "*cleanly*" with the word "clearly".
Coordination/ subordination/ correlative	e. g. *Everyone will meet troubles and problems in the way of reaching our goals, everyone will admit that studying is very difficult.* (16FM_009)	e. g. *Everyone will meet trouble and problems in the way of reaching our goals, and everyone will admit that studying is very difficult.*	Incomplete application of rules	The participant failed to apply the rules of subordinate sentence, so "*and*" is omitted in the second clause.

In this section, the description of interlingual and intralingual transfer is initially mentioned according to the categorization steps. The description shows that the writing errors caused by intralingual transfer are more than those of interlingual transfer, which are considered the most challenging linguistic features when writing in English. In addition, the three proficiency groups perform differently regarding the reasons causing writing errors. From the results, it can be concluded that the different proficiencies of the participants have achieved most of the English rules and related knowledge, and only some errors were caused by their interference with L1. From this perspective, it fits to the assumption that the participants we selected in this study belong to intermediate level students.

4.3 Questionnaire Statistics

4.3.1 Factor Analysis

In the pilot study, we investigated the number of constructs and measured the structure of the questionnaire. The factor analysis in the pilot study showed that Kaiser-Meyer Olkin (KMO) measure of sampling adequacy was factorable (KMO =.833) (see Table 3 - 11). However, the categories of items fell into three factors instead of five because two items belong to the scope of the same factor. In the main study, we employ Exploratory Factor Analysis (EFA) to identify complex interrelationships among items and group items that are part of unified concepts (Polit & Beck, 2012) and examine the validity and reliability of the questionnaire again, whose results showed that Kaiser-Meyer Olkin (KMO) measure of sampling adequacy was still factor able (KMO =.833) (see Table 3 - 11). Displayed coefficients were sorted by size, and small coefficients with an absolute value <.60 were suppressed. In the pilot study, Kaiser's eigenvalue-greater-than-one rule and Cattell's Scree test were employed to determine the appropriate factors to retain. With the above results, it could be seen that five factors were extracted, but the eigenvalue from the fourth and fifth factors were relatively small. Meanwhile, there were only two items in each of the factor, so the forth and the fifth factors were excluded from the factors.

As a result, the analysis was operated again with a three-factor solution, and reliability among items for three factors were adequate to high ($\alpha = 0.794$; $\alpha = 0.877$; $\alpha = 0.816$). The communalities of all extracted variables were higher than .60, which revealed that the extracted factors accounted for a high proportion of the variables' variance. A descriptive statistical analysis indicated that the mean scores of the 13 items ranged from 3.05 (item 2) to 4.26 (item 11) with standard deviations ranging from .568 to 1.054. The values for skewness were between –1.080 and .144 while the values for kuitosis were between –.756 and 2.320 (see Table 4 –2). It demonstrates the univariate normality of the response for they were far less than the cut-off values of +/–3.0 and +/–8.0 for skewness and kurtosis respectively (Kline, 2011). Through the investigation of items clustering around each factor, three factors were identified: Factor 1 accounts for 32.533% of variance; Factor 2 accounts for 22.875% of variance; and Factor 3 accounts for 10.991% of variance. Totally, the three factors explained 66.399 of the variance. Table 4 – 15 demonstrates the results of factor analysis, descriptive statistics and Cronbach's alpha of each factor.

Table 4 –15 KMO and Bartlett's Test

KMO Measure of Sampling Adequacy	.835	
Bartlett's Test of Sphericity	Approx. Chi-Square	1,683.914
	df	78
	Sig.	.000

4.3.2 The Three Topic Factors

There were totally three factors left after piloting all the items in the questionnaire. Initially, three items were loaded into Factor 1. Clearly, the three items (see Table 4 – 16) in the Factor 1 were all related to the students' internal reasons why students conducted such action when writing English compositions. The important action of studying English writing was driven by their intrinsic motivation or attitudes, such as pleasure, satisfaction, confidence and being comfortable in the writing process. These feeling are very critical for the consistent commitment of college students in their L2 writing because it seemed they realized their values with these feelings in L2 writing.

Table 4 – 16 Results of Factor Analysis, Descriptive Statistics and Cronbach's Alpha in Questionnaire

Component	Items	Loadings	*M*	*SD*	Skewness	Kurtosis	Eigenvalue	% of Total Variance	Cronbach's
Factor 1	Q9 I study English writing because I experience pleasure and satisfaction while learning it.	.673	3.47	.907	−.150	−.553	1.343	32.533	.794
	Q10 When asked to write a piece of work in English, I feel comfortable and confident.	.638	3.05	.953	.144	−.310			
	Q11 I find it interesting to express my ideas and emotions in English writing.	.739	3.73	.863	−.442	−.059			

(To be continued)

Component	Items	Loadings	*M*	*SD*	Skewness	Kurtosis	Eigenvalue	% of Total Variance	Cronbach's
Factor 2	Q12 When writing in English, I feel I am lack of vocabulary.	.640	3.97	.760	−1.080	2.320	1.111	22.875	.877
	Q13 When writing in English, the problem lies in making grammatical errors.	.704	3.54	1.001	−.453	−.652			
	Q14 When writing in English, I face problems on how to combine words in sentences.	.759	3.35	1.054	−.277	−.685			
	Q15 I feel I have a lot to say, but I don't know to deliver it in English in my composition.	.651	3.89	.858	−.804	.577			
	Q16 When writing in English, I usually use Chinese English in the composition.	.678	3.43	1.043	−.261	−.756			

(To be continued)

Component	Items	Loadings	*M*	*SD*	Skewness	Kurtosis	Eigenvalue	% of Total Variance	Cronbach's
Factor 3	Q17 After finishing my English writing, I face the problem in modifying the composition.	.617	3.70	.970	−.739	−.021	.546	10.991	.816
	Q18 I would like to get the direct feedback with corrections on my composition from my English teacher.	.732	4.26	.568	−.273	.790			
	Q19 Indirect feedback with some indications from English teacher can inspire me in improving the language accuracy in composition.	.724	4.20	.608	−.225	−.037			
	Q20 If my teacher can give me feedback in time, I can perform well in English writing.	.692	3.93	.842	−.503	−.268			

Factor 2 consists of 5 items that are closely related to the difficulties before, during, and after their English writing. This perspective is also responsible for exploring the reasons because some errors are committed by college students in their English writing. When students create their writing, vocabulary appears to be the primary problem they face when choosing appropriate words to combine correct sentences. The other critical issue in English writing for Chinese students is grammar. Most of Chinese students are afraid of making grammatical errors because grammar teaching is put on a priority state in their middle schools. Undoubtedly, because of incomplete development of their interlanguage, grammatical errors are inevitable, which cause worry and anxiety when composing the passage. Thirdly, English writing of Chinese students is affected deeply by their mother language, Chinese-English which is also called the interlingual errors. It is also one of two reasons which cause L2 writing errors, which will be discussed in depth in the later part of this dissertation. The last item in this factor requires higher capability in applying vocabulary and grammar well to modify the compositions as native-like.

Items for Factor 3 identify students' expectations in teachers' corrective feedback. Some of them prefer direct corrective feedback, while others think indirect methods can inspire students' cultivation in reflecting errors from their perspective. Different ways of corrective feedback may implicate different effects in L2 writing.

Table 4-17 Final Coding Scheme

Category Codes & Sub-items	Definition
Factor 1: WA	References to the emotions and feelings of English writing driven by internal rewards such as satisfaction and pleasure experienced by learners. Certain behaviors like confidence and comfortable which belong to intrinsic feelings about L2 writing.
Factor 2: WD	References to the difficulties committed by L2 writers in the process of writing. There are six aspects that are related to various difficulties before, during, and after writing the composition.
Vocabulary	Any references to the lack of vocabulary of students in L2 writing.
Grammar use	Any references to students' grammatical errors committed by L2 writers during English writing.

(To be continued)

Category Codes & Sub-items	Definition
Combine sentence	Any references to students' difficulties in combining words correctly in English sentences.
Accuracy	Any references to the difficulties of word choice for students in their L2 writing.
Deliver in English	Any references to the difficulties in the methods of delivering ideas and expressions in L2 writing.
Modifying after writing	Any references to the lack of ability to correct some errors or to polish the whole passage before submitting it.
Factor 3: CF	Any references to students' expectations on their teachers' feedback. It typically consists of two components: ways of feedback, and function of feedback.
Ways of feedback (items 18 & 21)	Any references to the ways of corrective feedback that teachers give on students' L2 writing.
Functions of feedback (items 19 & 20)	Any references to the expectations that students want to get from the feedback of their teachers.

With its 13 items, the questionnaire covers three dimensions in L2 writing: WA, WD and CF. A five-point Likert scale follows the statement: ① strongly disagree, ② disagree, ③ neutral, ④ agree, ⑤ strongly disagree.

Table 4 – 18 Pearson Correlation among Writing Variables

Factor	WA	WD	CF
WA	1		
WD	–.268**	1	
CF	.210**	.170**	1

Notes: WA = Writing Attitudes; WD = Writing Difficulties; CF = Corrective Feedback (**: $p < .01$).

To explore the construct validity of three factors in L2 writing, an investigation of correlations among the scales was conducted. Correlations generated from the three factors were commonly consistent with theoretical expectations. Table 4 – 18 shows the correlation among three factors: WA and WD are negatively correlated while WA and CF, WD and CF are positively correlated.

4.3.3 Students' Writing Errors and Writing Attitudes, Writing Difficulties, and Corrective Feedback

First, if we examine the correlation between students' writing errors and their WA, WD and CF, Table 4 – 19 can explain it with concrete statistics. The *Post Hoc* results of ANOVA demonstrate that High Proficiency Group (HPG) has better writing attitudes than Fair Proficiency Group (FPG) while Fair Proficiency Group (FPG) has better writing attitudes than Low Proficiency Group (LPG) [$F(3, 292) = 13.353$, $p < 0.05$]. Turkey's post hoc procedure indicates that students in FPG have more writing difficulties than HPG, while LPG has more writing difficulties than FPG [$F(3, 292) = 10.245$, $p < 0.05$]. Additionally, the students in FPG have quite a high recognition of teachers' feedback than HPG and LPG [$F(3, 292) = 2.895$, $p > 0.05$], but not significantly different in CF among these three groups.

Table 4 – 19 Results of ANOVA of Three Different Groups with WA, WD and CF

Factors	Three Different EPG	*M*	*SD*	*F* (3, 292)	*Post Hoc*
WA	*HPG* (n = 79)	3.73	.720	13.353	*HPG > FPG > LPG*
	FPG (n = 134)	3.40	.754		*FPG > LPG*
	LPG (n = 79)	3.12	.713		
WD	*HPG* (n = 79)	3.36	.726	10.245	*LPG > FPG > HPG*
	FPG (n = 134)	3.67	.788		*LPG > HPG*
	LPG (n = 79)	3.89	.608		
CF	*HPG* (n = 74)	4.09	.549	2.895	*FPG > HPG > LPG*
	FPG (n = 134)	4.20	.544		*HPG > LPG*
	LPG (n = 79)	4.02	.563		

Notes: WA = Writing Attitudes; WD = Writing Difficulties; CF = Corrective Feedback; HPG = High Proficiency Group; FPG = Fair Proficiency Group; LPG = Low Proficiency Group.

4.3.4 Predicative Effects on WA, WD and CF

Multiple linear regression was conducted to determine the best linear combination of English writing attitudes, writing difficulties, and teachers' corrective feedback for predicting English writing proficiency in China. Statistical assumptions, such as the normal distribution of residuals and non-linear correlation between predicated variables and residuals, were all met in the analysis. The means, standard deviations, and correlation coefficients can be found in Table 4 – 20. The regression method of "enter" showed that the combination of the three independent variables significantly predicted students' writing errors in L2 writing, F (3, 287) = 12.263, $p < 0.05$, with all of them significantly contributing to the prediction ($p < 0.05$) except corrective feedback of English teachers ($p > 0.05$) (Table 4 – 22). The beta weights, presented in Table 4 – 22, suggested that writing attitudes and difficulties contribute most to predicating students' English proficiency level. The R square value was 0.114, which indicated that the model explained 11.4% of the variance in students' writing proficiency. The standardized regression formulation is students' English writing proficiency = 0.185 × writing difficulties – 0.224 × writing attitudes – 0.028 × corrective feedback.

Table 4 – 20 Descriptive and Correlation Coefficients of Variables (n = 292)

	Variables	Descriptive		Correlation Coefficients		
		M	*SD*	1	2	3
DV	Writing Errors	2.00	.733	–.291 *	.256 *	–.047 *
IV	Writing Attitudes	3.41	.765		–.336 *	.193 *
	Writing Difficulties	3.65	.750			.133 *
	Corrective Feedback	4.12	.554			

Note: ** : $p < .05$.

Dependent Variable: students' Writing Errors.

Additionally, from the multiple regression results, it can be seen that WA has significant negative predictions on students writing errors while WD has significant positive predictions on it. Even though CF was found not to be a significant factor related to students' writing errors (see Table 4 – 22), one probable reason is that WA and WD can strongly influence students' writing errors. In other words, if a student has a good writing attitude and fewer writing difficulties, he or she probably has fewer writing errors and better WP.

Table 4 – 21 Results of ANOVA of Different Writing Proficiency with WA, WD and CF

Factors	Good EP ($N=79$)		Fair EP ($N=134$)		Poor EP ($N=79$)		F	*Post Hoc*
	M	SD	M	SD	M	SD		
WA	4. 02	. 549	4. 20	. 544	4. 03	. 563	13. 352	FPG > LPG
WD	3. 36	. 726	3. 67	. 788	3. 89	. 608	10. 245	
CF	3. 73	. 720	3. 4	. 754	3. 12	. 713	2. 895	FPG > HPG > LPG

Table 4 – 22 Multiple Regression Results of Writing Attitudes, Writing Difficulties and Corrective Feedback on Writing Errors

Model	Variables	β	t	F	R^2	ΔR^2	p	Tolerance	VIF	95% *CI*	
										LL	*UL*
1	Writing Attitudes	–. 224	–3. 665	12. 263	. 114	. 104	. 000	. 829	1. 206	. 988	1. 087
	Writing Difficulties	. 185	3. 054				. 000	. 846	1. 182	. 950	1. 101
	Corrective Feedback	–. 028	–. 483				. 630	. 918	1. 089	. 977	1. 035

Note: * : $p <. 001$.

4.4 Semi-structured Interview

For this part, two semi-structured interviews have been designed and distributed to two main groups in this research: English teachers and their students. This section will supply information which might offer insights into the actual L2 writing teaching and learning context. It mainly discusses the possible reasons for the errors, and also writing attitudes, motivation, learning difficulties of Chinese university students. Interview data were processed with the method of qualitative method (Yang, 2009). Meanwhile, based on the procedure of qualitative study, data have been collected, sorted and interpreted to achieve the goal to figure out the questions. In this semi-structured interview, teachers and students were assigned different questions, which can deeply explore the reasons for making errors.

4.4.1 Students' Perspective on Their Writing Errors

The six questions (see Appendix 6&7) for 14 students (see Table 3 - 13) were designed to explore the reasons and elements for making different linguistic errors. The questions are distributed from easy to difficult ones. Students can understand the questions very well, meanwhile, most of them can express their ideas explicitly.

First, they reported the frequency their English teachers assigned the writing homework. Surprisingly, two students said they had not been assigned the composition so far in the semester. In fact, compositions should be written once two weeks according to the syllabus of College English, but some of the teachers still thought it less important in acquiring English. Other students reported that they usually had their compositions once two weeks. Then, students reported the methods of scoring their compositions. Some of their teachers score the compositions by themselves while others put the composition in *Pigai. Org* (one of the well-known websites to score compositions automatically). Even though some compositions were commended on the Internet, English teachers also can point out the errors and mistakes and write suggestions on the side of the text. Among these, there are still some creative writing procedures to improve students' writing proficiency.

"... *We are usually divided into several groups. After writing the compositions, the group members will select one of the compositions and find out the errors and mistakes together, then hand it to our English teacher. Our English teacher will mark the errors and mistakes, then return it to the group. The group members will discuss based on the feedback of English teacher. Thus, these errors or mistakes may probably be corrected when writing for the next time.* " (Interviewee Hong)

The student Hong presents the different ways of his teacher to score students' compositions. On one side, each English teacher has at least 4 classes and about 200 students in all. It is impossible to score all the compositions once two weeks. Under such circumstances, group work might be a good idea. On the other side, the process for students to correct their compositions might be a good method to figure out the errors and how to avoid them the next time.

Interestingly, when asked whether it is necessary to teach grammars before writing the compositions, most high proficiency writers thought it unnecessary to mention that. Because, on the one hand, they thought they have acquired most grammatical knowledge during their high school. On the other hand, some students with weak basis in English would like their English teachers explain some grammar rules before writing.

"... *I don't think it is necessary to explain some grammar rules before writing. I believe if I can notice the errors by myself, it would be more impressive on me. The errors marked by my English teacher are usually searched on the internet or corpus to its using rules to avoid making mistakes next time.* " (Interviewee Zheng, SI)

"... *The student like me would prefer an English teacher explaining some grammar rules before writing because I had a rather weak basis on English.* " (Interviewee Li, SI)

For the two main questions in this part, the interviewees presented their point of view from different perspectives. The first question is what are the frequent errors you probably make, and the other is what possible reasons are responsible for these errors. The reason to conduct the interview is that you can explore a research question deeper. I learned a lot from the conversations with these college students.

"... *I seldom made spelling errors and sentence structure errors instead of grammatical and collocation ones. The reasons to contribute to the above errors are probably due to my unfamiliarity with some grammar or China English, which means the Chinese ways of thinking influenced our ways of expression.* " (Interviewee Chen, SI)

"... *I usually made errors in verb tense and word form. Sometimes I made spelling errors because of my unfamiliarity with these words. Alternatively, sometimes, I don't know how to use these words appropriately. The reasons which are responsible for the above errors are that in China, it is lack of learning context. Chinese students seldom communicate in English in their daily life. They only speak English in their class. Thus, it is impossible to improve the English language sense.* " (Interviewee Mao, TI)

"... *The most frequent error I made was spelling which is followed by grammatical errors. For the spelling errors, I think in college, English teachers do not require us strictly to memorize vocabulary, so the acquisition of it mostly depends on one's autonomy. Also, in high school, especially in order to achieve the goal to pass the national examination, we practiced the relevant knowledge every day. However in college we seldom do exercise in this aspect...* " (Interviewee Jiang, SI)

"... *I usually made errors in sentence structure for the ways of expression in China and English are quite different. I also has a problem in memorizing words, so the spelling is also the main error in my aspect. In solid collocations, the preposition was usually omitted because I am always confused with different prepositions in the collocation. For example, "be admitted to" is often omitted the preposition "to", or sometimes I usually change the preposition into another one. I still think English sentence structure is a little hard to grasp for there are some differences from Chinese sentence structure...* " (Interviewee Li, SI)

From the above conversation with interviewee, it can conclude that most students are aware of their writing errors and also try their best to overcome them. Undoubtedly, it needs time and writing practice to correct these errors. Regarding the possible reasons, most of them have the sense that the language differences arouse so many errors for Chinese L2 writers. Some of them think the learning context is quite important for language learning, and in China, college students have no such context. Even though students have their initial awareness of their errors and the possible reasons, the deeper reasons and the implications are still needed for their improvement in English writing. Therefore, explicit teaching in writing on grammar, sentence structures, and lexical selections is necessary.

4.4.2 Teachers' Perspective on Students' Writing Errors

Compared with students' interviews, conversations with teachers can reveal more details and supply deeper reflection from the teaching perspective. When referring to the critical points in the research, different teachers have their points of view.

"... *The errors students make are different, and it is impossible to deal with all the problems simultaneously. Therefore, at the beginning of their college time, basic knowledge like spelling and verb tense should be paid more attention to. Gradually, the passage structure would be a big problem to tackle. Of course, in their writing, there are lots of Chinese ways of expression which were influenced by the linguistic differences between two languages. The last point which is worth mentioning is the topic sentence and the detailed sentences. Regarding the possible reasons for make errors, I think it is certainly the L1 interference. This is normal, because we speak Chinese every day since we were children. The more important is that you can show your students native expression and practice until they are closer and closer to it.* " (Interviewee Hong, TI)

"... *My students usually made writing errors in sentence structure, part of speech, verb tense, spelling, punctuation, China English, coherence of the sentence and passages. Regarding the possible reasons for these errors: first, they are lack of systematic English writing training courses and related practice; second, they did not grasp the knowledge in grammar very well; third, when memorizing vocabulary, they just remember their Chinese meaning instead of its part of speech and usages; forth, their expression is influenced by negative L1 interference. Students are used to their Chinese way of thinking. When they write the composition, they usually think in Chinese and then translate it into English.* " (Interviewee Hua, TI)

"... *In my mind, the grammatical errors are the most frequent error types for my students, especially sentence structure. The reason for the above phenomenon is that Chinese and English are two different languages with different sentence structures, grammars, syntax. Notably, Chinese is their L1 which influenced L2 very much.* " (Interviewee Xin, TI)

"... *there are probably three kinds of errors for my students to make. The first is the passage's logic, which means they write what they want to write instead of thinking the coherence of the former part and the latter part. The second is that the supporting details are insufficient to support their topic sentence. Last but not least, there are some grammatical errors, spelling and other linguistic errors.* " (Interviewee Yang, TI)

"... *in the compositions of my students, lexical errors are the most frequent errors they made, such as word choice, word form, infinite, preposition and nouns. Syntactic errors are also emerging frequently, like subordinate errors and sentence structure. Regarding the reasons which contributed to the above errors, there are two points: first, all the errors, whether it is a lexical error or a syntactic error, are influenced by their L1 interference; second, in their past studying, students only memorized the vocabulary simply without understanding the deeper meaning of the words, thus, when using these words, they don't know the context clearly.* " (Interviewee Zhuang, TI)

In this part, some teachers clearly pointed out that Chinese college students' writing errors were aroused mainly by their L1 interference. For the next part, English teachers give some suggestions in overcoming these errors, which will also inspire the implications in Chapter 6 (see Section 6.2.1).

"... *for the above problems, I will have some suggestions for them. First, a systematic English writing course is quite necessary to explain writing purpose, structure and methods on different writing genres. Second, students should obtain solid, grammatical knowledge, especially in some complex sentences. Third, vocabulary teaching should be paid attention to for some words that have more than one meaning and are collocated with different prepositions or other words. Forth, it should train students' English thinking based on the analysis of Chinese and English linguistic differences. Last but not least, it should encourage students to analyze the texts in detail and learn to take advantage of these words or phrases in writing.*" (Interviewee Hua, TI)

"... *In the writing class, teachers can supply some cases of students and analyze the typical errors together with students, which can leave a deeper impression to students. At the same time, effective vocabulary teaching methods should be explored, such as helping students understand vocabulary, and memorizing them. Especially some high frequency words and phrases should be noted. Last but not least, grammars are still necessary to talk about in College English class.*" (Interviewee Zhuang, TI)

"... *In my mind, the effective way to overcome these errors is writing more and practicing more. I usually take one or two writing samples in English class to analyze the advantages and disadvantages. Meanwhile, the feedback will be presented on the screen, raising students' awareness of writing appropriate passages.*" (Interviewee Xu, TI)

"... *after writing, I will choose two or three compositions as the samples, which the students should do the proof reading. I believe when the students read the samples, they would like to compare the model writing with their own ones. Then the students may find their errors, which will be concluded by the teacher's summary.*" (Interviewee Yang, TI)

"... *Grammatical errors, like verb tense and predicate, are frequently occurring among students, which should supply feedback to those students. Regarding the sentence structure, first, I would like to give them a mini-lecture which is mainly about the transition of the sentence, which can raise their awareness of writing in unity. Then, when in reading class, I will show the transition of the sentence or the paragraph, and students might learn how to use them. Gradually, the errors in this aspect will decrease, and so to other errors.*" (Interviewee Xin, TI)

In summary, teachers have common sense in students' errors and ways to improve their writing levels and decrease writing errors.

4.5 Writing Instructions in the Non-English Major Class

Non-English majors need more time to practice writing in class. Even some teachers have no plan to teach writing every week. The writing was taught separately from speaking, reading, and translation in college. The participants in this study are all in their second semester of their first year in college. Their teachers usually assign the writing task after completing each unit of intensive reading class (two weeks for one unit). The textbook is called *College English Integrated Course* (the second version). The book has eight units, each with two texts on one topic. For each unit, there are four parts. The first part is the listening task that acts as a warming activity to introduce the unit's topic. The second part is the reading task for reading Text A in detail, which means the text should be learned in detail, including its division of the text, the main idea of each part, the underlying meaning of the sentence, the meaning and usage of words and phrases. Text A is followed by after-text exercises (about 11 pages, mostly paying attention to practising the words and phrases). The third part is Text B which is a home reading task. It is just for reading comprehension with multiple choice, translation, and language practice. Part Ⅳ is comprehensive language practice, and writing is only one page. Teachers only use less than ten minutes to deal with this part, because the textbook's essays are not fit to the requirement in CET – 4. English teachers would like their students to write compositions like in CET – 4 or 6, which will be counted in teachers' annual performance. Therefore, teachers are not interested in other writing genres, and only before the examination of CET – 4, the writing practice can be done fully.

Undoubtedly, I have no opportunity to experience the real writing process of the students in class for there is no time left for writing. All the writings are processed after class. Additionally, the teaching content seemed not so related to the students' need, or it could not be classified as useful, interesting and enlightening. Thus, it is very hard for teachers to supervise the writing process, not to mentioning the strategies before the writing, like brain storming, scaffolding, creative writing and group writing to stimulate students' interest in English writing.

In this chapter, the results of descriptive analysis, questionnaires and interviews of students and teachers have been presented and analyzed. In the descriptive analysis of writing errors, different tables and figures were supplied to show the tendency of errors changes in the participants. Meanwhile, we see each type of error in Chinese college students. In the questionnaires, the participants were asked different questions to examine their writing motivation, writing difficulties and other non-linguistic factors influencing their writing proficiency. The interviews for students and teachers traced can provide deeper reasons which caused such errors. More importantly, two fundamental conceptions, intralingual and interlingual were categorized and analyzed by their characteristics of language transferring with the concrete examples, which presented the reasons of errors types of Chinese L2 college students.

CHAPTER 5 DISCUSSION

This chapter presents the results of the data analysis which was conducted to answer the five research questions in the present study. Interesting findings were obtained regarding the characteristics of error types in the past eight years in Chinese L2 learners, so were possible linguistic reasons for those errors, and their writing attitudes during English writing. To the best of my knowledge, most similar studies focused on the same participants in a short period of time, and few studies could be found to do the experiments on different participants over a long time duration. Therefore, in some sections discussed below, it is difficult to find a comparable research to compare its findings with the results of the current research.

5.1 Writing Errors in Eight Years

Research Question 1: How many errors of each type occur in each group? What are the patterns of errors in Chinese L2 learners' writing? And what are the differences among proficiency level groups?

To answer this question, the descriptive data statistics have been calculated in Chapter 4 results. The findings showed that except the year 2013, which has a higher error number than others, the total number of the rest seven years were quite similar. The possible reason for this phenomenon is that as early as the year 2008 (the year the Beijing Olympic was held, which creates the atmosphere to learn English in China), the Education Ministry of PRC issued the English Curriculum Standards for Compulsory Education. From this year, the direction of English teaching has changed into a broad vision, that is, English class cannot only pay attention to English skills; higher quality like students' creativity, emotion, learning strategies, thinking ways should also be inspired and trained during teaching process, and most of schools started to learn English from the third year of their primary school (MoE, 2008). The early course learning of English equipped Chinese L2 students with a strong sense of comprehensive grasp of English language, not confined to speaking, listening and writing only. Because for many years, "the deaf and dumb English" has been criticized by the whole society in China. As an English teacher in college, I have my own feeling that in recent years, Chinese students' overall English proficiency has been improved a lot because they can express themselves freely even inevitably with some wrong expressions or errors.

Regarding the changes in total error numbers in each year in terms of proficiency levels, it can be seen clearly from Figure 8 that the overall trend in the three groups is decreasing even though the degree is different. The amplitude scope of the high proficiency level is the smallest, from about 40 to 100. Whereas, the other two groups obtain quite similar trend lines, which crossed three regions of the figure. The findings possibly indicate that the high proficiency students have the solid foundation of English knowledge, and there is no big difference among high proficiency group members in different years. At the same time, the degree of fair and low proficiency groups shaking to a large extent, meanwhile the two lines are quite the same except the year 2016 for it ranks the second highest in making errors of FPG except the year 2013. The above results may indicate that the instability of students' performance in fair and low proficiency groups, which, sometimes, depends on the theme of the topics or familiarity, and their existing English knowledge.

The last trend in this part is the changes of errors in terms of each category in the past eight years (see Figure 4 – 3). The figure depicts very clearly these five main error categories. Among these, the highest line indicates the most errors committed by students, while the middle line represents the medium, and the lowest represents the most minor errors. Obviously, semantic errors are the least one in them. Substance errors are aroused mainly by the differences between English and Chinese, for they belong to two different language systems. Regarding the reasons for making wrong spelling, we will discuss the possible reasons in Question 2. Few semantic errors occur, which attributes to the genre of the writing, because most of writings are expository writing and argumentative writing. Direct expression is the primary method to demonstrate the author's opinion, so few metaphors were adopted to accomplish the task. The second biggest problem for L2 learners is grammatical errors which includes lots of items under this category, like subject-verb agreement, verb tense, adjectives, adverbs, prepositions, plural forms, modal verbs, and link verbs. These grammars are the obstacles to acquiring L2 because the difference in such grammars is large between

Chinese and English language. Even though teaching English grammar is the most important part in school education, students still have many confusions and difficulties. The results can provide some implications for grammar teaching, which will be discussed later in Chapter 6.

Regarding the percentage of each type of error, it can be seen from Figure 4 – 4 that the use of substance errors was the most problematic category for the participants in this research (1,585 errors, 42%). The rest challenging types were grammar (1,306 errors, 34%), lexical words (532 errors, 14%), syntactic errors (337 errors, 9%), and semantic errors (21 errors, 1%). Among these, the frequencies of each category are different even though the frequencies between substance and grammatical errors are quite similar for they occupy the most part of the total errors. In the category of substance errors, three sub-type errors, like errors in capitalization, punctuation, and spelling, are included, which exhibit the percentage respectively 14% (224), 7% (111), and 79% (1,250) of the total substance errors. This could indicate that spelling is still a big problem for Chinese L2 students, especially for the participants in this study, because online computer final examination has been conducted for more than ten years in this university. When some students type their compositions in the computer, the screen brings a different feeling compared with handwriting on paper. With the technology development, some online composition, such as *Grammarly*, or *Pigai. org* (a Chinese online composition checking system) checking system appeared, which satisfied the needs of teachers in China, for there are over 50 students in each class.

The above findings are in line with the study of He (2009). The study claimed that spelling error is the most frequent in the category of lexical field, which has a different theory background on categorizing errors. The study showed that there are about 35.65% of spelling errors. Such phenomenon should arouse learners' attention because spelling errors are also committed by some high proficiency level students. He also stated the reasons for making so many spelling errors of Chinese learners. Firstly, the linguistic differences between English and Chinese, which we have mentioned in Chapter 4. Secondly, the complexity of English spelling referring to no correspondence between morpheme and phoneme, indicates that the letters in phonetic symbol or the combination of letters is much more than phoneme; and thirdly, the slip of handwriting and insensitiveness to English spelling are also committed to such errors.

The second biggest part of the error committed by Chinese L2 learners is grammatical errors, which is about 34% of the total error numbers. The evidence of grammatical errors indicated that the first year of non-English majors had difficulties in using correct grammatical structures and forms. However, these errors did not affect their communication since they could get themselves understood during their daily expression. Only a little part of errors caused miscommunication and ambiguity. Lots of studies conducted the experiment in grammatical errors.

Regarding the frequencies of each sub-type of errors, it can be seen clearly from Figure 4 – 4 that spelling is the most frequent error with a total of 1,250 errors, followed by word form, subject-verb agreement, verb tense, capitalization and sentence structure. The findings are in line with what we have reviewed, that is, spelling, grammatical items, and sentence structure are the primary sources of errors.

In order to show the characteristic of different proficiency groups, a statistical analysis is conducted to show the difference between them. The statistics (see Table 4 – 1) showed that the average error number of each composition in the high, fair and low proficiency group is 7.18, 12.78 and 15.81 respectively, which means that the average error in the low proficiency level is double than those of the high proficiencies group. The ANOVA shows that it is significantly different between high and low proficiency levels, also the same to fair and low proficiency levels. Regarding different error types, the average number of errors in the low proficiency group is higher than that of the high proficiency group, and the ANOVA presents that there is a significantly difference between the high, fair and low proficiency groups ($p < 0.05$). The results may indicate that the less errors in their compositions, the stronger competence they obtain to apply the linguistic items, and the higher scores they get in their compositions.

5.2 Relationship between Writing Errors and Writing Proficiency

Research Question 2: What is the relationship between Chinese L2 learners' writing errors and their writing proficiency?

To investigate the relationship between writing errors and writing proficiency, the statistical data of final examination score, composition score, error numbers, and each type of error numbers were conducted through SPSS. The correlation analysis reveals that error numbers is negatively correlated with composition scores, which means the higher the score compositions, the fewer the error numbers in students' compositions. Besides, regarding the relationship between English proficiency and error numbers, the results show a positive correlation, which suggests that the proficiency level of students decide the quantity of error numbers. What is more, the composition score was also examined with each type of error to see to what degree they are correlated with each other. The correlation analysis also reveals results further that composition scores are positively correlated with grammatical errors, substance errors, lexical errors, and syntactic errors, but no significance with semantic errors, which might indicate students' English proficiency can be improved with the development of studying and the increase of their cognition. Finally, to examine the relationship between final exam score and composition score, eight years data have been collected and examined through SPSS. From Table 4 – 4, it can be concluded that there is a significantly high positive relationship between the final score and the score of compositions (R final score-composition score = 0.838), which probably means that the level of one's English writing proficiency highly represents one's English level, because English writing is closely related to vocabulary, grammar, syntactic structure, and overall cohesion among sentences and paragraphs.

All the correlations examined with different data showed that writing proficiency is influenced closely by their overall English proficiency. Furthermore, according to Troia, et al. (2013), English proficiency played an essential role in student writing performance, which, in turn, correlates with student motivation in writing. So, the results indicate that students with higher writing proficiency are their good English proficiency. Therefore, L2 students might engage themselves in English writing since people spend more time and effort on courses that result in satisfaction and positive effect and avoid courses that generate dissatisfaction and negative effect (Zimmerman & Kitsantas, 2007). Additionally, it is impossible to deny that English writing has played a significant part in determining the competitiveness of an undergraduate student. However, due to the exam-oriented EFL writing instruction in Chinese university classes, most non-English major university students recognize English writing as a compulsory course that they should take for an exam rather than a course with useful knowledge or practical skills.

5.3 Linguistic Causes of Writing Errors

Research Question 3: To what extent are linguistic factors (interlingual or intralingual transfer) responsible for Chinese L2 learners' writing errors? Is there a difference among different proficiency groups?

The table (see Chapter 4, Table 4 – 12) of the frequency of interlingual and intralingual errors showed that most errors are intralingual transfer of errors. It is due to overgeneralization, false concept hypothesis, and incomplete application of language rules. From the table, the similarities of interlingual errors and intralingual errors made by the three proficiency groups can be identified. It also showed that in interlingual transfer of errors, the percentage is from high to low while the intralingual errors are from low to high. The three groups had not obvious differences in the perspective of interlingual and intralingual. As we have mentioned, there are about 80% of errors which belong to intralingual errors, and about 90% of intralingual errors are caused by their ignorance rule of restrictions, which probably means that the participants have grasped most of the rules in English, and they have passed the primary stage in L2 acquisition. This also fits to the natural condition that in this study, the participants belong to the intermediate level students in China. The result of the percentage in interlingual and intralingual errors concurs with the results reported in precious IL literature. On the other hand, the results also suggest that for college students, L2 English teachers should pay more attention to the authenticity of L2 in the perspective of accuracy, and complexity instead of simply grammar and vocabulary teaching, because they have passed the basic stage of language acquisition.

In order to examine the differences of the three proficiency groups in interlanguage scope, this study divides three proficiency levels according to their English proficiency. The policy to adopt such group number is that such division fits to the normal distribution, which has been mentioned in Chapter 3. The compared differences (one-way ANOVA) among three proficiency groups in interlingual and intralingual errors showed that there is a significant difference between interlingual errors among the three groups ($F = 1.824$, $p = .000$). In contrast, the difference is not significant in the perspective of intralingual errors. The results might indicate that the fewer the interlingual errors, the stronger their application in English writing, and the higher their compositions score.

5.4 Non-linguistic Causes of Writing Errors

Research Question 4: What is the relationship between Chinese L2 learners' writing errors and writing attitudes, writing difficulties and corrective feedback? What are the differences among different proficiency groups?

The *Post Hoc* results of ANOVA demonstrate that the High Proficiency Group (HPG) has better writing attitudes than the Fair Proficiency Group (FPG), while the Fair Proficiency Group has better writing attitudes than the Low Proficiency Group (LPG). *Turkey's post hoc* procedure indicates that students in FPG have more writing difficulties than in HPG while LPG has more writing difficulties than FPG. Additionally, the students in FPG have a high recognition of teachers' feedback than in HPG and LPG, but not significantly different in CF among these three groups. The results indicate that successful writing requires knowledge as well as active and consciousness of good writing behavior. Good writers also spend more time planning and revising their text as well as monitoring their writing process (Graham & Harris, 1992).

The multiple regression analysis suggests that WA and English proficiency are significant predictor of WP. This mirrors the other studies (Kiany & Nejad, 2001), which suggest that a higher level of L2 proficiency is related to higher L2 writing abilities. The finding argues against what Aliakbari stated that a certain level of L2 proficiency was not a must-be condition for L2 writing but required. English proficiency plays a very significant role in students' writing proficiency, which has been proved in the third research question with statistical analysis. Thus, if one has poor English proficiency, he/she might also has a problem in English writing. Meanwhile, this result also explains why L2 writers who lack motivation in their writing might have difficulty expressing his/her individuality (Tardy, 2005). Lots of studies show that motivation, writing attitudes, and writing difficulties can affect one's writing proficiency (Dornyei & Skehan, 2008; Wigfield, 1994; Zimmerman, 2008). These results support the statement that English proficiency is a significant factor influencing students writing proficiency as well as motivation, writing attitudes and behaviors.

The results of this research question support what some scholars found, if a student has high motivation or positive writing attitude, he/she might set high-level goals that lead to increase English writing proficiency. Motivation is usually regarded as the first and foremost element in SLA. This finding also explains why the students with low writing motivation acquire quite low scores in writing proficiency. Previous studies show a positive effect of writing attitudes on students' performance, which is apparent for challenging tasks (Arter, et al., 1994; Maehr & Stallings, 1972). Therefore, students with high motivation also show that they have high expectations in writing, more interest in writing, and the image of being a good writer. It also shows that there is no difference among students with medium and low writing attitudes. Therefore, the students with relatively high writing motivation seem more determined to engage themselves in writing. Furthermore, during this process, the students how their work hard, persistence, strong interest and higher expectations since one's perception of competence and the belief that whether he/she can control the desired outcomes may determine his/her expectations for success at a given task (Bandura, 1988). Last but not least, multiple regression results show that writing proficiency is a positive predictor of writing motivation. These results also suggest that the students with good EP and high WM are likely to be more engaged in L2 writing and will take measures to improve their writing ability. These findings also support previous arguments that highly proficient students are generally more confident and motivated to write (Lee, et al., 2018; Troia, et al., 2013).

5.5 Other Particular Variables Affecting Writing Proficiency

Research Question 5: What any other particular variables can affect Chinese L2 learners' writing errors?

According to the content of semi-structured interviews with Chinese English teachers and college students, there are still other particular variables that can affect students' writing proficiency. The first and foremost is the teacher, and some students express their like or dislike on the arrangement of English writing instructed by their English teachers. Their motivation and interest in writing were influenced to some extent based on their preference of their teachers' preference. These conclusions are consistent with some previous findings, which reported that the teacher was the most potent factor affecting students' motivation and interest in L2 writing (Oxford, 1998; Muhonen, 2004; Bahramy & Araghi, 2013; Quadir, 2017).

"... *compared with an English teacher in high school, the college English teacher is not so strict with us for they usually require us to upload the composition on the Internet. I believe lots of students don't take writing as a serious thing, because we cannot get the feedback directly. The feedback from the machine is not so believable...*" (Interviewee,

Hong)

"... *when I was in high school, English writing was assigned regularly, and the good compositions were shared in a class by our teacher. But in college, my English teacher randomly assigned the writing task. During this semester, my English teacher has never assigned the composition. I think this will impress the students that writing is not an important skill in English learning. Actually, English writing is important for college students, especially for those who want to get their postgraduate education or go abroad...* " (Interviewee, Li)

The above two interviewees claimed that they learned less than they did in high school in the perspective of English writing. This was contradicted by the objective of higher education which aims to improve students' capability in practice usage.

The reasons behind such phenomenon are that the teachers lack the sense that English is a compulsory teaching task that should be instructed with lots of practice. Alternatively, some teachers consider English writing can be temporarily trained before an exam.

"... *she only spared about ten minutes to explain the rules and regulations of English writing in class. They seemed to pay more attention to the textbook. Well, this may not be the responsibility of teachers, because college English has only three periods per week, which is not enough for teachers to accomplish all their tasks...* " (Interviewee, Wu)

While interviewees Mao and Zheng argued that if their teachers were highly concerned about writing instruction, they could be more motivated in English writing and have better writing proficiency.

"... *before the exam of CET-4 and CET-6, teachers usually spare several weeks to train us. They usually ask us to do timed writing in class and give us detailed corrective feedback after class. With such intensity, I felt my writing was improved a lot...* " (Interviewee, Mao)

"... *the training period provides us a series of writing skills, such as transition, cohesion as well as lots of writing genres, argumentative writing and expository writing. I can feel the passion of the teacher to train us. I really gain a lot from this...* " (Interviewee, Zheng)

From students' feedback, it can be seen that teachers' perception of English teaching before the exam suggested that they contributed a great deal to the students' exam-oriented mindset on. Actually, over the past decades, college English teachers failed to pay attention to increasing students' interest in writing (Boscolo & Hidi, 2007). This neglect harms students' motivation and interest in writing for the long run. Besides, teachers' expectations also impact students' motivation and confidence (Pidgeon, 1970).

Secondly, even though some teachers assigned writing tasks frequently, they gave feedback to frustrate students. Most teachers ask their students to finish their writing on an online checking system (Pigai. org), which can mark students' writing automatically. However, the online checking system provides feedback mainly on grammatical errors or wrong spelling, and it seems impossible to check the transition and cohesion of sentences or passages. The reason for teachers' preference in an online checking system is that English class is large. Therefore, in a work environment that is often overloaded, it is difficult for teachers to give individual feedback in large classes (You, 2004).

Finally, how teachers deal with teaching materials was considered unsatisfactory. Some students complained that the passages in the textbooks were generally outdated, old-fashioned, and lacked activities. This might diminish students' motivation and interest in English acquisition.

The other factor affecting the motivation of English writing might be the school administration. Some interviewees thought the school administration should have considered the demands of the students for they arrange English class in an inappropriate large size, with 50 to 80 in one class, which put much pressure on English teachers.

"... *Actually, I don't like the online checking system because I cannot give feedback directly to my students. However, assessing their compositions is time-consuming because I have four classes to teach with more than* 200 *students. So I have to only select about* 20 *compositions each time for each class to check by myself. Then I will arrange the team meeting to discuss the compositions together...*" (Interviewee Huang, TI)

Secondly, many universities in China require the certificate of CET-4 or CET-6 as a necessity to graduate, which pushes students to learn English writing to pass the exams. The result of such requirement, first, enhances students' ability to exam-oriented English writing but diminish their motivation and interest in freestyle writing, which harms the improvement of their writing in the long run. This situation is similar to what Deci, et al. (1999) argued: educational institutions often make students learn through external control, monitoring, evaluation, and artificial rewards, which make learning a chore rather than a joy. Pelletier et al. (2009) suggest that teachers mostly experience pressure from the standards stipulated by decision-makers as well as the non-engagement of students in the class which negatively influences their motivation to teach and the way they deal with students. William and Burden (1997) suggested that a successful school should judge their expressed education aims within the border national and cultural context of the country's educational system, for it may harm teachers' teaching as well as students' learning.

From interviewees' feedback, we can see that teachers and school administration also affect students' motivation and interest in improving their writing proficiency. Therefore, the implication for this is that decision-making should fit the regulations of human development. Otherwise, it will diminish the creation and motivation of students.

In this chapter, I mainly discussed the linguistic and non-linguistic challenges they faced when writing in English. The first two research questions focus on the descriptive of error types (mainly grammatical, substance, syntactic, lexical and semantic errors) and error numbers in the past eight years in L2 writing and the percentage of each error distributed in the total numbers. In the following research questions, the relationship between writing proficiency and error numbers is investigated through statistical data. It is presented that writing proficiency is negatively correlated with error numbers of the participants. The higher writing proficiency, the lower their error numbers, and vice versa. Among the non-linguistic factors, motivation, writing attitudes, writing difficulties, and corrective feedback play critical roles in increasing students' writing proficiency. In the next chapter, I shall move on to discuss and evaluate the implications these findings have for L2 writing pedagogy and research.

CHAPTER 6 CONCLUSIONS

This chapter demonstrates the main conclusion of this research in relation to its five questions, the main characteristics of error types that Chinese learners commit when composing in English, the possible reasons causing these errors, the non-linguistic factors to influence their writings, the comprehensive discussion of teachers, and students about the concrete questions in English teaching and learning. The implications of these findings for pedagogy (English writing instruction) are also discussed. I have also summarized the limitations of this study. This chapter concludes with recommendations for further researches in the future in the field of EFL writing skills and challenges.

6.1 Summary of Findings

Based on the theoretical frameworks of error analysis and interlanguage, this study investigated the frequencies and patterns of errors in L2 writing, and the linguistic and non-linguistic factors affecting writing errors. To depict an overview of L2 learners' writing errors, descriptive analysis was adopted to demonstrate the numbers of errors, the changes of error patterns, and the percentage of each type of error. Inferential analysis, with operating the software SPSS to get Spearsman and ANOVA of related files, was employed to show the relationship between writing errors and their writing proficiency, writing attitudes, writing difficulties and corrective feedback, and the differences among three proficiency groups. Last but not least, a semi-structured interview was conducted to explore deeper into the reasons of L2 writing errors. The combination of quantitative and qualitative study revealed the characteristics of L2 writing errors and the possible reasons to cause these errors.

Firstly, the findings of descriptive analysis of total errors in the past 8 years showed that except the year 2013, which has a higher error number than others, the total number of the rest seven years were quite similar. From this perspective, it may indicate that there are no significant differences in making a total number of errors among these participants. Besides, the quantitative data analysis showed the main characteristics of error types and different error types at different proficiency levels. Among these five main error categories, substance errors are the biggest challenge for Chinese L2 writers, among which spelling is a serious obstacle for them. Similar to other previous studies, grammatical errors are also the section for L2 students committing errors. The statistics showed that the average error number of each composition in the high, fair and low proficiency group is 7.18, 12.78 and 15.81 respectively, which means that the average error in the low proficiency level is double than that of the high proficiency group. The ANOVA shows that it is significantly different between high and low proficiency levels, also the same to fair and low proficiency levels. Regarding different error types, the average number of errors in the low proficiency group is higher than that of the high proficiency group, and the ANOVA shows a significant difference between the high, fair and low proficiency groups ($p < 0.05$). The results may indicate that the less errors in their compositions, the stronger competence they obtain to apply the linguistic items, and the higher scores they get in their compositions.

Secondly, regarding the correlation between students' writing errors and their writing proficiency, it can be seen that there is a negative significance between them through data analysis. When calculating statistically, L2 writing proficiency was confirmed to significantly account for the error numbers, final examination score, and each type of linguistic errors. Unsurprisingly, the low proficiency group made a greater number of errors than their fair, and high proficiency counterparts did. This observation was recurrent for each type of error. Meanwhile, the mean for the low proficiency group was much larger than that for the high proficiency group. Almost all these differences were found to be statistically significant. This finding indicates that the insufficient mastery of writing skills could be contributory and responsible for the large number of errors that low proficiency students make when writing in the L2.

Thirdly, when investigating to what extent linguistic factors are responsible for interlingual and intralingual errors, the statistics was calculated to find the reasons. Through data analysis, intralingual errors with about 80% of total errors for the participants belong to the intermediate level students for they have grasped the essential knowledge and skills in English learning. Through the results of compared differences in the three groups, the higher their proficiency are, the fewer errors they make.

Fourthly, question four discusses the relationship between students' writing proficiency and their writing motivation, attitudes, and writing behavior. The results showed that there is a positive significance between writing proficiency and writing motivation. The higher their proficiency, the higher their writing motivation, and vice versa. Students' writing proficiency was decided not only by their linguistic factors, but also non-linguistic factors. Lots of studies have proved that. The results implied that as an English teacher, emotional encouragement is necessary to increase students' interest in English writing. Meanwhile, teachers should provide necessary help when students meet difficulties in English writing.

Lastly, the semi-structured interview of teachers and students provides a more profound observation of the possible reasons of making errors and the feedback from front-line teachers. This section will supply information which might offer insights into the actual L2 writing teaching and learning context, which mainly discusses the possible reasons for the errors, and also their motivation, learning difficulties of Chinese university students. From the interview, it can be found that most students can realize their errors in their English writing, but it is still hard for them to correct these wrong forms. Most students are aware of their writing errors and also try their best to overcome. Undoubtedly, it needs time and writing practice. Regarding the possible reasons, most of them have the sense that the language differences arouse so many errors for Chinese L2 writers. Some of them think the learning context is quite crucial for language learning, and in China, college students have no such context. Even though students have their initial awareness of their errors and the possible reasons, the deeper reasons and the implications are still needed for their improvement in English writing.

6.2 Research Implications

6.2.1 For Teaching L2 Writing

The results derived from this research have, to a large extent, provided sufficient evidence that L2 writing is related to a bilingual process, as writers have two languages for their use (Cumming, 1990). The findings also show the complex and mixed elements involved in L2 writing.

Firstly, teachers should allocate sufficient class time to draw their students' attention on the importance of writing and arouse their interest to English writing as a process and to train them in the different writing genres. At the beginning of English teaching, the basic knowledge of English grammar should be taught with concrete examples.

Secondly, teachers also raise the awareness of students on the importance of spelling, for more than one third of errors is spelling errors. On the other side, the negative correlation of spelling errors and English writing proficiency shows that spelling errors, to a large extent, confine the improvement of writing proficiency. Meanwhile, students should broaden their vocabulary, especially the depth and width of high frequent words. It is reported that the most frequent words, about 1,000, cover 72.0% of general English, while the frequent words, 2,000, cover about 79.7% and 3,000 words covering 84.0%. Therefore, the acquisition of high frequency words is the most important and basic part. He (2009) also reported in his research that Chinese college students only obtain low quality in applying highly frequent words.

Thirdly, teachers should try their best to enhance students' overall English proficiency, because students' writing errors are closely related to it. For example, they are strengthening the reading input because reading extensively can broaden their vision in the practical use of English language.

Fourthly, teachers should emphasize the importance of raising the student's awareness of the differences between Chinese and English linguistic structures, especially the points which cause errors easily. Wherever there are differences between Chinese and English, it appears for Chinese students there are lots of word errors. The goal of this activity is to lessen the influence of negative transfer of the mother tongue. The suggestions for a problem are to strengthen the input of the target language. Raimes (1989) stated that relevant knowledge from good reading is the beginning to improve their writing proficiency. Sufficient input from reading English articles and stories can provide the understanding and the context of words, and also to word selection.

Fifthly, teachers should adopt different methods of examining students' compositions. Even though online checking system is popular in China, the survey showed that most students do not favor this assessment way. English teachers should adopt the combination of various ways to improve students writing. For example, the correcting marks can be set together between teachers and students, thus, students can understand clearly the feedback from teachers. Here are several methods for teachers to use in their writing checking. One is peer assessment which means students themselves check their peers' compositions and provide feedback. For example, the students can be divided into two groups freely. First, students should mark the errors with their signs, like grammatical errors, syntactic errors, lexical errors, etc. Meanwhile, teachers provide the following questions for students as references: ① Is there agreement between the subject and the predicate? ② Is verb tense correct? ③ Is the part of speech misused (like adjectives replacing adverbs or nouns)? ④ Are capitalization and punctuation correct? ⑤ Is word form appropriate? Peer assessment can relieve students' burden, which also raises students' awareness about errors or ideas, to alert student in their own writing. Second, group assessment. Teachers should provide instruction before assessing compositions, then the group members can check compositions via self-correction. Teachers raise related questions for students to think about: What is the theme of the composition? Is it clear? Does the beginning paragraph lead to the following idea? Is the main point clear? What is the relationship among paragraphs? Are there transition words or transitional sentences? Last but not least, the checking should be done by teachers. After one of the above checking methods, the number of errors need to be taken out or corrected has declined, especially for some basic errors and mistakes. Teachers only need to point out some errors in the theme and sentence level.

6.2.2 For L2 Learners

For L2 writing, students themselves should have positive attitudes and good habits towards it. For most of time, students are tired of dealing with test papers before the National Entrance Examination, so they need more time to feel the charm of English language. The first step to arouse students' interest is to let them apply English to practical use, like writing emails or diaries. Besides, listening to English songs and watching English movies are also effective ways to arouse students' interest and improve their English proficiency.

Students can arrange various activities by themselves. For example, English corner is always regarded as an easy and effective way to arouse students' interest. First, there is no limitation on the talking topics, and no teachers watch their action, so students are free to express their feelings to their peers.

The writing topic should be varied, especially at the beginning of their learning English stage. Students can write what they want, or write the hot spot at present. Regarding the content, words, or styles, no limitation attached to the requirement can inspire their innate genuine expression. Thus it can develop their writing ability for a long period of time. The national test writing model is only trained before the test. The long time training should decrease their interest of writing.

6.2.3 For School Administrators

School administrators play an essential role in training teachers' sense of utilizing strategies and improving student learning. From the findings of this study, there are several suggestions for school administrators.

First and foremost, as school administrators, before they make relevant policies or decisions, they should have clearly understand the purpose of EFL writing in Chinese setting. Besides, students' innate needs should be investigated and considered. For example, before releasing specific rules or policies, it is necessary to check students' attitudes through surveys, students' professional performance or teachers' assessments. Under the guidance of the above sense, decision-makers can weigh the gains and losses for implementing decisions or policies in advance and adjust their decision time to the immediate learning context.

Secondly, the current research indicates that schools should strive to create a favorable learning environment for teachers and students. Thus, textbook selection should be cautious with considering students' level under the guidance of National College English Guidelines. The renowned press should be taken into account at first, and then in a large number of textbooks, the textbooks should be closely related to students' reality and social development. School administrators should employ qualified teachers to set good learning standards for teachers are the prerequisite of a good education. School demonstrators should respect students' personalities and see the potential in all students.

Thirdly, school administrators should realize that the large class size and extra-class word hurt teaching effect, which can prevent teaching from applying useful approaches to writing instruction, paying close attention to students' individual needs, and planning EFL writing courses. The writing instruction of a college requires the guidance of a sound conceptual framework, such as the domain-specific nature of writing and the pedagogy of teaching writing (Morgan & Pytash, 2014). School leaders should understand the challenges teachers face in their EFL teaching (e.g., work overloaded) and satisfy teachers' vocational needs by providing opportunities for their professional development, especially in the field of teaching SLA. The professional development of teachers can lead to a successful school through different social and policy changes and potential challenges (Day & Gu, 2007; Loehr & Schwartz, 2006). School administrators should be aware of the importance of the context for teaching and create a favorable writing environment for faculties.

Last but not least, the motivation, effectiveness and a sense of commitment among teachers, a comfortable, positive, and inspired learning environment can nurture the students with quality of creativity, motivation, and self-efficacy.

6.3 Limitations

Though much effort has been put in drilling the error types of L2 writing and its possible reasons, lots of things cannot be conducted in this experiment due to the limitation of time and conditions. However, this limitation can evolve the further research topics for future studies.

Firstly, this research only analyzed the five most frequent errors with actual examples. Actually, there are many types of categorization in L2 writing errors which pay attention to different aspects of it. For example, Richards (1971a) categorized writing errors according to different ways of effect by errors, interlingual errors, intralingual errors and developmental errors. Corder (1974) categorized different writing errors according to the different stages of language system. They are pre-systematic errors, systematic errors and post-systematic errors, which, respectively, refers to the stages of development in mother language, interlanguage and target language. Therefore, the five types of writing errors cannot cover the total kinds of error types, and more categorization of writing errors can be adopted to reveal different rules and regulations of L2 writing errors.

Secondly, according to the results of data analysis, questionnaire and interview, the implication for teaching English writing can be concluded in improving writing and English teaching. However, due to the limited research experiences, the suggestions might cover all kinds of areas, schools and different teaching levels. As cited from Corder (1975), errors are inevitable during the writing process. Language learning is a process of making mistakes and correcting them. Error analysis plays an essential role in language acquisition. Even though this study has achieved some fruits, the researcher hopes that in the further study, the researcher can improve their research methods, broaden their research scope, and involve more participants.

Thirdly, this study only examined writing errors in one grade because of some limited situation, which will prevent the overall review of writing errors in different grades. Meanwhile, a learner corpus can be built to examine writing errors in Chinese and English to investigate the possible reasons to cause such errors.

Last but not the least, a longitudinal study has not been adopted to explore the development of L2 learners' interlanguage because limited data were saved and collected in the school computers, which might arouse the interest of researchers in future studies.

6.4 Future Studies

According to the results of data analysis, questionnaire and interview, future studies can be carried out in the following ways. The first direction goes to the theoretical framework of error analysis. In this study, we just adopted one theoretical framework of categorizing errors from James (1998), which mainly focus on five layers of L2 writing. The structure and discourse level of L2 writing were not investigated. Therefore, the further studies can adopt a detailed categorization of writing errors which is related to each level of L2 writings.

The second direction suggested in further study in writing errors can go to a corpus-based research. Compared with manual rating of writing errors, corpus-based method in error analysis has its advantages: first, a large learner corpus is expected to achieve. Because of limitation in rating, only 320 writings are adopted in this research. If a learner corpus could be built, the total population of L2 writings can be included in one corpus, thus, the reliability of the data analysis would be improved a lot. Second, a learner corpus can assist in pedagogical studies of writing errors, or provide raw material for SLA research, or serve as test beds for natural language processing system. Third, with a learner's corpus, the linguistic differences between mother language and target language can be compared and revealed, which can depict a clear picture of the differences of writing errors between native speakers and L2 learners.

Thirdly, it is advisable that more grades can be involved in the writing error analysis to compare the differences between different grades, which is investigated to what extent L2 learners are different in their different stages. Furthermore, a longitudinal study is expected to conduct to examine the development of interlanguage in a specific group of students.

This study sets out to fill the gap in the L2 writing literature and contribute to the development of error analysis and interlanguage in the field of L2 writing by investigating in depth both the error types and the possible reasons. It correlated non-linguistic factors that writers encounter when composing in English. By implementing a research with such challenges, this study hopes to draw the attention of EFL teachers so that school administrators, educators, and teachers can make appropriate rules and regulations to help learners overcome such difficulties, and at the very least help to minimize the obstacles and challenges that students encounter in their L2 acquisition.

ACKNOWLEDGEMENTS

First, I would like to express my sincere gratitude and appreciation to the College of Foreign Languages in Hainan Normal University. Without the support of college and college leaders, this book cannot achieve its publication goal. Besides, I am indebted to all the working staff who are committed to the publication of this book.

This book is composed based on my PhD dissertation. Therefore, I should express my gratitude to my supervisor, Professor Sunhee Kwon, for her professional guidance and continuous support and encouragement at every stage of my doctoral study. Her patience and consolation relieved much pressure from my heart while her insightful feedback and her academic aspiration inspired me a lot in the writing. Without her help, it couldn't be possible to achieve my goals in PhD journey.

I am also indebted to my four book examiners, Professor Hyowon Song, Professor Hayeun Jang, Professor Shinchul Hong, and Professor MinHoe Kim for their time to read my thesis and for their valuable comments on my book.

I am also grateful to my dear friends Gong Yichao, You Qidongmeng, Wang Yingxue, Wu Yan, Hou Jinrong, and Zhang Chengcheng, who accompanied me and provided me many suggestions in life and study, so I never felt scared or lonely with their help and encouragement.

My appreciation also goes to my colleagues who offered me generous help during my data collection and questionnaire stage. Without their help, I couldn't accomplish my task in time.

Additionally, my sincere and heartfelt thanks go to my mother, for her maternal concerns and cares during every step of my life. Even though she never went to school for a day, she provided me lots of meaningful lessons in my daily life, such as, if you want something, work for it. The special thanks also go to my father for his love and encouragement.

My deepest appreciation also goes to my husband, Mr. Yin Yiquan, for his understanding, support and patience throughout my doctoral studies. My sweet love also goes to my daughter and my son who might not know the meaning of their mother's study, but they encouraged me and showed their love to me. Without the support of my family, it wouldn't be possible to accomplish three years' doctoral study.

Last but not the least, I am grateful to all the people I met in Hainan and in Busan, who provided me many helps in life, study and work.

Yuhong Ma

March 3, 2023

REFERENCES

Agbay, N. G. & Reyes, Y. D. (2019). Scrutinizing interlingual and intralingual error: basis for English writing program. *The Educational Review, USA*, 3 (10).

Alivernini, F. & Lucidi, F. (2008). The academic motivation scale (ams): factorial structure, in variance and validity in the Italian context. *Testing, Psychometrics, Methodology in Applied Psychology*, 15 (4).

Al-Khresheh, M. H. (2010). Interlingual interference in English language word order structure of Jordanian EFL learners. *Proceedings of the European Journal of Social Sciences*, 16 (1).

Al-Khresheh, M. H. (2016). A review study of error analysis theory. *International Journal of Humanities and Social Research*, (2).

Anefnaf, Z. (2017). English learning: linguistic flaws. *Sais Faculty of Arts and Humanities*, USMBA, retrieved from https://www. academia. edu/33999467/English _Learning_in_Morocco_Linguistic_Flaws.

Anja, K. S. (2018). The development of German and English writing skills in a bilingual primary school in Germany. *Journal of Second Language Writing*, (39).

Arter, J., Spandel, V., Culham, R., et al. (1994). *The Impact of Training Students to be Self-assessors of Writing, Paper Presented at the Annual Meeting of the American Educational Research Association.* New Orleans.

Azzouz, A. (2013). *Interference of Syntactic, Lexical and Phonological Aspects from Arabic into English for Syrian University Students: a Cross-sectional Study in the HIL at Aleppo* (Unpublished doctoral dissertation). University of Aleppo.

Bahramy, M. & Araghi, M. (2013). The identification of demotives in EFL university students. *International Journal of Basic and Applied Science*, 1 (4).

Benathy, B. H., Trager, B. C. & Waddle, C. D. (1966). *Use of Contrastive Data in Foreign Language Course Development.* In Valdman (ed.). Trends in Language Teaching. New York: McGraw-Hill.

Bandura, A. (1988). Self-efficacy conception of anxiety. *Anxiety Research*, 1 (2).

Beardsmore, H. B. (1982). *Bilingualism: Basic Principles.* Tieto.

Boscolo, P. & Hidi, S. (2007). *The Multiple Meanings of Motivation to Write.* In Boscolo, P. & Hidi, S. (Eds.). Studies in writing and motivation (pp. 1-14). Elsevier.

Brown, D. B. (1994). *Principles of Language Learning and Teaching (3rd ed.).* New Jersey: Prentice Hall Regents.

Brudhiprabha, P. (1972). *Error Analysis: a Psycholinguistic Study of Thai English Compositions.* Thesis (M. A.): McGill University.

Bryman, A. & Bell, E. (2015). Business Research Methods, Oxford University Press, Oxford. In Azungah, T. & Kasmad, R. (2020). For Authors Qualitative research: deductive and inductive approaches to data analysis. *Qualitative Research*, https://doi. org/10. 1108/QRJ-D-18-00035.

Chau, T. (1975). Error analysis, constructive analysis and students' perception: A study of difficulty in second language learning. *IRAL*, 8 (2).

Chelli, S. (2013). *Interlingual and Intralingual Errors in the Use of Preposition and Articles.* Retrieved from http://dspace. univ biskra. dz:8080/jspui/bitstream/123456789/3571/1/Interlingual% 20or% 20Intralingal% 20Errors% 20in% 20the% 20Use%20of%20.

Chen, M. L., Flowerdew, J. & Anthony, L. (2019). Introducing in-service English language teachers to data-driven learning for academic writing. *System*, (87).

Chomsky, N. (1965). *Aspects of the Theory of Syntax.* M. I. T. Press.

Cohen, A. D. & Dörnyei, Z. (2001). *Taking my Motivational Temperature on a Language Task.* Minneapolis, MN: Center for Advanced Research on Language Acquisition, University of Minnesota. Retrieved 14 February 2021 from https://sites. google. com.

Corder, S. P. (1967). The significance of learners' errors. *International Review of Applied Linguistics*, 5 (1 -4).

Corder. S. P. (1974). *Error Analysis: Perspective on Second Language Acquisition.* Longman.

Corder, S. P. (1975). Error analysis, interlanguage and second language acquisition. *Language Teaching*, 8 (4).

Corder, S. P. (1981). *Error and an Interlanguage.* Oxford University.

Corder, S. P. (2000). *Error Analysis.* Longman Publisher.

Cumming, A. (1990). Expertise in evaluating second language compositions. *Language Testing*, 7 (1).

Cai, H. P. & Fang, Y. (2006). Investigation and analysis of the status quo of English writing teaching and learning. *Foreign Languages and Their Teaching*, 10 (10).

Dechert, H. W. (1983). *How a Story is Done in a Second Language*. In Graham Crookes Second Language Speech Production Research: A Methodologically Oriented Review, Studies in Second Language Acquisition. Cambridge University Press.

Deci, E. L., Koestner, R. & Ryan, R. M. (1999). A meta-analytic review of experiments examining the effects of extrinsic rewards on intrinsic motivation. *Psychological Bulletin*, 125 (6).

Diao, Z. M. (2014). Empirical study on the influence of negative transfer of Chinese on English writing of vocational college students. *China Adult Education*, (2).

Dörnyei, Z. (1998). Motivation in Second and Foreign Language Learning. *Language Teaching*, 31 (3).

Dörnyei, Z. (2001a). *Motivational Strategies in the Language Classroom*. Cambridge University Press.

Dörnyei, Z. (2010). Researching motivation: from integrativeness to the ideal L2 self. *Introducing Applied Linguistics: Concepts and Skills*, 3 (5).

Dörnyei, Z. & Csizér, K. (2012). *How to Design and Analyze Surveys in SLA Research?* In A. Mackey & S. Gass (eds.). Research Methods in Second Language Acquisition: a Practical Guide. Malden, MA: Wiley-Blackwell.

Dörnyei, Z. & Ottó, I. (1998). Motivation in action: a process model of L2 motivation. *Working Papers in Applied Linguistics*, (4).

Dörnyei, Z. & Skehan, P. (2008). *Individual Differences in Second Language Learning*. In Doughty, C. J. & Long, M. H. (eds.). The Handbook of Second Language Acquisition. John Wiley & Sons.

Dulay, H. & Burt, M. (1972). Goofican: an indication of children's second language learning strategies. *Language Learning*, 22 (2).

Dai, W. D. & Shu, D. F. (1994). Several research questions on contrastive analysis, error analysis and interlanguage. *The Foreign Language*, (5).

Day, C. & Gu, Q. (2007). Variations in the conditions for teachers' professional learning and development: sustaining commitment and effectiveness over a career. *Oxford Review of Education*, 33 (4).

Deng, J. (2002). Investigation into the current situation, problems and countermeasures of college English writing teaching. *Journal of South-west Institute For Ethnic Groups*, (4).

Denzin, N. K. & Lincoln, Y. S. (2005). *The Discipline and Practice of Qualitative Research*. Sociology. (3rd ed.). Sage Publications Ltd.

Edwards, R. & Holland, J. (2013). *What is Qualitative Interviewing?* Bloomsbury.

El-Aswad, A. A. (2002). *A Study of the L1 and L2 Writing Processes and Strategies of Arab Learners With Special Reference to Third-year Libyan University Students*. PhD dissertation, Newcastle University.

Ellis, M. (2022). Grammar. https://www. grammarly. com/blog/linking-verbs/.

Ellis, R. (1985). Sources of variability in interlanguage. *Applied Linguistics*, 6 (2).

Ellis, R. (1995). *Teaching and Learning Elementary Social Studies*. Boston: Allyn & Bacon.

Ellis, R. (1997). *SLA Research and Language Teaching*. Oxford: Oxford University Press.

Ellis, R. (1999). *The Study of Second Language Acquisition*. Shanghai Foreign Language Education Press.

Ellis, R. (2012). *Understanding Second Language Acquisition*. Shanghai Foreign Language Education Press.

Ferris, D. R. (2002). *Treatment of Error in Second Language Student Writing*. University of Michigan Press.

Fisiak, J. (1981). *Contrastive Linguistics and the Language Teacher*. Pergamon.

Fries, C. C. (1945). *Teaching and Learning English as a Foreign Language*. Ann Arbor, Michigan: University of Michigan Press. In Peter H. Fries, Charles C. Fries, Linguistics and corpus linguistics, *ICAME Journal*, (34).

Feng, L. & Gao, S. F. (2012). An empirical study on the effect of scoring methods in formative assessment of college English writing-comparative analysis of overall scoring and mixed scoring methods. *Journal of Beijing Jiaotong University (Social Science Edition)*, 11 (3).

Feng, M. Z. & Zheng, X. M. (2016). Using tasks to enhance English learners' reflective learning and writing competence among non-English majors in China. *Foreign Languages in China*, (6).

Gao, H. (2010). The current situation and thinking of the research on the evaluation of foreign and domestic second language writing in the UK. *Foreign Language Circles*, (2).

Gardner, R. C. (1985). *Social Psychology and Second Language Learning: The Role of Attitudes and Motivation.* Edward Arnold.

Gass, S. M. & Selinker, L. (2008). *Second Language Acquisition: an Introductory Course* (*3rd ed.*). Routledge.

George, H. V. (1972). *Common Errors in Language Learning.* Newbury House Publishers.

Gradman, J. (1971). The limitations of contrastive analysis predictions. *Working Papers in Linguistics*, 3 (4).

Graham, S. & Harris, K. R. (1992). *Self-regulated Strategy Development: Programmatic Research in Writing.* In Contemporary Intervention Research in Learning Disabilities. Springer.

Guan, S. H, Zhu, Q. & Huang, D. H. (2012). Research on the current situation of writing ability of English majors in science and engineering colleges. *Education Research Monthly*, (9).

Guo, X. H. & Ouyang, J. (2010). A new exploration of college English writing based on error analysis theory. *Foreign Language and Literature*, 26 (2).

Han, Z. H. & Tarone, E. (2014). *Interlanguage: Forty Years Later.* John Benjamins Publishing Company.

Hendrickson, J. M. (1987). *Error Correction in Foreign Language Teaching: Recent Theory, Research, and Practice.* In M. H. Long & J. C. Richards (eds.), Methodology in *TESOL*: a book of readings. Heinle & Heinle.

He, H. L. (2004). English composition selection strategy for non-English majors. *Foreign Language World*, (5).

He, H. Q. (2009) . Lexical error analysis in non-English major compositions-based on the corpus. *Foreign Language World*, 132 (3).

Honrado, F. B. & Biray, E. T. (2022). Error analysis in spoken English among grade 12 students. *International Journal of Educational Management and Development Studies*, 3 (1).

Hu, R. (1998). Interlanguage and foreign language teaching in China. *Foreign Language Teaching*, 3 (3).

Huang, J. B. & Yu, S. L. (2009). Review of domestic English writing research.

China Foreign Language, 6 (4).

Hwang, M. H. & Lee, H. K. (2017). Development and validation of the English writing strategy inventory. *System*, (68).

Jacobs, H., Zinkgraf, S., Wormuth, D., et al. (1981). *Testing ESL Composition: a Practical Approach*. Newbury House Rowley, MA.

Jakobovits, L. A. (1970). *Foreign Language Learning: a Psycholinguistic Analysis of the Issues*. Newbury House Publishers.

James, C. (1998). *Errors in Language Learning and Use: Exploring Error Analysis*. Longman.

Jang, X. & Xie F. (2007). Error analysis and the efl classroom teaching. *US-China Education Review*, 4 (9).

Jia, G. J. & Qiao, L. W. (2014). A study of error analysis on English major postgraduates. *Foreign Language World*, (3).

Jiang, P. & Wang, L. P. (2008). A follow up survey of argumentative writing errors of English majors. *Shandong Foreign Language Teaching*, (2).

Jung, M. (2013). Types of errors in college students' L2 writing in EFL environments. *Pan-Pacific Association of Applied Linguistics*, 17 (2).

Kafifah, N. & Aini, N. (2020). A comparative analysis of spoken error of students' utterances. *Pedagogy Journal of English Language Teaching*, 8 (1).

Karaca, M. & Iran, S. (2020). A measure of possible sources of demotivation in L2 writing: a scale development and validation study. *Assessing Writing*, (43).

Kaufhold, K. (2015). Conventions in postgraduate academic writing: European students negotiations of prior writing experience at an English speaking university. *Journal of English for Academic Purposes*, (20).

Keller, S. & Conradin, K. (2020). Semi-structured Interviews. Retrieved from https://sswm.info/planning-and-programming/decision-making/gathering-ideas/Semi-structured-interviews.

Kellera, S. D. & Fleckensteina, J. (2020). English writing skills of students in upper secondary education: results from an empirical study in Switzerland and Germany. *Journal of Second Language Writing*, 2020.

Kline, R. B. (2011). *Principles and Practice of Structural Equation Modeling*. Guilford Press.

Kramer, L. (2022). Grammar. https://www.grammarly.com/blog/pronouns/.

Krashen, S. (2003). *Explorations in Language Acquisition and Use: The Taipei*

Lectures. Heinemann.

Lado, R. (1957). *Linguistics Across Cultures: Applied Linguistics and Language Teachers*. University of Michigan Press.

Lado, R. (1964). *Language Teaching: a Scientific Approach in Students' Text*. McGraw-Hill: USA.

Langum, V. & Sullivan, K. P. H. (2017). Writing academic English as a doctoral student in Sweden: narrative perspectives. *Journal of Second Language Writing*, 2017 (35).

Lardinois, A. (2006). *The Polysemy of Gnomic Expressions and Ajax' Deception Speech*. In A. Rijksbaron & I. J. F. de Jong (eds.). Sophocles and the Greek language: aspects of diction, Syntax and Pragmatics, Leiden-Boston.

Lardinois, F. (2019). *Grammarly Goes Beyond Grammar*. Techcrunch. Archived from the original on January 15, 2021. Retrieved from https://techcrunch. com/2019/07/16/grammarly-goes-beyond-grammar/.

Larsen-Freeman, D. (2003). *Teaching Language: from Grammar to Grammaring*. Heinle.

Larsen-Freeman, D. & Long, M. (1991). *An Introduction to Second Language Acquisition Research*. Longman.

Lee, C. (2016). Second language learners' self-perceived roles and participation in face-to-face English writing consultations. *System*, (63).

Lee, I., Yu, S. & Liu, Y. (2018). Hong Kong secondary students' motivation in EFL writing: a survey study. *TESOL Quarterly*, 52 (1).

Lennon, P. (2008). *Contrastive Analysis, Error Analysis, Interlanguage*. In S. Gramley & V. Gramley (eds.), Bielefeld introduction to applied linguistics. Bielefeld: Aisthesis. Retrieved from http://www. homes. uni-bielefeld. de/sgramley/CA-ErrorAnalysis-Interlang-Lennon. pdf.

Li, C. Z. (2005). The application of error analysis theory in college English writing teaching. *Heilongjiang Higher Education Research*, (5).

Li, Y. Y., Zhao, Y. Q. & Kang, H. (2014). A literature review of the research on teaching methods and content of college English in China in the past decade. *Shandong Foreign Language Teaching*, 5 (4).

Lightbown, P. & Spada, N. (1990). Focus-on-form and corrective feedback in communicative language teaching: effects on second language learning. *Studies in Second Language Acquisition*, 12 (4).

Liu, F. (2013). Teach a man fishing—the enlightenment of the outcome of writing meta-cognition empirical research on teaching. *Foreign Languages*, 29 (S1).

Liu, Q. & He, L. (2017). Corpus-based autonomous learning model of English writing. *Audio Visual Foreign Language Teaching*, (6).

Liu, Y. & Tian, J. G. (2021). Error analysis of college students' spoken English. *International Journal of Languages, Literature and Linguistics*, 7 (4).

Liu, X. H. (2008). Case study in writing error analysis of non-English majors. *Foreign Language Journal*, 25 (2).

Liu, X. & Wang, M, et al. (2022). Intralingual errors in grammatical aspects of Chinese university L2 learners' compositions. *Social Science, Education and Humanities Research.* Proceedings of the 2022 3rd International Conference on Language, Art and Cultural Exchange (ICLACE 2022).

Littlewood, W. T. (1998). *Foreign and Second Language Learning.* Cambridge University Press.

Loehr, J. & Schwartz, T. (2006). *The Power of Full Engagement. Managing energy, not Time, is the Key to High Performance and Personal Renewal.* In Das Summa Summarum des Erfolgs. Springer.

Ma, X. L. (2013). Research on the teaching method of "Error Prompt" English writing. *China Journal of Education*, (S2).

MacNamara, T. (2000). *Language Testing.* Oxford University Press.

Maehr, M. L. & Stallings, W. M. (1972). Freedom from external evaluation. *Child Development*, 43 (1).

McIntosh, K., Connor, U. & Shelton, E. G. (2017). What intercultural rhetoric can bring to EAP/ES writing studies in an English as a lingua franca world. *Journal of English for Academic Purposes*, (29).

Miller, J. (2020). The bottom line: are idioms used in English academic speech and writing? *Journal of English for Academic Purposes*, (43).

Milin, Tracey. & Millin, Mark. (2018). English academic writing convergence for academically weaker senior secondary school students: possibility or pipe-dream? *Journal of English for Academic Purposes*, (31).

Ministry of Education (2008). *English Curriculum Standards for Compulsory Education.* Beijing Normal University Publishing Group.

Ministry of Education (2022). *The Guideline/Syllabus for College English.* Beijing Normal University Publishing Group.

Mitchell, R. & Myles, F. (1998). *Second Language Learning Theories*. London: Edward Arnold.

Morgan, D. N. & Pytash, K. E. (2014). Preparing preservice teachers to become teachers of writing: a 20-year review of the research literature. *English Education*, 47 (1).

Mou, Y. W., Zhu, L. P. & Shen, W. J. (2013). The impact of cross-cultural e-mail communication on students' English writing ability. *Modern Distance Education Research*, (1).

Mubarok, Y. & Budiono, T. (2022). An error analysis on EFL students' writing. *Englisia: Journal of Language, Education, and Humanities*, 9 (2).

Muhonen, J. (2004). Second language demotivation: factors that discourage pupils from learning the English language. (Graduation Thesis, University of Jyväskylä).

Naghdipour, B. (2016). English writing instruction in lran: implications for second language writing curriculum and pedagogy. *Journal of Second Language Writing*, (32).

Nemser, W. (1971). Approximative systems of foreign language learners. *IRAL*, 9. Retrieved from http://dx. doi. org/10. 1515/iral. 1971. 9. 2. 115.

Nemser, W. (1974). *Approximative Systems of Foreign Language Learners*. In J. C. Richards (ed.), Error analysis: perspectives on second language acquisition. Longman.

Nickel, G. (1971). *Papers in Contrastive Linguistics*. Cambridge University Press.

Norrish, J. (1983). *Language Learners and Their Errors*. Macmillan Press.

Nunan, D. (1992). *Research Methods in Language Learning*. Cambridge University Press.

Odlin, T. (1989). *Language Transfer: Cross-Linguistic Influence in Language Learning*. Cambridge: Cambridge University Press. The multiple effects principle. In S. M. Gass & L. Selinker (eds.), Language transfer in language learning. John Benjamins.

Oxford, R. L. (1998). *The Unravelling Tapestry: Teacher and Course Characteristics Associated with Demotivation in the Language Classroom*. Demotivation in foreign language learning. In TESOL'98 Congress, Seattle, WA.

Payne, A. R. (2012). *Development of the Academic Writing Motivation Questionnaire*. (Doctoral dissertation, University of Georgia).

Pelletier, L. G. & Sharp, E. C. (2009). Administrative pressures and teachers' interpersonal behaviour in the classroom. *Theory and Research in Education*, 7 (2).

Pidgeon, D. A. (1970). *Expectation and Pupil Performance*. National Foundation for Educational Research.

Pietro, R. J. (1973). Reviewed work: language structures in contrast. *Linguistic Society of America*, 49 (3).

Polit, D. & Beck, C. (2012). *Data Collection in Quantitative Research*. In Polit, D. & Beck, C., (eds). Nursing research, generating and assessing evidence for nursing practice, 9th edition, Wolters Kluwer Health/Lippincott Williams & Wilkins, Philadelphia.

Polit, D. F. & Beck, C. T. (2011). *Nursing Research: Generating and Assessing Evidence for Nursing Practice*. 9th edition, Lippincott, Williams & Wilkins, Philadelphia.

Popham, W. J. (1981). *Modern Educational Measurement*. Prentice-Hall.

Qiao, J. & Yu, G. (2017). The problems in the composition of College English Test and its complications. *Education Teaching Forum*, 254 (14).

Quadir, M. (2017). Let us listen to our students: an analysis of demotivation to study English in Bangladesh. *The English Teacher*, 46 (3).

Raimes, A. (1991). Out of the woods: emerging traditions in the teaching of writing. *TESOL Quarterly*, 25 (3).

Reichelt, M. (2009). Learning content in another context: English language writing instruction in Germany. *Issues in Writing*, 18 (1).

Richards, J. C. (1984). A non-contrastive approach to error analysis. *ELT Journal*, 25 (3).

Richards, J. C. (1974). A non contrastive approach to error analysis [reprinted from English Language Teaching, 25 (3), 1971. In Richards, J. C. (ed.)]. *Error Analysis: Perspectives on Second Language Acquisition*. Longman Group Limited.

Richards, J. C. & Schmidt, R. (2002). *Dictionary of Language Teaching and Applied Linguistics* (3rd *ed.*). Longman.

Rubin, J. (1975). What the "good language learner" can teach us. *TESOL Quarterly*, 9 (1).

Ryan, R. M. & Deci, E. L. (2009). Promoting self-determined school engagement: motivation, learning, and well-being. In K. R. Wenzel & A. Wigfield (eds.). *Handbook of Motivation at School*. Routledge/Taylor & Francis Group.

Ryan, R. M. & Deci, E. L. (2017). *Self-determination Theory: Basic Psychological Needs in Motivation, Development, and Wellness.* Guilford Publications.

Schofield, G. & Beek, M. (2005). Risk and resilience in long-term foster-care. *The British Journal of Social Work*, 35 (8).

Sciarone, A. G. (1970). Contrastive analysis—Possibilities and limitations. *International Review of Applied Linguistics in Language Teaching*, 8 (2).

Selinker, L. (1969). *The Psychologically Relevant Data of Second-language Learning*. In Pimsleur, P. and Quinn, T. (ed.). *The Psychology of Second Language Learning*. Cambridge University Press.

Selinker, L. (1972). Interlanguage. *International Review of Applied Linguistics*, 10 (3).

Selinker, L. (1974). Error analysis: source, cause, and significance. In J. C. richards (eds.). *Error Analysis: Perspective on Second Language Acquisition.* Longman.

Selinker, L. (1988). *Papers in Interlanguage.* SEAMEO Regional Language Center .

Selinker, L. (1989). CA/EA/IL: The experimental record. *International Review of Applied Linguistics in Language Teaching*, 27 (4).

Selinker, L. (1992). *Rediscovering Interlanguage*. Longman.

Selinker, L. & Lakshamanan, U. (1992). *Language Transfer and Fossilization: The Multiple Effects Principle*. In S. M. Gass & L. Selinker (eds.). *Language Transfer in Language Learning*. John Benjamins.

Senders, J. W. & Moray, N. P. (1991). *Human Error: Cause, Prediction and Reduction.* MA: Massachusetts Institute of Technology.

Shi, Y. & Meng, X. Q. (2013). Using error analysis theory to guide high school English writing. *Teaching and Management*, (21).

Silverman, D. (2020). *Qualitative Research*. SAGE.

Song, Y. (2014). A corpus-based study on the misuse of infinitive phrases in English writing. *Journal of Shanxi Normal University (Social Science Edition)*, 41 (S5).

Stetsenko, A. P. (2010). *Standing on the Shoulders of Giants a Balancing Act of Dialectically Theorizing Conceptual Understanding on the Grounds of Vygotsky's Project.* In Roth, W. M. (ed.). *Re/Structuring Science Education: Reuniting Sociological and Psychological Perspectives.* Springer.

Solano, P. A. C. (2014). Spanish interference in EFL writing skills: a case of

Ecuadorian senior high schools. *Canadian Center of Science and Education*, 7 (7).

Takac, V. P. & Berka, V. (2014). Motivation in foreign language learning: a look at type of school environment as a contextual variable, explorations. *English Language and Linguistics*, 2 (2).

The Ministry of Education. (2022). *Guideline for College English Teaching.* Foreign Language Teaching and Research Press.

Tian, Y. T. & Zhang, Y. Q. (2009). Textual errors in English composition of non-English majors: a rational combination of process approach and achievement approach. *Lanzhou University Journal of Science (Social Science Edition)*, 37 (S1).

Touchie, H. (1986). Second language learning errors their types, causes, and treatment. *Proceedings of the JALT Journal*, 8 (1).

Troia, G. A., Harbaugh, A. G., Shankland, R. K., et al. (2013). Relationships between writing motivation, writing activity, and writing performance: effects of grade, sex, and ability. *Reading and Writing*, 26 (1).

Ushioda, E. (2008). Motivation and good language learners. In C. Griffiths (ed.). *Lessons From Good Language Learners.* Cambridge University Press.

Ulicheva, A., Harvey, H., Aronoff, M., et al. (2020). Skilled readers' sensitivity to meaningful regularities in English writing. *Cognition*, (195).

Wiersma, W. & Jurs, S. (1990). *Educational Measurement and Testing.* Needham Heights, MA: Allyn and Bacon.

Wigfield, A. (1994). Expectancy-value theory of achievement motivation: a developmental perspective. *Educational Psychology Review*, 6 (1).

Williams, M. & Burden, R. (1997). *Motivation in Language Learning : a Social Constructivist Approach.* Cambridge University Press.

Wan, H. & Wu, J. (2006). An analysis of the misuse of conjunctions in college English writing. *Journal of Shanghai University (Social Science Edition)*, (6).

Wang, H. Y. (2010). Analysis of common errors in Chinese students' English writing and teaching countermeasures. *Teaching and Management*, (12).

Wang, M. H. (2014). A study of Mongolian students' English writing errors and the influence of their mother tongue. *Journal of Inner Mongolia Normal University (Education Science Edition)*, 27 (6).

Wang, W. & Wen, Q. (2002). L1 use in the L2 composing process: an exploratory study of 16 Chinese EFL writers. *Journal of Second Language Writing*, 11 (3).

Wang, W. L. (2015). Analysis of errors in college English writing of Mongolian non-English majors and teaching implications. *China Journal of Education*, (SI).

Wang, W. P. (2007). An empirical study of errors in's English writing. *China Adult Education*, (8).

Wang, Y. & Xuan, A. (2010). The influence of web-based interactive learning mode on the English writing proficiency and motivation of Chinese college students. *Computer-assisted Foreign Language Education*, (5).

Wang, Y., Xuan, A. & Chen, Y. J. (2006). Investigation and analysis of the status of English writing teaching in universities of science and engineering. *Foreign Language World*, 115 (5).

Wang, Y. Z. (2008). Analysis of common errors in college students' English writing and enlightenment. *Journal of Shaanxi Normal University (Philosophy and Social Sciences Edition)*, 37 (S2).

Wedell, M. & Liu, R. (2012). *Language Teaching & Learning From Theory to Practice*. High Education Press.

Widdowson, H. (2013). *Aspects of Language Teaching*. Oxford University Press.

Wilcox, K. C. & Jeffery, J. V. (2015). Adolescent English language learners' stances toward disciplinary writing. *English for Specific Purposes*, (38).

Wu, D. (2009). Metacognition and college English teaching: review and prospect. *Education Science*, 25 (2).

Wu, H. Y. & Zhang, J. (2017). Effects of different language environments on Chinese graduate students' perceptions of English writing and their writing performance. *System*, (65).

Wu, J. J. (2017). An empirical study of multimodal metaphor in college English writing teaching. *Journal of Jiangxi Normal University (Philosophy and Social Sciences Edition)*, 50 (4).

Wu, S. Q. (2008). Research on negative transfer of Chinese in English writing of Chinese non-English majors. *Journal of Capital Normal University (Social Science Edition)*, (2).

Wu, X. & Mauranen, A. (2020). Syntactic complexity in English as a lingua franca academic writing. *Journal of English for Academic Purposes*, (43).

Xiao, W. Y. (2011). An empirical study on metacognitive strategy training to improve students' English writing. *Foreign Language*, 27 (5).

Xiang, Q. Y. (2012). An empirical study on "Avoidance" in college English writing in the context of culture. *Journal of Jishou University* (*Social Science Edition*), 33 (3).

Xue, H. G. (2010). An empirical study on the impact of mutual exchange between Chinese and American college students on Chinese students' English writing ability under the network environment. *Foreign Language Teaching*, 31 (2).

Yan, S. & Kang, S. (2021). Interlingual syntactic errors in Chinese EFL learners' writing. *The Journal of Linguistic Science*, 98 (9).

Yang, L. (2013). *Qualitative Research in Applied Linguistics*. Foreign Language Teaching and Research Press.

Yeasmin, S. & Rahman, K. F. (2012). "Triangulation" research method as the tool of social science research. *Bup Journal*, 1 (1).

You, C., Dornyei, Z. & Csizer, K. (2016). Motivation, vision, and gender: a survey of learners of English in China. *Language Learning*, 66 (1).

You, X. (2004). "The choice made from no choice": English writing instruction in a Chinese university. *Journal of Second Language Writing*, 13 (2).

You, X. (2005). *Writing in the "Devil's" Tongue: a History of English Writing Instruction in Chinese Colleges*. PhD dissertation, Purdue University.

Yu, T. (2010). An empirical study of college English writing teaching based on Wiki cooperative writing system. *Research on Audio-visual Education*, (3).

Zafar, A. (2016). Error analysis: a tool to improve English skills of undergraduate students. *Procedia-social and Behavioral Sciences*, 217 (5).

Zhan, H. (2015). Frequent errors in Chinese EFL learners' topic-based writings. *English Language Teaching*, 8 (5).

Zhang, C. J. (2015). Empirical analysis of English writing errors and research on multimodal metaphor teaching. *Heilongjiang Higher Education Research*, (2).

Zhang, D. Z. (2002). *A Practical English Grammar*. Foreign Language Teaching and Research Press.

Zhang, L. X. (2008). Error analysis and independent collaborative modification—research on college English writing based on online corpus. *Foreign Language Audio Visual Teaching*, (6).

Zhang, T. (2008). Investigation and suggestions for the current college English writing teaching. *Education Exploration*, 207 (9).

Zhang, H. Y. (2012). The enlightenment of error analysis theory on the teaching of English writing for non-English major postgraduates. *Educational Theory and*

Practice, 32 (15).

Zhang, J. W. & Wang, Q. F. (2011). Trial analysis of error analysis theory and the improvement of English writing competence. *Teaching and Management*, (2).

Zhang, L. & Qiao, G. H. (2008). Error analysis in students' English writing. *Teaching and Management*, (12).

Zhang, L. Z. & Deng, H. Z. (2010). The impact of negative transfer of mother tongue on grammar errors in adult English writing. *China Adult Education*, (22).

Zhang, X. L. (2004). English major sophomore's English writing error analysis and enlightenment. *Journal of Sichuan University of Foreign Languages*, (2).

Zhang, W., Deng, L. F. & Zhang, L., et al. A survey on negative transfer. *IEEE/CAA J. Autom. Sinica.*

Zhao, J., Hao, J. & Gao, Y. (2010). An investigation into the current situation of college English writing. *Foreign Language Research*, 124 (6).

Zheng, C. & Park, T. J. (2013). An analysis of errors in English writing made by Chinese and Korean university students. *Theory and Practice in Language Studies*, 3 (8).

Zheng, X. Y. (2009). On the teaching and research of English writing: "skill encouragement" vs. "error discovery". *Shandong Foreign Language Teaching*, 30 (4).

Zhou, G. Q. (2011). Empirical study on errors of negative transfer of mother tongue in English writing—a sample study of non-English major students in North China University of Water Resources and Hydropower. *Adult Education*, 31 (8).

Zhou, L. R. (2018). Structural compression in academic writing: an English-Chinese comparison study of complex noun phrases in research article abstracts. *Journal of English for Academic Purposes*, (36).

Zhou, X. & Liu, J. (2012). Research on the teaching model of mutual assessment of college English writing—a group controlled experiment based on 60 students. *Science and Technology Bulletin*, 28 (12).

Zhu, Y. Y. (2011). Investigation and reflection on the development of English writing research in China—based on the statistical analysis of China's foreign language core journals (1980—2010). *Foreign Language Journal*, (6).

Zimmerman, B. J. (2008). Investigating self-regulation and motivation: historical background, methodological developments, and future prospects. *American Educational Research Journal*, 45 (1).

Zimmerman, B. & Kitsantas, A. (2007). Reliability and validity of self efficacy for learning form (SELF) scores of college students. *Journal of Psychology*, 215 (3).

APPENDICES

Appendix 1 The Writing Proficiency Test

Directions: For this part, you are allowed 30 minutes to write a composition on the topic. You should write the essay no less than 120 words but no more than 180 words.

Serial Number	Topics
1	*Campus Safety*
2	*Can Money Buy Happiness?*
3	*The Career that I'd Like to Pursue*
4	*Computer Games on Campus*
5	*How to Prevent Crimes?*
6	*Is Frustration a Bad Thing?*
7	*It Pays to be Honest*
8	*My Thoughts on Environmental Protection*
9	*Online Shopping*
10	*The Advantages of Getting a Good Education*
11	*The Negative and Positive Effects of Virtual Life*
12	*What Makes a Good Teacher?*
13	*Why People Fall Victim to Advertising?*
14	*Women Hold Up Half the Sky*

Appendix 2 Scoring Scheme for the Writing Proficiency Test

Principles and Standards in Scoring CET-4 and CET-6 Composition

Principles:

1. CET (College English Test) is conducted to check whether the candidate meets the requirements of English teaching and learning which is set out in the university English syllabus, and the evaluation of composition should be based on this criterion.

2. The CET composition is scored by the Global Scoring method. Instead of deducting points by the number of errors in the language points, the reader gives a reward score for the overall impression.

3. A comprehensive assessment of compositions is made in terms of content and language. Content and language should be united as a whole. The composition should express the content stipulated in the title, and the content should be delivered clearly through the language. The scoring should not only consider whether the composition is relevant, or fully express ideas, but also consider whether the ideas have been expressed very clearly and appropriately in English. Besides, whether linguistic errors will cause obstacles to understanding should be taken into account.

4. The scoring should be avoided a tendency to give a medium grade. The high level of writing should be given the high score, including the full score; the low proficiency composition should be scored lowly, including zero points. The scorer should not supply only a few intermediate scores in all the compositions reviewed.

5. All copies issued shall not be reproduced, or published. The above actions should be strictly prohibited. If found, the scorer will be investigated.

Criteria:

1. The full score of composition is 15 points.

2. The reading criteria can be divided into five levels: 2, 5, 8, 11 and 14. Each has one to two standard sample volumes.

3. According to the assessing criteria, the reviewer scores according to the sample volume. For example, if the article under review is considered to be similar to a score (e.g., 8 points), you can give it a score of 8; If you think that the article you are

reading is slightly better or worse than the score, you can add one point (i. e. 9 points) or decrease by one point (i. e. 7 points). However, no half points may be added or deducted.

4. Scoring criteria:

2 points—Unclear, disordered thinking, fragmented language or errors in most sentences, and most of which are serious errors.

5 points—Basic obey to the topic. The expression of thought is unclear and the consistency is poor. There are more serious language errors.

8 points—Basic obey to the topic. Some ideas cannot be expressed clearly. And the words are barely coherent; there are quite a few language errors, some of which are serious.

11 points—Be relevant to the topic. Clear thoughts, coherent words, but a small number of linguistic errors.

14 points—Be relevant to the topic. Clear thinking, smooth, coherent, basically no language errors, or only a few small mistakes.

(Note: blank writing paper, or composition has nothing to do with the subject, or only a few isolated words which can not express ideas, so 0 point will be given)

5. Insufficient number of words in the composition should be considered to deduct the score appropriately:

(1) If the subject sentence, the opening sentence and the closing sentence are given in the title or direction, the word number shall not be counted in the number of words written.

(2) If the prescribed content is not fully written, the points shall be deducted appropriately.

If judging the composition 0 point, it needs to be handled with caution.

Appendix 3 List of Codes Used to Analyse the Errors in English Writing

Types	Sub-category		Examples
Grammatical errors	Subject-verb agreement		e. g. *She come back home at six.*
	Verb tense		e. g. *Christmas coming soon.*
	Articles		e. g. *His daughter writes a card to a Santa.*
	Link verbs		e. g. *She a student.*
	Auxiliary verbs		e. g. *What not you like?*
	Adjectives		e. g. *I have not many time to spend at home.*
	Preposition		e. g. *We did not use to sit on tables when eating.*
	Adverbs		e. g. *She was disappointed so much.*
	Modal verbs		e. g. *I will must to study Norwegian.*
	Pronouns		e. g. *John decided to return the book at a library.*
	Prepositions		e. g. *When I was a millionaire, I could ask for anything not in the air.*
	Determiners	articles	e. g. "*a*", "*an*", and "*the*"
		demonstratives	e. g. "*this*", "*that*", "*these*", and "*those*"
		quantifiers	e. g. "*few*" and "*many*"
		possessives	e. g. "*my*", "*your*", "*his*", "*her*", "*its*", "*our*" and "*their*"
Substance errors	Capitalization		e. g. *I will buy benze.*
	Punctuation		e. g. *I liked them. they were so nice to me.*
	Spelling		e. g. *I want to go some intesting places to visit.*

(To be continued)

Types	Sub-category	Examples
Lexical errors	Word form	e. g. *Young people can be independence in the United States.*
	Word deficiency	e. g. *She is a beautiful.*
	Word abundance	e. g. *I have many lots of books.*
	Word selection	e. g. *Both sicks are kids.*
Syntactic errors	Coordination/ subordination	e. g. *Jasmine is afraid of dogs, she was bitten by a dog when she was young.*
	Sentence structure	e. g. *I dinner like to eat spaghetti.*
	Ordering	e. g. *The ball dropped the boy.*
Semantic errors	Ambiguity	e. g. *I saw the bank this morning.*
	Miscommunication	e. g. *He should love his woke who is belam to his job.*

Appendix 4 Items in Piloting Questionnaire (English Version)

Error Analysis and Research in Chinese College Students' English Writing

Dear students,

Thanks for your participation! The purpose of this questionnaire is to investigate the relationship between students' writing proficiency and writing motivation, writing attitudes, habits and corrective feedback. The questionnaire is composed of two parts: the first part has 25 items of different variables while the second one is demographic information. It can be assured that the data provided by you shall be used only for ascertaining and evaluating the above several factors. The data furnished and the identity of the respondent will be kept confidential. If you like, you can drop from this survey anytime for any reasons. For those who want to know the research results, you can leave your email address at the end of questionnaire. Thank you!

The following statements are about what you may or may not have experienced in the process of writing in English. Please give your answers honestly to guarantee the success of the survey.

In the following section, we would like you to tell us how much you agree or disagree with the following statements by ticking (√) a number from 1 *to* 5. *Please do not leave out any of the items.*

Strongly Disagree	Disagree	Neither Agree nor Disagree	Agree	Strongly Agree
1	2	3	4	5

(cited from You & Dörnyei, 2016; You, Dörnyei, Z. & Csizér, K., 2016; Alivernini & Lucid, 2008; Teng's writing motivational belief questionnaire 2016; Payne, 2012)

Part I

Students' motivation, attitudes, difficulties, behavior and feedback in writing.

Motivation:

1. English writing can be important to me because I think it will someday be useful in getting a good job.

2. English writing can be important to me because I think I'll need it for further studies.

3. I study English writing in order to get others' recognition as a good writer.

4. I study English writing to prove I can write as well as other students.

5. I study English writing because I need to learn it for examination.

6. I study English writing because I experience pleasure and satisfaction while learning it.

7. English writing is necessary for me because I don't want to get a poor score or a fail mark in English proficiency tests.

Attitudes:

8. When asked to write a piece of work in English, I feel comfortable and confident.

9. I find it interesting to express my ideas in English writing.

10. In English, writing is the most difficult of all learning skills.

11. It is not easy to find the ideas that help me to write in English.

Difficulties:

12. When writing in English, I feel I am lack of vocabulary.

13. When writing in English, the problem lies in making grammatical errors.

14. When writing in English, I face problems on how to combine words in sentences.

15. I feel I have a lot to say, but I don't know to deliver it in English in my composition.

16. When writing in English, I usually use Chinese English in the composition.

17. When writing in English, I face the problem in modifying the composition.

Behavior:

18. When writing in English, first I think in Chinese, and then I write in English.

19. I use an English/Chinese, Chinese/English dictionary when writing in English.

20. I use check my compositions for some errors before I submit them.

21. When writing in English, I write the structure of the sentence in Chinese, and then I translate it into English.

Feedback:

22. I would like to get the direct feedback with corrections on my composition from my English teacher.

23. Indirect feedback with some indications from English teacher can inspire me in improving the language accuracy in composition.

24. If my teacher can give me feedback in time, I can perform well in English writing.

25. I would like my English teacher to underline all the errors in my composition.

Part Ⅱ Personal Information Part

Please choose one item which is fit for your reality, and tick it.

● Male/Female

● Freshman/Sophomore

● Age:__________

●Have you ever been to English speaking countries? If yes, how long?

☐ yes (__________months) ☐ no

● Your major: (Please noted: ____________________________)

● The length of learning English: (Please noted: __________years)

Appendix 5 Items in Piloting Questionnaire (Chinese Version)

中国大学生英语写作的错误分析与研究

同学您好！非常感谢您的帮助！本问卷旨在分析和研究中国大学生英语写作中存在的困难。参与者将被要求完成一份中英文问卷（如果英文水平较高，建议直接阅读英语原文），用时大约 5 分钟。问卷包括两部分，第一部分则是关于英语写作动机、态度、行为习惯等，第二部分是关于个人信息，这份问卷完全保密，答案亦没有对错之分，我们关注的是您的个人观点，请根据您的实际情况填写。本问卷结果仅供学术研究之用，个人信息也会得到妥善保管，敬请放心。您的支持对本研究能否取得成功至关重要，再次对同学们的配合表示感谢！

下表中有五个等级，根据你对所述句子的赞同程度，分为从极不赞同到非常赞同，为确保调查问卷的准确性，请按实际情况填写。

极不赞同	不赞同	不确定	赞同	非常赞同
1	2	3	4	5

第一部分：学生英语写作的动机、态度、困难、行为习惯、反馈等。

写作动机：

1. 我学习英文写作是为了以后得到一份更体面的工作。

2. 英语写作对我来说很重要是因为以后深造时会需要。
3. 我学习英语写作是为了得到别人对于我是擅长写作者的认可。
4. 我学习英语写作是为了证明我可以写得和其他同学一样好。
5. 我学习英文写作是因为考试（期末考试、英语四六级、考研）需要。
6. 我学习英文写作是因为在写作过程中能体会到愉悦和满足感。
7. 英语写作对我来说是必须要做好的事情，因为我不想在英语水平测试中得低分。

写作态度：
8. 当被要求用英文写作时，我感到很有信心。
9. 用英文来表达自己的思想和情感是一件很有趣的事情。
10. 在英语中，写作是所有技能中最困难的一项技能。
11. 用英文写作时，不容易找到可以帮助我写作的灵感和想法。

写作困难：
12. 用英语写作时，我感觉很缺乏词汇量。
13. 用英文写作时，我的问题主要是出现很多语法错误。
14. 用英文写作时，我不知道如何组织句子里的单词。
15. 用英文写作时，我总感觉有很多话要说，但又不知道如何表达。
16. 写英语作文时，我通常会用中式英语来表达。
17. 写完作文后，我不知道怎么去修饰（修改）作文。

写作行为习惯：
18. 写英语作文时，我都是先用汉语思考，然后用英文写下来。
19. 写英语作文时，我会查阅英汉或者汉英字典。
20. 交作文之前，我通常会检查文章中是否有错误。
21. 写作文时，我都是先用汉语写句子结构，然后再翻译成英文。

写作反馈：
22. 每次老师批改作文时，我都希望老师能把错误的地方以及如何改正写出来。
23. 我只需要老师指出作文中的错误即可，这样更能激发我自己主动学习的欲望。
24. 如果每次老师能及时给出作文错误的反馈，我的写作能有更大的进步。

25. 我希望老师每次都能把作文中所有的错误标注出来。

第二部分：个人信息部分

请就以下问题打“√”或根据您的实际情况填写。

● □男　　□女

● □大一　　□大二（请注明：____________）

● 年龄（周岁）：________

● 您曾经去过英语国家吗？如果是，在那里停留多长时间？

□是　　□否

● 您的专业：（请注明：____________）

● 学英语的年限：（请注明：______年）

Appendix 6　Items in Semi-structured Interview (English Version)

Questions for students

Below are the interview questions that will be given to gain information about factors that cause students make errors in writing.

1. How many times a week does your English teacher assign the composition?

2. How does your teacher deal with these errors in your writing? Underlined, give feedback or face to face correction?

3. Do you think it is necessary for teachers to explain some grammatical rules before writing an essay?

4. Do you usually check the compositions for some errors before submitting the composition?

5. Which errors do you think you make the most?

6. What do you feel when you make errors in writing English sentences?

Questions for teachers

1. What types of errors do your students usually make in their writing?

2. Among the types of errors in writing such as spelling, grammar, sentence structure and vocabulary, which is the most frequent error made by students? Can you rank the errors from the most to the least?

3. What are the reasons, do you think, responsible for making errors?
4. How do you help your students to minimize the errors in English writing?
5. Do you think these methods you use effective? Why or why not?

Appendix 7 Items in Semi-structured Interview (Chinese Version)

学生受访问题

以下问题为采访问题，主要用来探究影响学生写作偏误的因素和原因。

1. 你们的英语老师每周布置几次写作作业?
2. 你的英语老师如何处理你作文中出现的错误? 是画下划线，给出反馈还是点对点纠正?
3. 你认为有必要在写作文之前先解释一些语法规则吗?
4. 你提交作文之前会检查作文中的错误吗?
5. 你认为你最容易犯哪类错误?
6. 当你用英文写作时犯了错误，你感觉如何?

教师受访问题

1. 你的学生在英文写作时经常犯哪类错误?
2. 在这些错误中，比如拼写错误、语法错误、句子结构错误、单词错误中，哪类错误出现得最多? 你能把它们排个序吗?
3. 你认为学生英文写作中犯的这类错误的原因是什么?
4. 你是如何帮助学生减少他们写作中的错误的?
5. 你认为这些方法有效吗? 为什么?

Appendix 8 An Example of Transcription in an Interview (English Version)

Interview 1 with Wang

Nov 13, 2021

Interviewer: Yuhong MA

1. Yuhong: How many times does your English teacher assign the composition?
2. Wang:
3. Yuhong: How does your English teacher deal with the writing errors in your compositions? Underlined, giving feedback or face-to-face correction?
4. Wang:
5. Yuhong: Do you think it is necessary to explain some rules or regulations before writing the compositions?

...

Appendix 9 An Example of Transcription in an Interview (Chinese Version)

受访者：黄同学
2021 年 11 月 13 日
采访者：马玉红
1. Yuhong：你们的英语老师每周布置几次写作作业？
2. Wang：
3. Yuhong：你们的英语老师如何处理你作文中出现的错误？画下划线，给出反馈或者点对点纠正？
4. Wang：
5. Yuhong：你认为有必要在写作文之前解释一些语法规则吗？
……

Appendix 10 Questionnaire Consent Form

Consent for participation in the study

Research Topic: An Investigation of Errors and Interlanguage in Chinese L2 Writing

I consent to my participation in the above survey for the topic. I give my permission to the researcher to use my questionnaire results which are taken during the survey for research purposes.

Name/Signature: Date:

I, the researcher, have explained the purpose of this book and have requested the cooperation of the above participants in this research questionnaire. I have guaranteed that any information taken from the questionnaire will be just used for scientific research, no other business utility.

Name/Signature: Date:

Appendix 11 Interview Consent Form

Consent for participation in the study

Research Topic: An Investigation of Errors and Interlanguage in Chinese L2 Writing

I consent to my participation in an interview for this research. I give my permission to the researcher to use my interview script which are taken during the interview for research purposes.

Name/Signature: Date:

I, the researcher, have explained the purpose of this survey and have requested the cooperation of the above participants in this research interview. I have guaranteed that any information taken from the interview will be just used for scientific research, no other business utility.

Name/Signature: Date:

Appendix 12 The Cutting Point of Three Different Proficiency Groups

Grade	Proficiency Groups	Numbers	Maximum	Minimum	Cutting Point
2013	High	11	90	68	67
	Fair	18	67	48	
	Low	11	47	25	47
2014	High	11	92	70	69
	Fair	18	69	50	
	Low	11	49	25	49
2015	High	11	91.5	71	70
	Fair	18	70	52	
	Low	11	53	28	52
2016	High	11	95	72	72
	Fair	18	71	54	
	Low	11	53	24	54
2017	High	11	96	68	68
	Fair	18	67	50	
	Low	11	49	29	50
2018	High	11	99	72	72
	Fair	18	71	50	
	Low	11	49	30	50
2019	High	11	96	70	70
	Fair	18	69	51	
	Low	11	50	29	51
2020	High	11	96	76	76
	Fair	18	75	55	
	Low	11	54	25	

Appendix 13 Items in Questionnaire of the Main Study

Error Analysis and Research in Chinese College Students' English Writing

Dear students,

Thanks for your participation! The purpose of this questionnaire is to investigate the relationship between students' writing proficiency and writing motivation, writing attitudes, habits and corrective feedback. The questionnaire is composed of two parts: the first part has 25 items of different variables while the second one is demographic information. It can be assured that the data provided by you shall be used only for ascertaining and evaluating the above several factors. The data furnished and the identity of the respondent will be kept confidential. If you like, you can drop from this survey anytime for any reasons. For those who want to know the research results, you can leave your email address at the end of questionnaire. Thank you!

The following statements are about what you may or may not have experienced in the process of writing in English. Please give your answers honestly to guarantee the success of the survey.

In the following section, we would like you to tell us how much you agree or disagree with the following statements by ticking (√) a number from 1 *to* 5. *Please do not leave out any of the items.*

Strongly Disagree	Disagree	Neither Agree nor Disagree	Agree	Strongly Agree
1	2	3	4	5

Part Ⅰ Personal Information Part

Please choose one item which is fit for your reality or fill in the blank.

1. Your Student's ID: ____________
2. Your class: ______________________
3. Your major: (Please noted: ______________________)
4. Male/Female
5. Freshman/Sophomore

6. Age: ___________

7. Have you ever been to English speaking countries? If yes, how long?

□yes (________months) □no

8. The length of learning English: (Please noted:________years)

Part Ⅱ Students' Writing Attitudes, Difficulties, Corrective Feedback

9. I study English writing because I experience pleasure and satisfaction while learning it.

10. When asked to write a piece of work in English, I feel comfortable and confident.

11. I find it interesting to express my ideas and emotions in English writing.

12. When writing in English, I feel I am lack of vocabulary.

13. When writing in English, the problem lies in making grammatical errors.

14. When writing in English, I face problems on how to combine words in sentences.

15. I feel I have a lot to say, but I don't know how to deliver it in English in my composition.

16. When writing in English, I usually use Chinese English in the composition.

17. After finishing my English writing, I face the problem in modifying the composition.

18. I would like to get the direct feedback with corrections on my composition from my English teacher.

19. Indirect feedback with some indications from English teacher can inspire me in improving the language accuracy in composition.

20. If my teacher can give me feedback in time, I can perform well in English writing.

21. I would like my English teacher to underline all the errors in my composition.

Appendix 14 Items in Questionnaire of the Main Study (Chinese Version)

中国大学生英语写作的错误分析与研究

同学您好！非常感谢您的帮助！本问卷旨在分析和研究中国大学生英语写作中存在的困难。参与者将被要求完成一份中英文问卷（如果英文水平较高，建议直接阅读英语原文），用时大约5分钟。问卷包括两部分，第一部分是关于英语写作动机、态度、行为习惯等，第二部分则是关于个人信息，这份问卷完全保密，答案亦没有对错之分，我们关注的是您的个人观点，请根据您的实际情况填写。本问卷结果仅供学术研究之用，个人信息也会得到妥善保管，敬请放心。您的支持对本研究能否取得成功至关重要，再次对同学们的配合表示感谢！

下表中有五个等级，根据你对所述句子的赞同程度，分为从极不赞同到非常赞同，为确保调查问卷的成功，请按实际情况填写。

极不赞同	不赞同	不确定	赞同	非常赞同
1	2	3	4	5

第一部分：个人信息部分

请就以下问题打“√”或根据您的实际情况填写，以便我们更好地了解您之前提供的信息。

1. 学号：____________
2. 班级：____________
3. 您的专业：（请注明：____________________________________）
4. □男　　□女
5. □大一　　□大二（请注明：____________________________________）
6. 年龄（周岁）：________
7. 您曾经去过英语国家吗？如果是，在那里停留多长时间？
   □是　　□否
8. 学英语的年限：（请注明：________年）

第二部分：学生的写作态度、写作困难和纠正性反馈

9. 我学习英文写作是因为在写作过程中能体会到愉悦和满足感。

10. 当被要求用英文写作时，我感到很有信心。

11. 用英文来表达自己的思想和情感是一件很有趣的事情。

12. 用英语写作时，我感觉很缺乏词汇量。

13. 用英文写作时，我的问题主要是在作文中会出现很多语法错误。

14. 用英文写作时，我不知道如何组织句子里的单词。

15. 在英文写作时，总感觉有很多话要说，但又不知道如何表达。

16. 写英语作文时，我通常会用中式英语来表达。

17. 写完作文后，我不知道怎么去修饰（修改）作文。

18. 每次老师批改作文时，我都想老师能把错误的地方以及如何改正写出来。

19. 我只需要老师指出作文中的错误即可，这样更能激发我自己主动学习的欲望。

20. 如果每次老师能及时给出作文错误的反馈，我的写作会有更大的进步。

21. 我希望每次老师都能把作文中所有的错误标注出来。